Battered Women in the Courtroom

JAMES PTACEK

Battered Women in the Courtroom

The Power of Judicial Responses

Northeastern University Press · Boston

Northeastern University Press
Copyright 1999 by James Ptacek

Library of Congress Cataloging-in-Publication Data

Ptacek, James.
    Battered women in the courtroom : the power of judicial responses / James Ptacek.
        p.   cm.—(The Northeastern series on gender, crime, and law)
        Includes bibliographical references and index.
    ISBN 1-55553-390-6 (pbk. : alk. paper).—ISBN 1-55553-391-4 (cloth : alk. paper)
        1. Family violence—Law and legislation—United States.   2. Abused women—Legal status, laws, etc.—United States.   3. Restraining orders—United States.   4. Judicial process—United States.
    I. Title.   II. Series.
    KF9322.P78   1999
    345.73'025553—dc21   98-48853

Designed by Christopher Kuntze

Composed in Trump by Coghill Composition in Richmond, Virginia. Printed and bound by The Maple Press Company in Binghamton, New York. The paper is Sebago Antique Cream, an acid-free sheet.

Manufactured in the United States of America

03   02   01   00   99   5   4   3   2   1

To Alice Ptacek
in loving memory of Joseph Ptacek
to my sisters and brothers
and to Alex and Joey

Contents

Preface

We live in a time of tremendous social change concerning responses to woman battering. Since the mid-1970s substantive efforts have been made across the United States to criminalize battering and to aid abused women. Despite serious problems with these new laws, most of the research on criminal justice responses to battering has focused on the police, and relatively little has focused on the courts. It is crucial to examine the ways that judges respond to women who are claiming their rights under these laws.

Given the reluctance of district attorneys to prosecute batterers and the difficulties many women have with trusting remedies offered under criminal law, in many communities civil restraining orders are currently the most common form of legal sanction against battering.[1] Surprisingly, little research on domestic violence restraining orders has been done. This study examines the role of judges in the process of obtaining restraining orders in the lower criminal courts. I do not evaluate the effectiveness of restraining orders in modifying the behavior of violent men. Rather, I examine issues that stand logically prior to such a direct test: What do judges do with their authority in restraining order hearings? How do judges interpret their role in responding to woman battering? What effect do judges have on women seeking restraining orders? Understanding the variability, complexity, and actual processing of restraining orders is essential if we are to assess their potential utility in stopping woman battering.

This investigation of women, violence, and the courts centers on three levels of analysis. The first level concerns the *historical negotiations between feminist political movements and the state* that produced the current law on restraining orders in Massachusetts. The second level of analysis concerns *the effects of men's violence on women's "negotiation of daily life,"* to use the phrase of Rebecca Emerson Dobash and Russell Dobash.[2] Addressing the range of violence and abuse women report to the courts is essential if we are to make sense of judges' responses. Finally, the *courtroom negotiations between women and judges* in restraining order hearings form the main body of the study.

Battering, I argue, is best understood in the context of gender, class, and racial inequality. In the chapters that follow, attention to these intersecting inequalities informs discussions of the research, history, politics, and institutional responses relating to battering.

Although comparisons between "good" and "bad" courts in terms of judicial responses might be useful, I instead focus on two courts that are regarded as generally supportive of women's legal rights and that are located in communities that differ racially and economically. Given a widespread skepticism about the utility of restraining orders, I thought it would be useful to study courts that appear to take them seriously and that might therefore offer insights into their potential as an institutional remedy. I assumed (correctly) that even in these courts, substantial differences between judges in their treatment of these cases would surface.

The focus of the study was developed through discussions with women in the shelter movement, feminist attorneys, court advocates, judges, and criminal justice researchers. While they cannot be responsible for my misjudgments, a number of individuals deserve acknowledgment.

Tina Nappi, Bonnie Zimmer, and Danielle London conducted telephone interviews with abused women about their court experiences. I am grateful for the skill and compassion they brought to these conversations. Bonnie Zimmer, my life partner, brought an extensive understanding of violence and trauma to her participation in this study. I am deeply indebted to her faith in the research project. A host of activists and advocates in the Boston area shared their insights into judicial responses to battering, including Sarah Buel, Chris Butler, Joan Stiles, Anne Richmond,

Laurie Salame, Carla DiMare, Lois Frankel, Molly Chaudhuri, Samantha Wallack, and Bridget Spann.

Shulamit Reinharz, who chaired my dissertation committee, possesses an excitement about research and feminist scholarship that guided me throughout the project. I have benefited greatly from her vision and tireless support. Kersti Yllö, Karen Hansen, and Gila Hayim also served on my dissertation committee, where they were extremely supportive of the kind of qualitative approach I wanted to pursue. Kathleen Daly, Eileen McNamara, Jim Hardeman, and Andrew Klein also offered critical advice on the research.

Arlie Hochschild and Bob Connell generously responded to drafts of my work on men's violence against women. They will see much evidence of their own theories of gender, power, and emotionality in this study. Todd Crosset challenged me to sustain my focus and spirit through the daily dramas of field research. His friendly support has been essential. Pam Pacelli helped me enormously during a difficult stretch in the writing process. Edward Gondolf, Ted German, Ken Ormes, and Mary Gilfus offered spirited feedback on my writing. I must also thank Susan Schechter, Etiony Aldarondo, Fernando Mederos, Beth Richie, Oliver Williams, Michele Bograd, Chuck Turner, Ellen Pence, Deb Cohan, Albert Cardarelli, and Susan Ostrander for their observations and encouragement.

At Northeastern University Press, Claire Renzetti and Bill Frohlich were delightful to work with, offering patience and enthusiasm during the book process. In my department at Suffolk University, I have been sustained by my wonderfully friendly colleagues, especially Alexandra Todd, Carolyn Boyes-Watson, Steven Spitzer, and Sharon Kurtz.

A number of judges were welcoming of my questions and facilitated my access to court documents. In my interviews with them, confidentiality was neither requested nor offered. Nonetheless, in an attempt to move the discussion of judicial responsiveness beyond individual personalities and onto the judiciary as an institution, I have chosen to identify none of these judges by name. The only contemporary judges named in this study are those who were involved in public scandals, appeared in the newspaper, authored articles, or gave public testimony before the Massachusetts Legislature.

Lastly, I must acknowledge my appreciation for the women who participated in the telephone interviews. I hope I have done justice to their thoughtfulness and eloquence.

This research was supported in part by a dissertation fellowship from the Harry Frank Guggenheim Foundation.

Battered Women in the Courtroom

We may assume that the old doctrine, that a husband had a right to whip his wife, provided he used a switch no larger than his thumb, is not law in North Carolina. Indeed, the Courts have advanced from that barbarism until they have reached the position, that the husband has no right to chastise his wife, under any circumstances. § But from the motives of public policy,—in order to preserve the sanctity of the domestic circle, the Courts will not listen to trivial complaints. § If no permanent injury has been inflicted, nor malice, cruelty nor dangerous violence shown by the husband, it is better to draw the curtain, shut out the public gaze, and leave the parties to forget and forgive.

JUDGE SETTLE, in *State v. Oliver* (1874)[1]

1

Judges and the Social Entrapment of Battered Women

Is woman battering worthy of the court's attention, or is it re-garded as merely a "trivial" matter? Historically, there has been a dramatic difference between the written law and the law in practice regarding violence against wives. In 1874 Judge J. Settle affirmed that Richard Oliver was indeed guilty of assault and bat-tery on his wife. Richard Oliver arrived at home drunk one morn-ing, and during breakfast he threw a cup and coffee pot on the floor after objecting to his wife's cooking. He then brought in two

3

"switches" or branches and whipped her, stopping only after witnesses intervened. His wife—her name is not recorded in the case—suffered "bruises on her arm, which remained for two weeks." Neither of the branches was as thick as a man's thumb, according to the facts presented at his trial. Judge Settle affirmed the guilty finding of the lower court, stating that the "rule of thumb" doctrine was not law in North Carolina. The case is regarded as establishing in that state "that a husband has no legal right to chastise his wife under any circumstances."[2]

But there is another finding in this case. Judge Settle claims that "motives of public policy" and "the sanctity of the domestic circle" weigh against state involvement in "trivial complaints." Richard Oliver, he finds, demonstrated "both malice and cruelty"; but the court is prepared to tolerate men's violence against women, he appears to say, in cases where injuries are not permanent or where dangerousness, malice, or cruelty are not shown. This decision offered judges wide discretion as to the meanings of "trivial" and "dangerous" concerning men's violence against women and thus considerable latitude in applying the law.

Some 112 years after Judge Settle gave his ruling, the meaning of what is and is not "trivial" about battering was made a public issue in Massachusetts. In March of 1986, Pamela Nigro Dunn went to court to obtain a restraining order against her husband, six weeks after their wedding. In an affidavit submitted with her request, she wrote:

I'm a prisoner in my apartment. He locks me in and takes the phone cord out. He choked me and threatened to kill me if I try to leave. He made me work only where he works. . . . My life is in danger so long as he is around.[3]

She was given an order by Judge Paul P. Heffernan prohibiting her husband, Paul Dunn, from contacting her. In a hearing 12 days later, she was verbally chastised by Judge Heffernan for arranging for a police officer to escort her to her apartment so that she could gather her things. With both Pamela Dunn and Paul Dunn before him, Judge Heffernan said the following:

This is pretty trivial. . . . This court has a lot more serious matters to contend with. We're doing a terrible disservice to the taxpayers here. You want to gnaw on her and she on you fine, but let's not do it at the taxpayers' expense.[4]

Telling Pamela that she didn't need an escort, Heffernan told her to "act as an adult."[5] The judge also addressed an advocate from the district attorney's office when she tried to speak on Pamela Dunn's behalf: "You don't understand my point of view worth one cent. You heard me tell this lady that she didn't need the police," he said.[6] Heffernan even criticized the police officer who supported Pamela Dunn's position, saying, "You've been duped in this case. I don't mind saying so for the record."[7]

Pamela Dunn's fears were seen as "trivial" by the judge. But her fate at the hands of her husband made her story front-page news, linking her name with that of Judge Heffernan. In August of 1986, less than five months after this hearing, Pamela Nigro Dunn was brutally murdered by her husband. According to news reports, she was abducted at gunpoint by her husband at a street corner. Nine hours later she was found face down in a puddle at a town dump; she had been shot, stabbed, and strangled.[8] Pamela Nigro Dunn, who was five months pregnant, was 22 years old. Six months later, Paul Dunn was convicted of first-degree murder and sentenced to life in prison without parole.[9]

The memory of Pamela Nigro Dunn's death remains alive among many women in Massachusetts. Her vicious killing triggered an investigation of her efforts to obtain help from the courts, especially Judge Heffernan. A public scandal arose when the judge's remarks to Pamela Dunn became front-page news. What was at issue was not whether Heffernan had issued the restraining order; he obviously had. What was at issue was how Pamela Dunn had been treated in the courtroom. Were women's fears of violence being taken seriously? Were women being routinely harassed when they sought protection from the courts? What were judges doing with their authority in these hearings? What messages were the courts giving to abusive men? How dramatic were the differences between the written law and the law in practice?

This murder had a profound impact on feminist organizing in Massachusetts. It spurred efforts to train advocates to assist battered women in the courts, and women's shelters, law schools, undergraduate colleges, and law firms have worked to place advocates in every courthouse in the state. In the wake of this murder, community activists pressured the state to examine judicial misconduct and gender bias in the courts. Ironically, the scandal that arose over judges corresponded with a rise in women seeking restraining orders, possibly due to greater publicity of women's rights under the law.

The local news media have still not forgotten this case. Daily news of women's murders at the hands of a husband, former husband, partner, or former partner in the Boston area routinely include mention of whether the woman had sought a restraining order and whether inadequate law enforcement may have played a contributing role in each tragedy.

This story also continues to haunt judges. Seeing hundreds of abused women each year in restraining order hearings and reading the daily news, they fear the potential consequences of making a mistake. Seven years after Pamela Dunn's murder, a local judge said on the radio, "No judge wants to be the one who didn't grant a restraining order to the woman found face down in the morning."[10]

This is a sociological study of how judges treat abused women in the courtroom. The focus is not on high-profile trials of celebrities or on cases of extreme or fatal violence. Instead, this study investigates the much more common, everyday interactions in which women request restraining orders and risk appearing "trivial" with their complaints. Do judges express irritation, impatience, and even hostility toward women seeking the protection of the courts? Or do judges use their authority to express concern for women's safety and mobilize resources on their behalf? And how are abused women affected by these responses?

Civil restraining order hearings represent some of the most common negotiations between women and the state over freedom from violence. Restraining orders or court orders of protection are now available in all 50 states.[11] In 1996, over 50,000 requests for restraining orders were filed in Massachusetts courts. More than 600 women go to court every week in Massachusetts to seek protection from violent partners or former partners.[12] Women call the police even more frequently than they appear in court. But in Massachusetts, as in most other states, only judges have the authority to order a man to leave a residence for an extended period of time. Only judges have the authority to award temporary child support and temporary custody of children. Only a judge can send a man to jail for violating an order. The bulk of social scientific research on criminal justice responses has focused on the police. What is needed is further research on the role that judges play in women's efforts to escape violence. This study examines what judges do with their authority in these courtroom encounters.

Often people ask, "Isn't the restraining order just a piece of paper?" I have heard this comment from abused women, from judges, from police officers, and from lawyers. Abusive men threaten women with this remark. Behind this common phrase, I believe, lies a crisis of judicial authority. If judges are seen as tolerating men's violence against women, courts lose legitimacy. Do abusive men violate restraining orders with impunity? Are judges processing them with only token gestures of authority? Do women experience these orders as merely empty promises? One of the most common sources of referral to the courts for restraining orders is the police. Are the police encouraging women to go to the courts for an order that is meaningless? If the legal remedies contained in restraining orders are merely "empty rights," then surely judicial authority is deserving of investigation.

A restraining order, I argue, represents an interactive process, a negotiation between women and the state over protection from violent and abusive men. The goal of the study is to provide a sense of the process, context, and meaning of restraining order hearings, both to abused women and to judges.

Given how often women are asking for the protection of the courts, it is crucial to identify the ways that judges either encourage or discourage women from claiming their rights under the law. This requires an understanding of what battering is and what dilemmas are posed by state responses to violence against women.

Battering as Social Entrapment

Just what is meant by the term *battering*? A new concept can throw fresh light on a problem; it can even help make a previously hidden problem become public. In the history of feminist activism on men's violence against women, a number of new terms have been created, including *sexual harassment, wife rape,* and *femicide*. Each of these terms reconfigures how events in women's lives are viewed in the public imagination.

In the past two decades of public attention being paid to crimes against women, a variety of different definitions of *woman battering* have emerged. The distinction between *incident-based* and *control-based definitions* is particularly important to a study of court responses to women.[13] Incident-based definitions of battering focus narrowly on physical harm—on discrete episodes of violence that violate criminal laws on assault and that may produce medically recognizable injuries.

And indeed, measured in terms of physical harm and criminal assault, intimate violence is a major threat to women's health. Battering may be the most common cause of injuries that women present in emergency rooms.[14] A recent national study of 31 hospital emergency departments found that assaults by intimate partners or former partners account for over 45 percent of women's violence-related injuries, where an assailant is identified.[15] Research also indicates that many abused women seek medical attention for less obviously related problems such as depression, anxiety, sexual problems, or "vague medical complaints." Battering may be the most important context for women's alcoholism and suicide attempts. Rape is also significantly related to battering: one study of hospital rape cases found that nearly a third of the women seen in the hospital for rape had documented histories of battering.[16] In Diana Russell's ground-breaking study of wife rape in San Francisco, most of the women who had suffered wife rape had also been battered.[17]

And yet the problem of woman battering must be measured by more than physical consequences, as extensive and terrible as these are. Battering undermines women's ability to participate freely in social life—even after leaving violent partners. This aspect of social control is the focus of another range of definitions. "I'm a prisoner in my apartment," Pamela Nigro Dunn wrote, when seeking help from the court. Men who batter women intend to isolate them and to undermine their mobility and sources of support. Batterers frequently pull telephones out of the wall, slash women's car tires, warn women not to talk with friends and relatives, and threaten women when they call the police and go to court. Damage to women's relational lives is a primary consequence of battering.[18]

Control-based approaches define battering more broadly as a form of domination, only parts of which violate the law and only traces of which would be visible to the nurse and physician. The experience of "coercive control," rather than criminal assault, is central to these approaches.[19] In this view, battering is characterized by a web of coercive tactics that a man uses against a woman, including physical and sexual violence, threats of violence, psychological abuse, and manipulation of economic resources. This perspective has been developed by the battered women's movement, drawing from the experiences of abused women.[20] Here, the power of battering resides not only in the physical force men use but also in the social isolation they impose on women with their threats, in the indifference of powerful institutions, and in the cultural authority granted to men in a sexist society.

Historian Linda Gordon summarizes this distinction between incident-based and control-based approaches:

> One assault does not make a battered woman; she becomes that because of her socially determined inability to resist or escape: her lack of economic independence, law enforcement services, and quite likely, self-confidence.[21]

Gordon describes battering as a social dynamic in which institutions are directly implicated. Individual women are assaulted by individual men, but the ability of so many men to repeatedly assault, terrorize, and control so many women draws on institutional collusion and gender inequality. Even the self-confidence of abused women has social roots, in Gordon's analysis.

A range of studies have identified the inextricably social aspects of women's struggles with violent men. This research examines the role powerful institutions play in women's ability to resist and escape violence. These institutions include social work agencies,[22] medicine,[23] law,[24] the courts,[25] and the police.[26] The contributions of poverty and racism to women's victimization are beginning to be addressed.[27] In addition to social scientific research, theoretical and political writings by feminists of color have named how racism, colonialism, and political marginalization intensify violence against women.[28]

In this study battering is investigated as a form of *social entrapment*. The term *entrapment* has been applied to battering by Evan Stark and Anne H. Flitcraft, and it is also used in a somewhat different way by Beth Richie.[29] But three elements are common to these authors: (1) a focus on the social isolation, fear, and coercion that men's violence creates in women's lives; (2) attention to the indifference of powerful institutions to women's suffering; and (3) identification of the ways that men's coercive control can be aggravated by structural inequalities of gender, class, and racism. Extending this usage, *social* entrapment emphasizes the inescapably social dimension of women's vulnerability to men's violence, women's experience of violence, and women's abilities to resist and escape. This approach links private violence to community responses and offers a way of connecting poverty, racism, and political disempowerment to women's abilities to survive violent relationships.

Seeing battering as social entrapment helps to reveal both the possibilities and pitfalls of criminal justice interventions. The courts represent just one of many institutions involved in what Gordon calls the "system of male power"[30] that is the basis of battering. And yet in the United States today, no institution has greater authority to redress this injustice on a daily basis. Seeing battering as social entrapment gives heightened significance to judicial responses. How do the courts affect women's ability to resist or escape violence? What judges do with their authority can break through this social isolation; what judges do can also worsen women's entrapment.

Violence and the State

Contemporary definitions emphasize that "the state" really names a complex of governmental and quasi-governmental institutions operating at federal, state, and local levels. As a key element of state power, the criminal justice system is itself such a loosely integrated set of institutions that even within a single state confusing relationships exist between various courts and between the courts and their related police departments. With the recent sensationalizing of crime in campaigns for political office, new conflicts have emerged within criminal justice institutions and within state legislatures over crime and punishment. This disarray is so pronounced that some criminologists refer to a "criminal justice *nonsystem*."[31] When speaking of "the state" as a single entity, then, it should be clear that this is an oversimplification.

And yet there are elements of state power that carry through all these levels and all institutions of criminal justice. The early twentieth-century social theorist Max Weber placed violence at the heart of his definition of the modern state. He made the connection in this manner:

Today the relation between the state and violence is an especially intimate one. In the past, the most varied institutions . . . have known the use of physical force as quite normal. Today, however, we have to say that the state is a human community that (successfully) claims the *monopoly of the legitimate use of physical force* within a given territory.[32] (Emphasis in the original)

In this passage Weber was discussing physical coercion as used by the military or the police. As part of its establishment of authority, the state has a monopoly over the legitimate use of violence, Weber claims. And yet while the importance of violence to the modern state is an essential observation, a number of contemporary theorists question whether the state really possesses a "monopoly" over legitimate force.

Research on men's violence against women indicates that it is endemic to modern societies. Surveying patterns of wife beating, rape, child sexual abuse, and sexual harassment in the workplace, Sylvia Walby argues that there are similarities in the motivations among male offenders, similarities in the consequences of such violence for its victims, and similarities in how such violence affects women's lives more generally. She further finds cultural legitimation for these forms of violence. Most important, Walby also finds commonalities in the limited nature of state intervention to stop violence against women, except in the most extreme cases.

Viewing violence against women as a structural dimension of modern society and as legitimated through the inaction of police and judicial state apparatuses, Walby challenges Weber's theory of the state. "I propose to abandon the notion that the state has a monopoly of legitimate coercion in a given territory," Walby states.[33] Donald Black makes a parallel argument in his theory of "crime as social control." Black sees battering, rape, and violence driven by racial hatred as forms of social control, as crimes committed deliberately against defined groups by people who see their actions as legitimate. Following Black's logic, it is this sense of legitimacy or self-righteousness on the part of men who batter that accounts for the lack of remorse that so frequently accompanies their violence, even in cases of fatal violence.[34] Pointing to the tolerance and indifference of the law and public officials to much of this crime, Black concludes that "in modern society the state has only theoretically achieved a monopoly over the legitimate use of violence."[35]

These theories of violence and the state are important to a study of the courts. Clearly, violence is central to the authority of the modern state; this is dramatically visible in the operation of the criminal justice system. But at the same time, the state does not hold a monopoly on the "legitimate" use of violence. Indeed, the history of feminist efforts to criminalize violence against women in the United States has been an attempt to force the state to challenge the legitimacy of battering, rape, and incest.

Over the past 150 years, American feminists have made numerous attempts to draw the power of the state into conflict with the coercive power of violent husbands. In 1848 in Seneca Falls, the first Women's Rights Convention produced a "Declaration of Sentiments" that included reference to the injustice of the legal power of a husband "to deprive [his wife] of her liberty, and to administer chastisement."[36] Elizabeth Pleck has documented that between 1868 and 1896, there was extensive feminist organizing around "crimes against women," including demands of stiffer criminal penalties for wife beating, rape, and incest.[37] Contemporary feminist efforts to transform legal responses have a long history, and this history indicates that the state has been reluctant to intervene in men's violence against women.

Dilemmas of State Intervention Against Battering

History also teaches us that competing agendas can be furthered by the same criminal justice "reforms." State action responding to gender politics is simultaneously marked by the politics of class and race. In 1905 the Oregon state legislature passed a law that established a new punishment for "wife beaters"—20 lashes at a "whipping post." The law was promoted not by women's activists but by the governor and a wealthy merchant, both men. None of the legislators were women. It passed into law, despite arguments that it would be used against not all batterers but only poor men. And in fact, during the six years before it was repealed, only three men were whipped under the law in Portland: one was unemployed, and two were immigrant Russian laborers. Noting the class scapegoating that occurred under the law and the evidence of battering among men of all classes, historian David Peterson del Mar concludes that "Oregon's whipping post law probably better served Oregon's men than its women."[38] Racial bias in arrests for battering has also been documented in nineteenth-century Pennsylvania and South Carolina, as well as in Oregon in the early twentieth century.[39] State responses to violence against wives, then, have historically been shaped by social divisions not only around gender but around class and race.

Herbert Blumer warns that "a social problem is always a focal point for the operation of divergent and conflicting interests, intentions, and objectives."[40] What is relevant about this for a study of judges and battered women is that their courtroom encounters have been staged in a highly politicized cultural atmosphere. Structural inequalities within American society, and within the state itself, pose obstacles and dilemmas to the rights of abused women. Fears of men's violence, fears of state violence, and the visibility of gender, class, and racial antagonism have combined to present a series of dilemmas to abused women seeking help, to judges, and to movements for social justice.

Abused women may fear that by calling the police and going to court, their actions may lead to more violence by their husbands or boyfriends. They may worry that the police won't believe their stories and that judges won't understand their predicaments. Women of color may have themselves experienced racially discriminatory treatment by the police or the courts and may therefore be ambivalent about using the violence of the state against men of color. They may fear police mistreatment of their abusers, owing to racial bias, in communities with histories of police brutality.

Judges may also fear that whatever they do—or don't do—may inspire an abusive man to commit more violence. With public exposure of crimes against women, judges have learned how retaliatory some men can be when their authority is threatened; judges may fear for their own safety. They may lack the training, the resources, and the coordination with police departments, shelters, and batterers' programs to offer meaningful remedies to women.

There are also dilemmas here for movements for social justice. Among feminist activists in the United States and elsewhere, there are sharp differences of opinion on the best course of action for the state to take, given the limitations of criminal justice responses and the patriarchal character of the state itself.[41] There are concerns about a backlash against women and about efforts to transform state responses draining energy from all other feminist activism. Attempts at reforming police and court practices have resulted in some problematic consequences for women. Mandatory arrest policies for domestic violence have often led to "dual arrests," meaning the arrest of the women who called the police along with their alleged abusers.[42] Some judges also issue "mutual restraining orders," ordering both women and their abusive partners to stay away from one another, despite the fact that this practice goes against the guidelines of the law.[43] Both "dual arrests" and "mutual restraining orders" may indicate resentment of the new laws and anger toward abused women.

Anglo-American feminists and feminists of color in the United States have disagreed over strategies to end violence. Angela Davis states that African American feminists were conspicuously absent from participation in the rape crisis movement of the 1970s, owing to the legacy of racial mistreatment of black men by the judicial system and the reliance of this movement on law enforcement strategies.[44] Some feminists of color have prioritized police accountability in their approaches to stopping battering.[45]

The prominence of woman battering as a public issue has also attracted the support of "get tough on crime" politicians and conservative lobbying groups, which have historically been hostile to feminist views of social justice. One example of this was on display recently in Massachusetts, when proponents of capital punishment added a new kind of homicide to the list of crimes that could lead to execution: murder in violation of domestic violence restraining orders. While the bill was narrowly defeated, it was an attempt to exploit public concern with battering to pass the death penalty in the state legislature.

These dilemmas have been raised to indicate how complex and conflicted the current climate is regarding state intervention. They provide a context for examining how the courts are responding to battering. Five main questions guide this study. First, what can be learned about state intervention from the public scandal over "judicial harassment" of battered women in Massachusetts? Second, what types of violence and entrapment are women reporting to the courts? Third, what do judges do with their authority in restraining order hearings, after reading and hearing women's testimony? Fourth, how do judges see their role in these negotiations with abused women? And fifth, what effect do judges have on women's efforts to free themselves from violence? Framed against the history of feminist efforts to change state responses, it is hoped that this detailing of court processes will illuminate both the potential and limitations of current judicial responses to abused women.

Nationally, we say it is the prevalence and effects of violence on individuals and society with which we are concerned. Yet we cannot ignore or promote poverty among our citizens and reduce violence at the same time.

ANGELA BROWNE[1]

2

Political Moves: Class, Race, and Research on Woman Battering

For many years economic deprivation and racial discrimination have been known to make women vulnerable to violence. Yet the implications of this connection have barely been developed in social science research. In fact, the literature on battering has generally neglected class and race. This chapter outlines the politics of this neglect.

After twenty-five years, feminist organizing has established woman battering as an issue of gender politics. Research on woman battering has grown in response to this powerful political movement. In an important sense, studies of this topic have been conducted in a culture that has been highly politicized—successfully so, from the perspective of feminist organizing.

I want to begin with the assumption that gender politics has been an essential inspiration for research on woman battering. But other social conflicts also influence studies of violence against women: class politics and racial politics. Among those studying battering, decisions about whether to address the class and racial dimensions of this violence also carry political weight. In the United States, the gap between rich and poor has increased over the past several decades,[2] and the nation remains sharply divided by race. I think it is fair to assume that researchers are aware of these inequalities, even if the depth of their understanding varies considerably. Researchers—and institutions that support and fund research—choose whether to address racial and class dimensions of battering against the background of this awareness.

Personal Background

If the perspective of the researcher is relevant to this discussion, it is important that I detail my own. I have been working on the problem of woman battering for over 15 years. In addition to research and teaching in this area, I worked for eight years at Emerge, a Boston-area counseling and educational agency for men who batter. Over this period, I coled batterers' counseling groups and conducted trainings for criminal justice, human services, mental health, and hospital personnel.

The direct service work at Emerge gave me an understanding of the self-perceptions of violent men and of the range of violent and other abusive behaviors that characterize battering.[3] Working collaboratively with battered women's shelters taught me about the consequences of violence, the connections between racism and woman abuse, and the toll that hostile and indifferent institutional responses take on women's safety and well-being.

These are strengths that I bring to a study of judicial responses to woman battering, but other aspects of my background represent significant weaknesses. As a man who studies violence against women, my most serious limitation is that I have no personal experience of terror. As a white man, I have a further lack of personal experience with the harsh effects of racism. This is particularly a weakness given that I have chosen to study the experiences of both black and white abused women. As a grandchild of Polish Catholic and Czech Catholic immigrants, I grew up in two virtually all-white communities near Milwaukee, Wisconsin—a white ethnic working-class neighboring town and a more professional-managerial class suburb. The fact that my family was able to move to a different town already says much about race and life chances. Milwaukee is one of the most racially segregated metropolitan areas in the nation.[4] Racism reduces the competition that white citizens of Milwaukee face for housing and jobs. My white racial identity, forged in settings where sharp class divisions create "differences" between whites and African Americans, puts me at a disadvantage for interpreting black women's experiences with the courts.

Nonetheless, much research and policymaking about woman battering have failed to take into account the relevance of race and class to women's experiences of violence. Because this lack of attention to class and racial dimensions of battering is so pronounced and so consequential for social action, I chose to study one court in a multiracial poor and working-class area of Boston and one court in a predominantly white, working- and middle-class city. This was done to bring the issues of racism and class division "from margin to center," a research strategy inspired by bell hooks,[5] Patricia Hill Collins,[6] Kimberlé Williams Crenshaw,[7] and the battered women's movement in the Boston area.[8]

Political Moves

I fear that silence on class, race, and battering has been costly to progress on social justice. These interlocking dimensions are misrepresented in popular writing and in political campaigns. The failure to address class and race seriously, I argue here, has had negative consequences for women who have the greatest difficulty resisting and escaping violence.

But in a fiercely divided society, public discussions of class, race, and violence entail risks. Wittingly or unwittingly, those who name these interconnections arouse powerful racist images, even when their goals are to displace them. Social scientists, especially scholars of color, have noted a collective reluctance to write about these matters. Patricia Hill Collins[9] observes that criticism and censure have greeted black feminist writings on violence against women. In their research on race, crime, and urban inequality, Robert J. Sampson and William Julius Wilson state that "criminologists are loath to speak openly on race and crime for fear of being misunderstood or labeled racist."[10] In his recent book on race, poverty, and criminal justice, Michael Tonry writes:

Several times from the late 1970s onward, I tried to commission essays on race and crime for *Crime and Justice*, a book series I edit for the University of Chicago Press. . . . Most qualified scholars turned me down cold. Two took on the subject and later withdrew because it was just too controversial.[11]

The fear that even well-intended research can be used by others to further racist agendas is openly expressed. In *Ethnicity, Race, and Crime*, Darnell Hawkins lays out the goals of his edited collection with a cautionary note:

As during the past, the public and scholarly discourse on the subject of ethnicity, race, and crime itself can be used to justify ethnocentrism, bigotry, and discriminatory policies and practices. Such discourse can also lead to the eradication of myth, pseudo-science, and stereotypes.[12]

And not all research on race may be well intended. Charges of racism are currently being leveled both against and between researchers concerning the issue of race and IQ. The publication of *The Bell Curve: Intelligence and Class Structure in American Life* by Richard J. Herrnstein and Charles Murray[13] has generated no fewer than six collected volumes of often harshly critical responses, many of which claim that essentialist forms of racism continue to lurk behind the facade of science.[14]

Racism presents real obstacles to stopping violence against women. Black feminist activists have described how difficult it is to name the problem of battering in communities already besieged by hostile publicity.[15] Asian American advocates for abused women are also burdened by well-grounded fears of racist attacks on their communities, driven in part by hateful images of Asian men.[16] There are further parallels with ethnic hostility. Latina activists have been told that raising the issue will reinforce racist stereotypes of Latinos and create divisiveness.[17]

It is not my intention to minimize these risks. Indeed, a serious understanding of racism and ethnic discrimination is necessary to make sense of the social entrapment that defines battering. Rather, I wish to raise other risks that may follow from neglecting the interconnections among poverty, racism, and violence in women's lives.

In a divided society, decisions by domestic violence researchers about whether to address class and race might be seen as *political moves*—that is, decisions influenced by awareness of social inequality. Decisions concerning what to study, who to study, and how to study in this area are affected in no small measure by politics. Research on battering, in turn, has the potential—for good or bad—to shape political perceptions of women, men, class, race, and ethnicity.

The discussion in the remainder of this chapter is in five parts. I begin with a discussion of two myths about battering and social status. Next, I review the evidence indicating that poverty makes women more vulnerable to battering. This includes a discussion of femicide and the severe differences in vulnerability to murder between black women and white women. Following this I describe how despite this evidence—which is not new—class and race have been placed at the margins of the research literature on battering. The patterns and possible rationales for these political moves are detailed. Finally, I relate this absence of attention to the politics of welfare and criminal justice, both of which have tremendous relevance to woman battering.

Misperceptions of Battering: The "Class Myth" and "Universal-Risk Theory"

If a myth is understood as a fiction, then two powerful myths about race and class have been identified in the literature on battering. The first has been called the "class myth."[18] This is the false notion that woman battering, or family violence generally, is *limited to working-class or poor families.* Many books about abused women challenge this class myth by stating that such violence is found in all social classes and across all racial divisions.

The conflation of race with class is part of this myth. Belief in the class myth hinders an understanding of just how widespread violence is in women's lives. It even blocks personal awareness of abuse, as revealed in this account by Jennifer Hunt:

Before I joined [the Abused Women's Advocacy Project], whenever I thought of battered women or abused children, I never thought that it happened to middle-class people. I was pretty uneducated. I thought it only happened to minorities and poor people. I thought it happened to those poor kids down the street or only in alcoholic families. When I began to do public service, I didn't understand how abusive my relationship was.[19]

Clearly, the class myth remains powerful, despite relentless attempts to challenge it by feminist activists, researchers, practitioners, and public figures. Deeply held "gut" feelings that poor people, working-class people, or people of color generally represent the "dangerous classes" live on. In trainings on battering I conducted for health care professionals, social workers, and criminal justice officials, I often said that men seeking batterers' counseling in my agency included doctors, psychologists, and computer industry professionals. The emotional reaction this consistently drew from my largely white training audiences revealed the power of this deeply felt class myth. It was as if these professionals said, "You mean this happens between people like us?"

Now that the class myth has been challenged, especially by feminists, a second misperception has arisen. If the class myth falsely limits women's risk, this second myth falsely denies differences in women's vulnerability. This misperception has been called "universal-risk theory" by Martin D. Schwartz[20] and "classless intimate violence" by Angela Moore.[21] Schwartz defines this myth as the notion "that all women are equally situated in a patriarchal society and thus equally likely to be victimized by wife abuse."[22] Schwartz sees this myth as the creation of liberal and radical feminists, but at the same time his analysis draws on concerns about ignoring race and class that have been raised by many feminist authors, including Susan Schechter[23] and Michelle Fine.[24] While he sees some political advantages to universal-risk approaches, according to Schwartz "empirical studies of every possible design have shown that there is more battering in low-income, low-economic-status families."[25] Schwartz suggests that there may be class-specific forms of violence against women, with professional-managerial-class men committing these crimes for different reasons and in different contexts than working-class men. Class position also provides men with different resources for controlling women. While not disputing that battering is a serious problem in middle-class households, Schwartz sees universal-risk theories as obscuring the impact of economic deprivation on men's violence against women.

Angela Moore also acknowledges the practical appeal of theories of battering that ignore race and class. Such theories can help mobilize women from many backgrounds against a common problem, she states. But like Schwartz, she finds the idea of battering as a "classless" phenomenon to be unsupportable:

To argue that intimate violence is not distinguished by socioeconomic status is inconsistent with the extant literature. . . . Women on the lower end of the economic scale are at greater risk of victimization than their counterparts at higher levels. Intimate violence is more prevalent and tends to be more frequent and severe among women with lower socioeconomic status.[26]

Moore also argues that the impact of arrest for domestic violence varies with employment status. In a study of arrest for domestic violence in Milwaukee, for example, arrest deterred further violence among employed men but seemed to increase domestic violence among unemployed men.[27] Moore concludes that battering is mediated by class.

Both the class myth and the universal-risk myth misrepresent the social patterns of battering. Battering does occur in the United States among people in every class, every race, every religion, and every ethnicity. But it is not evenly distributed throughout the class structure. These issues have been generally neglected in research, but where work has been done, the myths have been disproved repeatedly. In terms of public consciousness about battering, however, there seems to be an either-or supposition operating behind these myths: *either* battering occurs only among the poor and working class, *or* class is irrelevant; *either* battering is a problem only for women of color, *or* race (better, racism) is irrelevant.

Twenty-five years' worth of research and activism—and a string of celebrity battering cases—have shown the class myth to be false. As a social problem, battering—and men's violence against women in general—is not limited to poor and working-class communities. And yet as common as battering is in women's lives, research based on self-reports of violence indicate that social class is terribly relevant to women's vulnerability. The evidence in favor of rejecting the myth of universal risk, since it is much less commonly discussed, is worth examining.

Are All Women Equally at Risk for Battering?

Flawed and incomplete as it is, evidence has shown for some time that economic deprivation places women at greater risk for battering. The 1975 National Family Violence Survey conducted by Murray A. Straus, Richard J. Gelles, and Suzanne K. Steinmetz found violence against women by men in high- and low-income categories. But the rates of men's violence differed dramatically when these categories were compared. The rate of "violence between couples" in poor families was 500 percent greater than in families with incomes over $20,000.[28] Many problems have been raised with the definitions and methods employed in this study.[29] Yet as serious as these criticisms are, the class patterns in women's victimization identified here have been found in many other studies.

Data from the National Crime Surveys, conducted by the U.S. Department of Justice, reveal a significant relationship between income and wife assault. Martin D. Schwartz analyzed the data collected between 1973 and 1982. Although women in both high- and low-income categories reported violent assaults by their husbands, more than two and a half times as many poor women reported assaults as did women with family incomes over $15,000.[30] These surveys have been sharply criticized for underreporting violence against women.[31] In 1992 new questions were added to the survey (now called the National Crime Victimization Survey) to better elicit responses on domestic violence and rape. While the survey remains less comprehensive than the questionnaires used by feminist researchers such as Diana E. H. Russell,[32] Mary P. Koss,[33] and Liz Kelly,[34] the revised questions greatly increased the number of women reporting violent crimes. Nevertheless, the rate of intimate violence reported by women with family incomes of less than $10,000 was twice the rate for women with incomes from $20,000 to $30,000 and four times the rate for women with incomes over $50,000.[35]

Recent studies of intimate violence in the lives of women on welfare further establish class patterns. In a probability sample of 734 women receiving welfare assistance, University of Massachusetts researchers found that 19.5 percent reported incidents within the past year that met the state's legal definition of domestic violence.[36] To offer a rough comparison between these figures and those from other research, the figure of 19.5 percent is 73 percent higher than the "overall violence" against wives reported in the 1985 Gelles and Straus survey.[37] Asked if they had *ever* experienced such violence, 64.9 percent of the Massachusetts women said they had.[38] Again, to offer a rough comparison, this figure is three times the rate of wife beating reported in Diana E. H. Russell's random sample of women in San Francisco.[39] As high as this last figure appears, lifetime rates of battering between 50 and 60 percent have been found in other studies of women receiving welfare in Massachusetts, Illinois, Washington, and New Jersey.[40]

Poverty is dangerous because it undermines women's control over their lives and therefore their safety. Recent trends in urban poverty pose particular risks for women who are single mothers. In their study of mostly white and Puerto Rican poor mothers in Worcester, Massachusetts, Ellen L. Bassuk and her colleagues described the connection in this manner:

Many poor women survive by building extensive support networks. Unfortunately, factors such as the low-income housing crisis, rampant violence and drug abuse, and the collapse of institutional supports in inner-city neighborhoods have eroded these networks and have added homelessness to the risks that impoverished families face.[41]

If poverty exposes women to violence, violence also exacerbates poverty. Judging from admissions to homeless shelters in Massachusetts, New York, and Oregon, battering is a major cause of homelessness.[42] And according to women who receive welfare, men who batter frequently sabotage women's participation in job-training programs and their ability to succeed in new jobs.[43]

If a significant relationship between battering and poverty appears unmistakable, the issue of race is much less clear. Ways of classifying "race" are inconsistent across studies. "Racial differences" are frequently reported without addressing whether the supposed differences are really indications of class position rather than racial category. Where both race and class have been addressed in research on battering, some studies found that when economic deprivation is controlled, few racial group differences remain. But studies of race and battering, of which there are relatively few, also offer inconsistent findings.

Most of the research that addresses race focuses on differences between white and black women. For instance, Straus, Gelles, and Steinmetz reported in their first national survey that black women were assaulted almost 400 percent more often than white women.[44] But in a separate article by Straus and Cazenave, when the data were controlled for income, the portrait was more complex. Rates of "wife slapping" were lower for black women than white women at the $12,000 to $20,000 income level. Black and white women's rates of assault were similar for "severe" violence, except at the $6,000 to $12,000 level, where rates were higher for black women. Cazenave and Straus suggested that the higher rates of abuse for black women at this income level may be due to unmeasured aspects of racial oppression.[45]

Lettie L. Lockhart's study of 300 black and white women in a southeastern city used different categories for social class and found different results. Rates of wife assault between black and white women were the same, but the class distribution within each racial group was different. A larger proportion of middle-class African American women reported violence from their partners in comparison to white middle-class women.[46]

Studies of Hispanic women are conflicting. It must be noted that *Hispanic* is a broad term that lumps together people of diverse nationalities and widely varying racial identities. Diego Castro, who prefers the term *Latino* or *Latina*, notes the inaccuracies of such a simplistic categorization:

Both terms, "Latino/a" and "Hispanic," pose significant problems for the millions of people who are homogenized through their use. The people these terms lump together prefer to identify themselves by their country of origin.[47]

Research has so far addressed only some of the issues of race and national origin hidden within these terms. Murray A. Straus and Christine Smith compared wife assault between Hispanic (black and white) and non-Hispanic whites, drawing from the 1985 National Family Violence Survey and an oversample of Hispanic families. While they found rates of wife abuse to be twice as high in Hispanic families, when the results were controlled for economic deprivation, age, and urban residence, these differences were no longer significant.[48] A Los Angeles survey by Susan B. Sorenson and Cynthia A. Telles compared violence between Mexican American and non-Hispanic white households. While rates of "spousal violence" were almost the same when comparing non-Hispanic whites with Mexican Americans born in Mexico, higher rates were found among Mexican Americans born in the United States. The authors suggest that the strain of adjusting to U.S. culture may weigh heaviest on nonimmigrant generations of Mexican Americans.[49]

And some studies find no racial or ethnic differences whatever. The same 1995 National Crime Victimization Survey that found rates of victimization dramatically higher for low-income women states that "women of all races and Hispanic and non-Hispanic women were about equally vulnerable to violence by an intimate."[50]

Such studies, few as they are, suggest that structural factors associated with race in the United States, especially class inequalities, are more powerfully related to violence than racial categories themselves. This is consistent with studies of class, race, and criminal violence generally.[51]

Class, Racial, and Ethnic Contexts of Femicide

Murders of women by men who are their partners or former partners have played a prominent role in community campaigns against battering. In Massachusetts, virtually every major reform of criminal law, civil law, or criminal justice practice relating to battering has been made in response to such killings, which have been publicized by feminists as an organizing strategy. Diana E. H. Russell coined the term *femicide* to highlight the misogyny that drives this most extreme form of violence against women.[52]

It is important to place these murders not only in their gendered context—which is essential—but also within the context of class and race.

Battering may be the single most common cause of injury to women,[53] but intimate violence is the leading cause of death for young black women.[54] A recent report on female homicide in New York City over the five years from 1990 to 1994 illustrates this. The New York City Department of Health reports that although black women and men comprise 25 percent of the city's population, black women account for 52 percent of female homicide victims. White women and men make up 46 percent of the population, but white women represent 16 percent of all female homicides. Of all killings of women where perpetrators were identified, 49 percent were intimate partners. Homicides of Hispanic women were slightly higher than their proportion of the population, and the number of killings of Asian women was lower than proportionate.[55] Like the term *Hispanic*, the category *Asian* collapses together people from a host of nationalities in a simplistic fashion.

Curiously, the Department of Health's 15-page report says nothing whatever about the class dimensions of these murders. But in her comments on this report, New York City writer Marcia Smith places these deaths in a social context:

Because African-American communities as a whole—women and men, young and old—are experiencing the multiple effects of economic and political disenfranchisement, ranging from joblessness to substance abuse, from crises in housing and education to the impact of welfare reform, violence against women is not seen by many political leaders as a priority. Nor is it seen as integral to other community concerns.[56]

In Massachusetts, where at least 40 percent of female homicides are killings by current or former intimate partners, the homicide rate for non-Hispanic black women is eight times the rate for non-Hispanic white women. For Asian women, the rate is four times higher than for white women; for Hispanic women, the homicide rate is over three times higher than for white women. The official report of the Massachusetts data makes it clear that domestic homicides are highly concentrated in poor urban areas.[57]

Researchers attempting to make sense of these rates of homicide emphasize different social dimensions of race. Robert J. Sampson and William Julius Wilson emphasize the concentration of poverty in urban black communities.[58] Darnell F. Hawkins identifies ideological barriers to intervention in black communities, including the historical devaluation of black life in the United States, racist stereotypes of African Americans as somehow inherently violent, and racially discriminatory treatment of black communities by the criminal justice system.[59] Evan Stark states the problem is not "race" but racism.[60] In any case, the evidence on battering and on homicide, incomplete and flawed as it is, conflicts with the idea that all women are at equal risk for intimate violence.

All forms of violence against women do not follow the same pattern. Wife rape remains one kind of violence that apparently transcends class patterns entirely. In her random sample of women in San Francisco, Diana E. H. Russell gathered data on the prevalence of both wife rape and wife beating. Russell found class differences in wife beating consistent with those described above; lower-class women were substantially overrepresented among those reporting battering. However, this pattern was strikingly *absent* among women reporting wife rape: neither income, occupation, education, race, nor ethnicity was strongly related to the occurrence of wife rape. Commenting on these findings, Russell concludes, "It appears that wife rape, and possibly by implication other forms of rape by intimates as well, may be more evenly distributed in the population than other crimes of violence."[61]

The evidence to date on battering and femicide, however, reveals significant class patterns in women's victimization. As the research cited above demonstrates, this pattern is found in government studies and in independent research, in studies conducted by scholars of color and in research by white scholars, and in research done by feminists and by individuals who do not so identify. As researchers, activists, and citizens, we need to find new ways to talk about class, racism, and violence that names their interconnections without making these divisions worse. Patricia Hill Collins suggests a "both/and" way of framing race, class, and gender interconnections as an alternative to more simplistic "either/or" dichotomies.[62] Following her example, it may be useful to say that it is *both* true that battering can be found in virtually every community *and* that there are social circumstances—such as poverty and racism—that make it difficult for women to effectively resist or escape violence.

Political Moves: The Neglect of Class and Race in the Literature on Battering

Just how much attention has been given to class and race in the research on battering? According to two major databases in the social sciences, very little.

SocioFILE is a computer database containing abstracts of articles in over 2,000 journals in the social sciences. Over the 23 years from 1974 through 1996, which marks the rise of battering as a public problem, SocioFILE lists over 1,000 articles containing either *battered women* or *domestic violence* in their titles or abstracts. Of these articles, 42 articles mention *class*, and 49 articles mention *race* in either their titles or abstracts (4.0 percent and 4.7 percent of the 1,038 articles, respectively). This means that over 90 percent of the articles on battering in this database do not even mention race or class in the descriptions of their studies. Race and class are apparently marginal issues in the sociological literature on battering, at least in this large database.

The major database for the psychological literature reveals a similar pattern. PsycLIT contains abstracts from over 1,300 journals. From 1974 through 1996, 672 articles in psychologically oriented journals mention *battered women* or *domestic violence* in either their titles or abstracts. Of these, 13 mention *class* (1.9 percent), and 19 articles mention *race* (2.8 percent). Thus, the psychological literature on battering also appears to exclude race and class from its main focus.

Even those articles that name class or race are not necessarily research studies: they may be theoretical papers, reviews, or commentary. These patterns of exclusion can be described by the five types of political moves that researchers seem to make.

Ignoring Class, Race, Poverty, and Racism Altogether

Ignoring class and race appears to be the dominant political move and one that I made in a previously published study. Angela

Moore criticized Kersti Yllö and Michele Bograd's edited volume, *Feminist Perspectives on Wife Abuse*, for giving "little consideration . . . to the differential distribution of violence by race, class, and economic status."[63] I was a contributor to this book, and I agree with Moore's criticism. This collection, which I still think is important, unfortunately does not give the reader much understanding of how poverty and racism affect violence against women. Moore concludes that "to disregard the impact of socioeconomic status decontextualizes intimate violence."[64] Only recently have studies been published on domestic violence in the lives of women on welfare.

Studies of race or ethnicity have been conducted even less frequently than those that address class. One review of the literature between 1977 and 1987 found only 13 publications on battering that referred to black women and men.[65] In a 1997 review, Etiony Aldarondo and his colleagues found only 17 studies of wife assault that included significant numbers of women of color. Aldarondo describes this state of affairs as "shameful."[66]

Discussing Class or Race but Only at the Margins of the Investigation

Where researchers address race, they do so often in the context of racial differences or individual characteristics, without much acknowledgment of racism as a political process that divides communities. Similarly, class is present in surrogate form as socioeconomic status, occupation, or education, which do not entirely capture class divisions in the United States.

Addressing Race but Ignoring Class

When researchers study race separately from class, their research findings become difficult to interpret. What do the statistics on femicide in New York City mean without a sense of a class context? How exactly does skin color so severely mark risk for domestic homicide? To say that race delimits life chances in the United States does not mean that racial groups are monolithic: indeed, reducing a whole category of people to a single characteristic is the logic of racism. Sampson and Wilson note that black homicide in San Francisco is triple the rate of black homicide in Baltimore—to emphasize that "racial differences" in victimization cannot be understood apart from economic and other structural circumstances.[67]

Addressing Class but Ignoring Race

Some research studies of battering emphasize class but fail to discuss race. But the role that racism plays in creating black and Hispanic poverty is relevant to battering. The issue is not just that African Americans are "overrepresented" among the poor, which in any case is highly exaggerated in the public mind.[68] Rather, in many urban areas, black and white poverty represent distinct kinds of isolation and disempowerment. According to Robert J. Sampson and William Julius Wilson, 70 percent of poor white New Yorkers live in *nonpoverty neighborhoods*—that is, they live in economically mixed communities, alongside work-ing-class and middle-class people. In contrast, 70 percent of poor black New Yorkers live in *poverty neighborhoods.*[69] Poverty among African Americans is heavily concentrated, and this has implications for isolation from political power, health care, jobs, and community resources.[70] It is not difficult to suppose that all of these dimensions of isolation may contribute to the entrap-ment of battered women. In every community, women develop strategies to resist or escape their abusers. But when hospitals close in politically marginalized communities, this complicates women's efforts to seek help. When white racism limits the neighborhoods that people of color can live in, women's options to leave are narrowed. When businesses close and jobs leave poor communities of color, women lose economic opportunities that could help them gain independence. To treat class but not race is to ignore the effects of racial segregation on women's lives.

Furthermore, the effects of racism are not simply a function of class position. Racial discrimination against African Americans extends across the class structure. African American philosopher and social critic Cornell West reports that in his first 10 days at Princeton University, he was stopped by police three times for "driving too slowly."[71] This phenomenon has been so widely re-ported by African American men of all classes that the alleged offense has been called DWB—Driving While Black. This, too, has repercussions for abused women of color, who must consider whether to trust the police in communities that have a history of racist police practices.

*Moving Class, Race, Poverty, and Racism from the Margins
to the Center of the Investigation*

This is the least common move among researchers. I am aware of only three books consisting of research on race and battering in the United States. Two are collections edited by Robert L. Hampton—*Violence in the Black Family: Correlates and Consequences* (1987) and *Black Family Violence: Current Research and Theory* (1991).[72] The third is the recent study by Beth Richie, *Compelled to Crime: The Gender Entrapment of Battered Black Women* (1996).[73] In a variety of ways, each of these books argues that carefully conducted research on race and class is essential to social action against violence.

Research on battering and social inequalities must also involve "studying up," to use Laura Nader's phrase.[74] While there has been sensationalized media coverage of celebrity batterers, oddly little research on battering has been conducted among the economically privileged. For instance, investigative reporter Seymour Hersh recently stated that President Richard Nixon beat his wife, Pat Nixon. "There was a serious empirical basis for believing [Nixon] was a wife beater, and had done so—at least hospitalized her a number of times," Hersh said.[75] If the Pulitzer Prize–winning journalist has his facts correct, his account raises questions about the class-specific dimensions of battering. What are the costs of speaking out about abuse for economically privileged women? What resources do abusive men use against women at this class level? What are the social arrangements that support and conceal this kind of violence in elite circles? And what relationships exist between the private violence and the public politics of abusive men? Research on battering has ignored these dimensions of class entitlement.

Explaining Political Moves: Why Has the Research Literature Neglected Class and Race?

What accounts for the political moves of researchers? Based on the writings of those few who have addressed these issues and on discussions with researchers and activists, I offer the following speculations.

Concern with the Class Myth

The class myth is driven, in part, by powerful racist images of men of color, especially African American men and Latinos, as violent. Challenging the class myth may be one way to challenge racist beliefs, but it has perpetuated the invisibility of the experiences of poor women and women of color. There is also the question whether silence on class and race is sufficient to counter bigotry. In their important study of racial politics, Michael Omi and Howard Winant insist that "opposing racism requires that we notice race, not ignore it."[76]

Concern with the Gendered Dimensions of Violence Against Women

Over a quarter of a century after the "second wave" of feminism arose in the United States, the terrain of gender politics remains highly charged. Because of the continuing resistance to feminist perspectives on violence against women—indeed, at a time that some feminists have characterized as one of "backlash" against women—a focus on the gendered dimensions of battering may be displacing attention to issues of class and race. The problem here is that in a multiply divided society no political move is pure and that moves inspired by attention to gender will inevitably have consequences for economic class and racial politics. Feminists of color have for many years raised questions about prioritizing one form of oppression over others. Johnnetta B. Cole warns against "the tendency to 'level oppressions,'" by which she means suggesting "that all women are equally oppressed."[77] Cole cautions that *failing* to recognize differences poses its own barriers to working toward common goals.

Fear That Research on Race and Class Will Be Misused by Bigots

Political campaigns highlighting issues of "crime" have historically drawn on images of vulnerable (white) women for demagogic effect. In 1964 Barry Goldwater raised the issue of crime in his unsuccessful presidential campaign by claiming, "Our wives, all women, feel unsafe on our streets."[78] In recent years, some politicians have deliberately perpetuated racist notions that men of color are somehow inherently or uniquely violent and pose tremendous danger to white women. During the 1988 presidential campaign, the image of William Horton—dubbed "Willie" by white political commentators—became omnipresent in the media.[79] Horton is an African American who was convicted of kidnapping, assault, and rape against a white couple after failing to return from a weekend furlough while serving a sentence in Massachusetts for murder. In an effort to associate Massachusetts Governor Michael Dukakis with the crimes that Horton committed while on furlough, the campaign manager for George Bush stated he would make Willie Horton's name a household word. Campaign commercials featured the Horton case and portrayed Dukakis as "soft on crime." This racialized image of violent crime had a long afterlife: between 1988 and early 1993, there were 148 references to Horton in the *Congressional Record*.[80]

This cynical exploitation of white racism no doubt continues to affect public discussions of criminal justice, paralyzing serious attention to class, race, and criminal victimization.[81] Yet again, paralysis by researchers offers no antidote to such demagoguery. In a study of race and crime, Gary LaFree states that

while criminologists have largely ignored connections between race and crime during the past three decades, the involvement of African Americans in the legal system has reached crisis proportions. The story of Willie Horton clearly illustrates how racial stereotypes operate in the absence of more objective analysis.[82]

Belief That Studies of "Classless" or "Raceless" Violence Mobilize White Professionals and Communities Against Battering

This rationale might be expressed by the common saying, "a rising tide lifts all boats." In a fiercely divided society, it may be that many research projects address battering in broad, even "classless" terms in order to arouse the attention of policymakers, media gatekeepers, medical and mental health professionals, and other researchers—groups that are predominantly white. Kimberlé Williams Crenshaw observes:

There is . . . a thin line between debunking the stereotypical beliefs that only poor or minority women are battered, and pushing them aside to focus on victims for whom mainstream politicians and media are more likely to express concern.[83]

The logic here may be that if battering is addressed seriously by white elites, this will help mobilize white middle-class communities and that the effects will eventually be felt in communities of color and the poor. But a "rising tide" may not lift all boats. Recent policy changes involving welfare and criminal justice are profoundly affecting African American women and men in ways that have direct relevance to battering, as is discussed below.

Insufficient Life Experience or Training in Issues of Class and Race

The overwhelming majority of sociologists and psychologists are non-Hispanic whites.[84] I mentioned at the beginning of this chapter how my own background in virtually all-white communities near Milwaukee impairs my understanding of racial oppression; this could be termed "insufficient life experience." And indeed, scholars and activists of color have been prominent among those willing to address class, race, and battering. But surely it is possible for white researchers to learn how to study these matters responsibly.

Many additional explanations can probably be found for the marginalization of class and race in the literature on battering. Researchers and research funders may simply wish to avoid controversy. Perhaps they don't see how class and race are relevant to their topics. White racism and condescending attitudes toward poor and working-class people may be involved. The relative absence of women and men of color, poor people, and working-class people in the academy also affects the selection of research topics. Finally, politically marginalized academics and practitioners may lack support for their research.

Woman Battering and the Politics of Welfare

If the past twenty-five years have seen a huge increase in research on battering, this period also witnessed a transformation of urban poverty in the United States. During the 1970s, racial segregation in housing and the relocation of manufacturing out of the inner cities of the Northeast and the Midwest concentrated poverty in new ways in African American and Puerto Rican neighborhoods.[85] For example, in the New York metropolitan area between 1970 and 1980, the rate of poverty among African Americans rose from 21 percent to 30 percent. In the Chicago metropolitan area, the rate of poverty among African Americans rose from 20 percent to 28 percent. During this period, the social contract between the state and the poor was rewritten, the most visible symbol of which is the welfare "reform" bill signed into law by President Bill Clinton in 1996. White racism has played a historic role in undermining antipoverty programs in the United States.[86] Recent research indicates that white opposition to welfare is rooted in strong negative beliefs about black welfare mothers.[87]

Some of the politicians who have been most fervent about repealing welfare have at the same time tried to position themselves as "getting tough" on domestic violence. But as Angela Browne asks at the outset of the chapter, how can one ignore or promote poverty and stop violence at the same time? The disconnection of battering from its social context is essential for such contradictory political stances to be sustained.

Ruth Brandwein investigated the relationship between battering and welfare assistance in a study of 3,000 women in Salt Lake City.[88] Brandwein found two patterns to welfare use by abused women. A sizable number of women first received welfare within a year *after* a report of domestic violence. Brandwein speculates that these women may have left their abusers and thus needed temporary assistance to survive without them. A second pattern involved women who received welfare within a year *before* calling the police. Brandwein reasons that seeking welfare may have been a move toward independence for these women, which may have caused their partners to retaliate with violence. This interpretation is consistent with studies indicating that leaving or even attempting to leave relationships places women at risk.[89] Both patterns suggest that welfare offers a way out of abusive relationships. And yet, due in part to limited research on these interconnections and to lack of visibility of the issue of battering in political debates over welfare "reform," the economic resources available to abused women have been diminished with the passage of the new restrictions.[90]

Woman Battering and the Politics of Criminal Justice

Over the past twenty-five years, feminist organizing has led to dramatic changes in criminal justice responses to battering. Civil restraining orders are now available in every state, new laws have been passed to give police greater powers of arrest, and "gender-bias" studies of the courts have been conducted in many states to address, among other things, judicial mistreatment of abused women. But during this same period of time, other sweeping changes in criminal justice are posing dilemmas for abused women who are marginalized by poverty and racism.

Between 1980 and 1995, the overall prison population in the United States more than tripled,[91] and during this time the race of those admitted to state and federal prisons has gone from majority white to majority black.[92] This increase in incarceration, and its racial dimensions, have not been caused by an increase in violent crime generally or in crime by African Americans in particular. Victimization rates over this period have been more or less flat.[93] Instead, this sharp rise in imprisonment has been the result of changes in law enforcement practices and sentencing "reform," especially concerning drugs. The "war on drugs," launched by the Reagan administration at a time when drug use was in general decline, severely increased the penalties for drug use and drug sales. Even though drug abuse rates are not dramatically different between white and black Americans, the "war on drugs" has been conducted most aggressively against black communities. In a recent study of these policies, Michael Tonry states:

Urban black Americans have borne the brunt of the War on Drugs. They have been arrested, prosecuted, convicted, and imprisoned at increasing rates since the early 1980s, and grossly out of proportion to their numbers in the general population or among drug users. By every standard, the war has been harder on blacks than on whites; that this was predictable makes it no less regrettable.[94]

According to a report by the National Criminal Justice Commission, this misguided effort at crime control has damaged the economic futures of a large proportion of men and women, hurt the economic health of communities of color, undermined the credibility of criminal justice institutions in black and Hispanic neighborhoods, and needlessly socialized large numbers of young men within the violent world of prisons.[95] Tonry believes the policymakers responsible for this failed effort at crime control "should be held morally responsible for the havoc they have wrought among disadvantaged members of minority groups."[96] In fact, Tonry recommends that crime-control policies should be subject to "racial impact" reviews, much as is done in the case of educational policies, housing ordinances, and employment practices.[97]

What are the consequences of this "get tough on crime" approach for battered women of color? After all, the criminal justice system conducting the "war on crime" is the same system that many battered women turn to for assistance. Feminists of color contend that hostile and racially discriminatory police practices undermine domestic violence strategies.[98] At the end of a decade that has seen riots over police brutality in Los Angeles and Miami and reports that police officers beat and raped a Haitian man in New York City, it is evident that policing remains a site of political conflict in communities of color. Recently a New York Congressman spoke about a dual system of policing:

There are two systems of policing. . . . One follows the book and probably is second to none in the world when it comes to the majority white community. But you have a separate system in the minority community where the policemen . . . ignore the procedures they are supposed to uphold. . . . The white power structure, the white community, is not upset enough about it.[99]

It is worth noting that the immediate impact of the "war on drugs" on women of color has been especially severe. Between 1986 and 1991, the number of African American women in prison for drug crimes increased 828 percent. This is twice the rate of increase for African American men and three times the rate of increase for white women.[100] And abuse is prominent in the lives of many of the women in prisons and jails: Beth Richie reports that at least half the women behind bars at Riker's Island in New York City have been battered.[101] A recent report on crime policies describes this tension between aggressive prosecution of drug crimes and police unresponsiveness toward victimization by violence:

Many minority communities in America feel both *overpoliced* and *underprotected*—overpoliced because of the massive intervention of law enforcement in the inner city to fight the war on drugs, and underprotected because the drug trade flourishes with the same vitality as before, and because police are often slow to respond to 911 calls from minority neighborhoods.[102]

Politically driven changes in criminal justice, then, are being made in multiple directions, not all of which may help to stop violence against women. Awareness of the city's own history of racial conflict over police practices has led Boston's battered women's shelters to caution against mandatory arrest policies for domestic violence.

Summary

Research on battering is political, even when researchers seek to avoid controversy entirely. Because the gender politics of the literature of woman battering has been well documented, my concern here is to highlight the costs of a treatment of battering that largely ignores class and race, at a time when social divisions seem to be deepening. Addressing the interconnections among gender, class, and racial politics is the promise of feminist theory and social action. My argument calls for research on battering that moves the experiences of the most economically and politically marginalized women to the center of the analysis. Class is important because class position has a significant bearing on women's vulnerability to battering and femicide. Race is important because racism creates poverty and poses unique barriers to women's help-seeking. Race is also important because racial politics has been a powerful force in the dramatic changes in welfare assistance and criminal justice policies, changes that may make it even more difficult for women to resist and escape violence. It is the case *both* that battering is a core threat to women's freedom and health generally in the United States *and* that poverty and racism increase women's vulnerability to violence.

Angela Browne argues that "we cannot ignore or promote poverty among our citizens and reduce violence at the same time."[103] It must also be clear that we cannot ignore or promote racism among our citizens and reduce violence at the same time.

A social problem does not exist for a society unless it is recognized by that society to exist. . . . Social conditions may be ignored at one time yet, without change in their makeup, become matters of grave concern at another time.

HERBERT BLUMER[1]

3

The Reconstruction of a Public Problem:
Judicial Responses to Woman Battering
in Massachusetts

American attempts to criminalize violence against wives go back as far as the seventeenth century in Massachusetts Bay Colony. Since then, public action against what is now called *woman battering* has gone through a number of cycles of appearance, disappearance, and reappearance. Seen in this context, recent efforts by feminists to alter state responses to battering are part of a long political struggle over the right of husbands to use violence and the right of wives to be free of it.

Sociologist Herbert Blumer argues above that social problems go through periods of rise and decline in the public eye. The rise and fall of *public attention* to a problem, such as woman battering, often has little to do with changes in the occurrence of the problem itself. In a way, Blumer's perspective reframes the familiar question, "If a tree falls in the forest, but no one hears it, does it make a sound?" To Blumer, the question is: If widespread human suffering is taking place, but no one is talking about it publicly, no one is organizing around it, newspapers and legislatures are silent about it, and the affected individuals are unaware of how common their experiences are, then is it a social problem? Blumer's answer is no. Such a problem may have social roots, but his meaning of a social problem is concerned with public action in response to the problem. A social problem is in a sense created, then, when private or previously hidden forms of suffering, such as woman battering, are brought to public attention. For Blumer, the rise of a public problem is a dynamic and ever-conflicted process of definition and redefinition that values subjective perceptions of a problem more than its objective reality. Do the courts fail to protect battered women because a few judges are "bad apples" or because of a deeper patriarchal bias in the judiciary? More than anything else, how the problem is defined influences what will be done about it.

Blumer's perspective on the creation and waning of public attention to problems gives rise to a series of questions concerning judges and woman battering. First, what is the history of woman battering as a public problem? This history is reviewed briefly, with particular attention to demands for state responses to violence against wives. Next, how did the "judicial harassment of battered women" become a public problem in Massachusetts? This issue is examined as it was reported on in the *Boston Globe*, with a focus on the conflict and accommodation between feminist activists and the state. And finally, what lessons for social change can be drawn from this public furor over judicial responses to battering?

Historic Efforts to Alter State Responses to Battering

According to Elizabeth Pleck, at three periods in U.S. history significant attempts were made to change laws regarding violence against women in families. Massachusetts was an important site of reform in each case. The first occurred in the seventeenth century: "From 1640 to 1680, the Puritans of colonial Massachusetts enacted the first laws anywhere in the world against wife beating."[2] In 1641 the Massachusetts Bay Colony passed a law that stated the following:

Everie marryed woeman shall be free from bodilie correction or stripes by her husband, unless it be in his owne defence upon her assault.[3]

The prohibition of "bodilie correction or *stripes*" meant that blows such as those inflicted with a whip were forbidden against wives. Pleck notes that the inspiration for this new law "had nothing to do with the prevalence of domestic violence."[4] Businessmen living in the colony demanded a written constitution to protect their liberties in relation to the British crown, and this law, reflecting the religious principles of its Puritan author, was part of the new legal code. In fact, there is evidence of resistance to the gendered nature of this newly codified "right." Pleck notes that "a few years later the law was amended to prohibit husband beating as well."[5] While the law was rarely enforced, records from Plymouth County suggest that wife beating was brought before the courts more often in the 1660s and 1670s than it was in the first half of the eighteenth century. According to Pleck, the religious morality behind the law gave way to state tolerance and indifference toward wife beating as the community grew more pluralistic.[6]

The second period of legal reform occurred in the nineteenth century. Over the course of that century, state appellate courts issued contradictory rulings on a husband's right of "moderate chastisement" of his wife. The courts in Mississippi supported this right; courts in five states, including Massachusetts, denounced wife beating; and the North Carolina Supreme Court issued rulings that went in both directions. A number of states passed statutes prohibiting wife beating, and some provided for the whipping of batterers as a penalty. Still, Pleck notes that "wife beating, even if a criminal offense, was nonetheless considered appropriate behavior for nineteenth-century American husbands."[7] And when police records are examined to determine who was arrested for wife beating, class and racial patterns appear. Police records in Pennsylvania list mostly immigrant men from Germany, Ireland, England, Hungary, and Italy; records from Charleston, South Carolina, identify black men almost exclusively.[8] Police were apparently unwilling to arrest nonimmigrant white men.

As early as the 1850s Susan B. Anthony and Elizabeth Cady Stanton were campaigning against wife beating and arguing that women "should have the right to divorce their husbands on the grounds of cruelty or habitual drunkenness."[9] Linda Gordon notes that while wife beating played an important role in women's political organizing in the nineteenth century, "it was addressed primarily indirectly, through temperance, child-welfare, and social purity campaigns."[10] Nonetheless, Elizabeth Pleck found that between 1868 and 1896 there was feminist organizing on behalf of battered women in rural Texas and San Diego. In Chicago during this time, feminists offered legal aid to women and children victimized by incest and rape and demanded that laws be changed to make the punishments for such crimes more severe.[11]

Boston was an important site of both black and white women's political organizing against violence during the late 1800s. Black women focused on different dimensions of violence against women. African American leaders within the women's rights movement, including Ida Wells-Barnett, Frances Ellen Harper, and Frederick Douglass, came to distrust white feminists, Anthony and Stanton in particular, because of their racist appeals for white women's suffrage.[12] The women's club movement among African American women agitated against the terrors of lynching and of the rape of black women by white men. The first national conference of black women's clubs took place in Boston in 1895. In the 1890s the African American journalist and author Ida Wells-Barnett published pamphlets analyzing lynching and rape in the context of race, gender, and economic oppression. She challenged white feminists to see the lie behind the justifications of lynching as a means of protecting white womanhood from black men.[13]

The most striking historical parallels to the present involve white feminist Lucy Stone. In Boston in 1876, Stone began publishing a weekly listing of "crimes against women" in the *Wom-*

an's Journal, which she coedited with her husband, the
abolitionist Henry Blackwell. This column detailed national and
local news accounts of wife murder, wife beating, rape, and incest. The following commentary by Stone appeared on June 16,
1877:

CRIMES AGAINST WOMEN
The frequency with which the most revolting crimes are committed
against women is appalling. Still more appalling is the fact that the punishment for this class of crimes is light in the extreme, and that, among
those who make and execute the laws, there is no moral sense which
takes cognizance of their real atrocity. . . .
    It remains for women to correct the public sense, in regard to this
crime against their sex. . . . Women who are neither judges nor even
jurors in such cases, or any other women who are denied all right to help
make or execute the laws, can yet create a public sentiment that will go
far to support justice, and to punish crime as it deserves. . . .
    The instances here reported, are only a few of many similar ones
which crowd our daily papers, and which show the need of a redeemed
public sentiment in regard to this great crime.[14]

Stone justified this listing by pointing to an increase of such
crimes in newspaper reports.[15] She drew inspiration from English
suffragist Frances Power Cobbe. In 1878 Cobbe published an article entitled "Wife Torture in England" that called for an end to
the legal encouragement given to violent husbands. At that time,
English common law gave a man the right "to give his wife moderate correction . . . by domestic chastisement," the same right
that men had over their children and apprentices.[16] Following
Cobbe's lead, in 1879 Lucy Stone circulated a petition in Massachusetts, urging new legal protections for abused wives:

PROTECTION OF WIVES
*To the Senate and House of Representatives of the State of Massachu-
setts;*
    The undersigned, citizens of Massachusetts, respectfully represent;
    That the laws at present do not give adequate protection to wives,
especially among the poorer classes, against aggravated assaults and cruelty of their husbands. Your petitioners therefore pray that you will provide by statute, that whenever a husband is convicted by any Court of
an aggravated assault upon his wife, the Court, on her application, shall
have power to authorize her to live separate from her husband, and to
enjoin him not to visit her without her consent, and to give her the custody of any of her minor children, and to order him to pay to the Court,

or the Overseers of the poor, such weekly sum as may be reasonable for the support of her and of her minor children; or that you will pass such other act as may better protect wives from personal injury.[17]

The petition proposed, in other words, legislation containing three key elements: it would have enabled women to apply to the local court for legal separation, legal custody of their children, and an order requiring child support and spousal support payments by the abusive husband. This legislation was introduced in Massachusetts in 1879, 1883, and 1891, suffering defeat all three times.[18] All these elements of relief are currently available through restraining orders in Massachusetts and other states.

Although Stone's bill failed, before the end of the century some of the laws that feminists campaigned against were changed. By the end of the 1870s, the "privilege" of woman battering no longer found legitimation in the written law of most states.[19] But the legacy of men's entitlement did not end there. Although it has been formally illegal since the 1870s, battering was not seriously prosecuted as a crime until the 1970s.[20]

What happened to this activism around "crimes against women"? Elizabeth Pleck observes that Stanton and Anthony began to deemphasize these issues after 1870. Their protests against violence had been a means to argue for temperance and women's right to divorce, which they saw as larger issues. Already criticized for their attacks on marriage, they gradually decreased the attention they gave to issues of violence to avoid alienating further support for their main concerns. Lucy Stone, who actually opposed divorce, saw the failures of male legislators to pass protective legislation as evidence of the need for women's suffrage; after the 1891 defeat she made no further attempts to initiate legislation. By the end of the century, as the movement for women's suffrage grew stronger, attention to battering, rape, and incest diminished. These came to be viewed as controversial issues that could undermine this momentum.[21]

The complexity of this period of women's history defies brief summary. Organizing around women's rights continued among white women and African American women. It did not stop entirely with the ratification of the Nineteenth Amendment in 1920, which gave women the right to vote.[22] But after the 1890s, activism around "crimes against women" left the public stage. Pleck concludes:

Only after another eighty years would feminists renew their sisterhood with victims of crimes against women, to refute once again popular stereotypes and to challenge the conspiracy of silence.[23]

The 1970s: Institutional Collusion by the Police and the Courts

The third period of legal reform began in the early 1970s. At that point, there were few shelters for battered women in the United States. Then in 1973 Rainbow Retreat began housing women in Phoenix, Arizona, and in 1974 Haven House opened in Pasadena, California. By 1978, the U.S. Commission on Civil Rights identified over 300 shelters, hotlines, and legal advocacy projects in the country.[24] By 1989, there were 1,200 shelters, safe-home networks, or battered women's projects in the United States, offering refuge to 300,000 women and children a year.[25] In communities across the country, shelters became symbols that women were not safe in their own homes and that the idea of the family household as a haven in a heartless world misrepresented many women's experiences.

From the immediate work of aiding women and children fleeing violent men, battered women and other feminist activists soon turned their attention to changing the institutions that colluded with violent men.[26] Notable among these institutions was the criminal justice system.

Police responses in the 1970s were characterized by indifference to women's terror and fear. Women's calls to the police were assigned low priority. There are accounts of police ignoring such calls or delaying their responses to women's pleas for help. When police officers did show up at the homes of women seeking protection, frequently the police would do little other than sending a man away to "cool off" and perhaps take a walk around the block. Arrests were rarely made.[27] In fact, some police training materials explicitly stated that officers should avoid arresting batterers. The 1975 training bulletin of the Oakland, California, Police Department offered the following instructions:

Normally, officers should adhere to the policy that arrests shall be avoided . . . but when one of the parties demands arrest, you should attempt to explain the ramifications of such action (e.g, loss of wages, bail procedures, court appearances) and encourage the parties to reason with each other.[28]

Women of color often received worse treatment from the police than working-class and professional- and managerial-class white women. It was not until lawsuits were filed and won against police departments and courts in California and New York that both the law and its enforcement began to change significantly. In 1976 a class-action suit was filed in Oakland on behalf of "women in general and black women in particular," naming five black women as plaintiffs. The suit charged that the police ignored their calls for help, responded in a threatening manner, and failed in their legal duties to uphold the law that indicated that arrest was warranted. This lawsuit argued that black women received inferior treatment compared to white women, in violation of the equal protection clause of the Fourteenth Amendment. The Oakland Police Department agreed to a settlement three years later that included changes in policy on emergency calls and arrests of batterers.[29]

In New York in 1976, a class-action suit was filed against the New York City Police Department and the New York Family Court. The suit alleged that the police failed to make arrests of battering husbands and that court personnel refused women access to the court. In a decision ruling against dismissal of this lawsuit, a New York judge acknowledged the contradiction between the written law and the law in practice this case revealed:

Anglo-American laws treated a man's physical abuse of his wife as different from any other assault and, indeed as an acceptable practice. If the allegations of the instant complaint—buttressed by hundreds of pages of affidavits—are true, only the written law has changed; in reality, wife beating is still condoned, if not approved, by some of those charged with protecting its victims.[30]

An agreement was reached in this case in which the police department promised substantial changes in its policy concerning responding to calls, arresting batterers, and informing women of their rights to obtain orders of protection from the family court.[31] Until the end of the 1970s, then, the pattern of responses from institutions of criminal justice was one in which women's complaints of abuse were trivialized and ridiculed, women's injuries were ignored, women's terror and fear were invalidated, and women were blamed by the police and the courts for the violence they suffered. Racial and class discrimination against women was part of this pattern of responses.

Since the end of the 1970s, there have been significant institutional responses to the needs of abused women, ranging from local community projects to new state legislation to federal government policy guidelines. Hundreds of shelters and safe-home networks have been created. At the initiative of feminist activists, shelter workers, community groups, and legal services attorneys, new state legislation was passed across the nation in the late 1970s and early 1980s that offered both civil and criminal remedies to abused women.[32]

One of the legal remedies created for abused women during this period was the domestic violence restraining order. In 1976 Pennsylvania became the first state to pass legislation authorizing judges to issue such orders, which are also called *orders of protection*.[33] And in 1978—99 years after Lucy Stone's first attempt—the Massachusetts legislature passed a law offering new civil and criminal remedies to victims of intimate violence.

The initiative for the new legislation in Massachusetts came from the Battered Women's Action Committee (BWAC), a group of grassroots activists. According to one member of this group, Katherine Triantafillou, this group of women understood that no law could ever eradicate the problem in itself.[34] Seeking to force the process of social change in a range of institutions that were colluding with violent men, the BWAC wrote a piece of legislation designed to publicly name the problem of woman abuse and use the authority of the law to direct a major educational campaign in the Commonwealth. They also sought to design temporary remedies that would immediately stop the assaults and enable women to make a transition toward autonomy. In a recent interview, Triantafillou said she had not been aware of Stone's attempts to introduce similar legislation in Massachusetts in the late 1800s.[35] Like so much of women's history, it had been invisible prior to recent feminist scholarship.

The Abuse Prevention Act offered new civil and criminal remedies for victims of domestic violence and mandated changes in traditional police and court responses to abused women. Offering women a legal instrument that was free and immediately accessible, the law placed new responsibilities on the courts and police. The Act addressed physical violence, psychological battering, and also forced sexual relations at a time when most states still exempted husbands from accusations of rape by their wives.[36] By including the term *household member,* the law additionally made protection available to individuals in lesbian and gay relationships.

Under the Abuse Prevention Act, family members and household members, including former partners and former cohabitants, are entitled to obtain relief. This was amended in 1991 to extend to individuals in present or past dating relationships. Six basic kinds of orders can be sought under the law, at the discretion of the complaining party:

- *Refrain from abuse order* This directs the defendant not to harm or threaten the complainant.

- *No contact order* The defendant can be ordered to stop contact with the complainant and, if requested, with the complainant's children unless authorized by the court. Contact can be specified on the order to include phone calls, letters, and messages through third parties. The defendant can be further prohibited from coming near the workplace of the complainant.

- *Vacate order* The defendant can be ordered to move out of the residence and remain away from it.

- *Temporary custody order* For children under the age of 18 years, the party seeking the order can obtain temporary custody, so long as this is not already being sought through family court.

- *Temporary support order* If a legal obligation to support the children exists, the defendant can be ordered to pay temporary child support. Temporary spousal support is also a right under this law, if a legal obligation exists.

- *Restitution order* Where the complainant has suffered losses as a result of the abuse, such as injuries requiring hospital costs or damaged property, the defendant can be ordered to pay compensation for these losses.

Katherine Triantafillou, one of the authors of the legislation, observed that after an initially supportive response to the new law in 1978, there followed a period of "institutional lethargy" in its application until feminist challenges to the state's response arose again in the mid-1980s.[37]

1986: "Judicial Harassment of Battered Women" as a Public Problem

Over the past two decades, the problem of battering has gone through two closely related cycles of public attention in Massachusetts. The responsiveness of the courts has been central to both episodes. This dynamic process of problem reconstruction can be observed in the pages of the *Boston Globe*, an important forum where battering has been discussed as a public problem. Even more, the *Globe* has used its authority to define the problem. Figure 3.1 presents the number of *Globe* articles mentioning woman battering or domestic violence from 1979 to 1996. The two most dramatic increases in news coverage took place in 1986 and 1992. Each of these increases coincides with a shift in how the problem was defined. I first examine the dominant definition that the *Boston Globe* focused on in 1986—the "judicial harassment of battered women"—and then turn to the *Globe's* focus in 1992.

For those familiar with the glacial speed of change in the judiciary, 1986 was more like an avalanche. Beginning in August of 1986, the problem of judicial mistreatment of battered women was so vividly publicized in the *Boston Globe* that the Massachusetts lower criminal courts were forced to take dramatic and unprecedented actions. Within four months from the *Globe's* first story on judicial misconduct, the crisis of public trust in the Massachusetts courts had become so serious that two judges withdrew from hearing domestic violence cases, a third judge was stripped of most of his authority, the state Judicial Conduct Commission began new investigations, separate inquiries were initiated in two courts, and the state's highest court appointed a commission to study gender bias in the court system as a whole.

Three main categories of actors were engaged in the creation of this public problem: feminist activists, the state, and the *Boston*

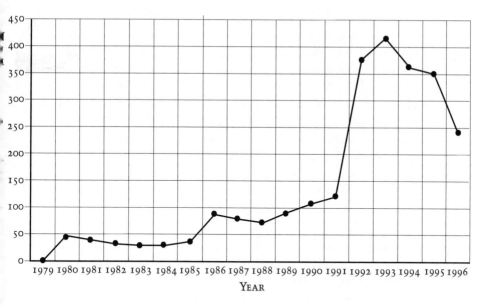

Figure 3.1

The Rise and Fall of Boston Globe *Coverage of Battering*

Source: *Boston Globe* Archives, Boston Globe Electronic Publishing, Inc., 1997.

Globe. The feminist activists were advocates for battered women who worked in shelters or other domestic violence projects. The "state" includes the judiciary, the governor's office, and the legislature in Massachusetts, as well as other local politicians. The *Globe* represents one of the key public arenas in which this problem reconstruction took place and one of the key institutional players, and feminist insights into battering were apparent among its journalists. Moreover, feminists were also part of the state itself: advocates served in the Women's Legislative Caucus and on the Battered Women's Working Group, a subcommittee under the governor's office.

The public events of 1986 in Massachusetts actually had their origins in the previous year. The initial documentation of judicial misconduct was done in a 1985 report prepared by the Battered Women's Working Group. This body, a committee of the Governor's Anti-Crime Council, developed an imaginative study of the law in practice concerning restraining orders. The Working

Group, made up of representatives of battered women's shelters, feminist attorneys, legal services representatives, police officers, and other service providers, set up a phone line at the State House to record calls presenting evidence of mistreatment of women seeking judicial protection from abuse under the state law. The study design called for each complaint to be witnessed by either a shelter worker, a legal advocate, or an attorney. Within six months, 250 incidents from around the state had been compiled.

The study documented "widespread patterns of noncompliance" with the law on the part of the police, court clerks, and judges.[38] The following documentation from the study illustrates the nature of the complaints:

Case #0063: Woman went to district court for temporary restraining, vacate, and custody orders against her abusive boyfriend. Judge would not grant custody; he told her, "most people get married and do not have illegitimate children. These things don't happen to them."

Case #0040: When a woman was called to the bench after requesting a restraining and vacate order the judge asked her:
   Does your husband drink?
   Does he gamble?
   Does he run around with other women?
When woman replied no, the judge asked her what reason then, did she have to be in court? Woman stammered and began to cry—advocate ended up speaking for woman. Judge has a reputation of being difficult and asking unrelated personal questions.

Case #0113: Judge granted husband and wife mutual restraining orders against each other. Judge told them to go home and behave themselves. Woman was visibly bruised, had two black eyes and many cuts and scratches on her face. Outside the court room the husband threatened to kill the wife. The woman did not feel it was safe to return home; she went into shelter.[39]

The most common acts of noncompliance attributed to judges were incorrect applications of the law, a biased or racist attitude toward women, inappropriate denials of a temporary restraining order, and inaccurate advice or ignorance of the law. While this study is dated December of 1985, it was not released to the public under an agreement between the Working Group and Chief Justice of the District Courts Samuel E. Zoll. In return for not releasing the report, the Working Group was told there would be trainings of criminal justice officials.[40]

In August of 1986, Pamela Nigro Dunn was shot, stabbed, and strangled by her husband. She had gone to court four times to seek protection from him. Although she had been issued a restraining order, she had been mistreated by the judge who issued it, according to the parents of Pamela Dunn, who filed a complaint with the state Judicial Conduct Commission after her death. The day the killing was reported, a page-one story appeared in the *Boston Globe* with the headline "Domestic Violence Difficult to Prevent: Legal Orders Called Largely Ineffective."[41] The Working Group study was mentioned in the story.

In Massachusetts, all court hearings are tape-recorded; this enabled *Globe* reporter Eileen McNamara to listen to the interactions between Pamela Dunn and Judge Heffernan after her death. Drawing from these taperecordings, McNamara wrote a number of page-one stories on the "judicial harassment" of battered women.[42] The press accounts began with Judge Heffernan, but other judges were also identified as displaying a hostile demeanor to abused women. Through this press coverage, the *Boston Globe* legitimized the problem that had been initially raised by advocates. Over a period of four months, the Globe ran 22 front-page stories on this problem. The headlines listed in Table 3.1 give a sense of the intensity of this news coverage.

In a front-page story entitled "Judge Criticized After Woman's Death," *Globe* reporter Eileen McNamara quoted Judge Heffernan scolding Pamela Nigro Dunn in the presence of her husband:

"You want to gnaw on her and she on you, fine, but let's not do it at the taxpayers' expense." . . . In court recordings of her four appearances before Heffernan, the judge can be heard dismissing her fears, insisting she did not need police protection and chastising her for "doing a terrible disservice to the taxpayers" by taking up the court's time when it "has a lot more serious matters to contend with."[43]

McNamara also reported the reaction of advocates for battered women to the killing of Pamela Dunn, two of whom said that Heffernan's treatment of Pamela Dunn may have contributed to her death. Such treatment of women was routine at Somerville District Court, advocates claimed.

This story created public outrage over judicial responses to battering. Pamela Dunn's murder galvanized battered women's ad-

---

TABLE 3.1

BOSTON GLOBE 1986 FRONT-PAGE HEADLINES
"Judicial Harassment of Battered Women" as a Public Problem

"Judge Criticized After Woman's Death" (9/21/86)

"Plans for Probe of Judge Reported" (9/26/86)

"Friends Say Charges Malign Judge, Abuse-Case Controversy Seethes Around 'A Sensitive Person' " (10/5/86)

"Zoll Comes to Defense of Judge, Victim's Family Irate" (10/11/86)

"Two Judges Withdraw from Cases, Won't Hear Domestic Abuse Matters Pending Probe" (10/15/86)

"State Report Found Poor Enforcement of Abuse Prevention Law" (10/30/86)

"Judge Tempone Said to Top Complaint List" (11/2/86)

" 'No Quick Fix' in Abuse Cases, Judge Rules" (11/13/86)

"Dorchester Judge Stripped of Right to Hear Most Cases" (11/14/86)

"Panel Expected to Back More Power over Judges" (12/19/86)

---

vocates in the Boston area, who felt their complaints about the courts had gone unheard. A protest demonstration was held outside Somerville District Court. Within a week it was reported that a Judicial Conduct Commission investigation was underway. Not everyone was outraged: friends and colleagues on the bench came to Heffernan's defense, suggesting his remarks were "out of character."[44] When Chief Justice Zoll wrote a letter to the parents of Pamela Dunn that was interpreted as defending Judge Heffernan, a protest was staged outside Zoll's home.[45]

But Heffernan was not the only judge whose treatment of battered women made the front page. Eileen McNamara was following up on allegations that these practices were widespread. Evidence of abusive conduct involving another judge at the Somerville Court was soon reported. According to battered women, prosecutors, and private attorneys, Henry A. Tempone, the presiding justice at Somerville District Court, was routinely abusive in domestic violence cases. One front-page story quoted Judge Tempone, based on a taperecording of a restraining order hearing:

"I don't feel I have a right under the 209A [restraining order] statute to make a decision about whether this man has a right to see his own child," [Judge Henry A.] Tempone told the woman, dismissing her protests that her husband has a violent temper with the comment that "even Dillinger could have made a good father. Is that before your time? How about Manson, then?"[46]

Judge Tempone had been mentioned more frequently than any other judge in the complaints documented in the Working Group study. After Judge Tempone first appeared on the front page, Chief Justice Zoll initiated an investigation of the Somerville court. When he announced his probe of these two judges, Zoll said he was seeking to preserve "the public's confidence in the courts."[47] Judges Heffernan and Tempone "voluntarily" withdrew from hearing domestic violence cases until the probe was completed.[48]

Before the end of the year, a third judge made the front page. Judge Paul H. King, presiding justice at Dorchester District Court, refused to issue a vacate order to a woman whose beating was confirmed by the police:

"There is no quick fix in the Dorchester court," [Judge Paul J.] King told the 30-year-old woman as he issued an order that prohibited her husband from beating her but permitted him to remain at home. "I read the *Boston Globe*, too, ma'am." . . . He denied the woman's request that her husband be temporarily evicted because, he said, "I don't believe she was beaten. I didn't see any bruises; most women bruise pretty easily. . . . I don't believe in breaking up families. . . . My wife tells me I hate women," he said with a laugh. "I don't hate women. I just hate what they do sometimes."[49]

In essence, Judge King was saying that women seeking restraining orders were liars. In a front-page *Globe* interview, King said that he suspected this woman had read about restraining orders in the *Globe* and had learned how easy it was to obtain one. "I figure she read them and thought, 'Here's a quickie way to get him out of the house,'" he told the *Globe* reporter. He criticized the law on restraining orders, saying that such orders are often used "to get a leg up in a divorce." King further acknowledged he had not read the guidelines issued by Chief Justice Zoll about domestic violence cases but added that if he had read them, he would not feel constrained by them.[50]

After reading the interview with Judge King in the *Globe*,

Chief Justice Zoll immediately barred King from sitting in Dorchester Court and removed most of his authority to hear cases.[51] Amid public concern over the practices at the Dorchester Court, an investigation was ordered by the Supreme Judicial Court, the highest court in the state. More individuals began to report cases of judicial misconduct to the Judicial Conduct Commission. The state legislature gave new emphasis to long-standing attempts to make the workings of the Judicial Conduct Commission public. And in the wake of this scandal, the Supreme Judicial Court commissioned a gender-bias study of the Massachusetts courts— something the Women's Law Association had requested for some time.[52]

The public spotlight on judicial hostility toward battered women created enormous pressure for official responses. And in this scandal, the *Globe* served both as a public forum and as an instigator. In addition to the front-page articles, the *Globe* printed four editorials on judicial mistreatment of battered women. One editorial, entitled "Judicial Accountability," criticized the "conspiracy of silence" among judges, prosecutors, and defense lawyers "that allows some judges to engage in misconduct with near impunity."[53] In the space of a few months, the power of the press forced changes that activists had sought for years.

However, the length of time taken by the state's highest court to act on the cases of the three judges raised even more questions about the credibility of the judiciary. When public officials assume responsibility for a problem, they generally take control in ways that reframe the issue or undermine the impetus for change. Judge Tempone's case was resolved the most quickly; he was pressured into retirement.[54] But it was over two years before the Supreme Judicial Court reprimanded Judge Heffernan for what they called his "rudeness, discourtesy, sarcasm, and hostility." And since the court saw his intimidating demeanor as unintentional, this reprimand was the extent of the sanctions imposed on the judge. In its reframing of the problem, the court criticized the news media for its "inaccurate reporting" of the case.[55]

The case of Judge King took even longer to come to a decision. This is all the more surprising since King was alleged to have tyrannized for many years not only battered women but also welfare recipients, court clerks, police officers, and African American defendants. Nonetheless, it was over four years before the Supreme Judicial Court censured Judge King's conduct, a decision that allowed him to continue to serve on the bench.[56]

Other signs of resistance to change within the judiciary were apparent. Whether the demeanor of judges toward women was the result of individual style or institutional culture was a matter fiercely argued by judges in a number of public forums. In 1987 the Massachusetts Senate Judiciary Committee, responding to pressure from the judges' lobby, backed a bill that would make it more difficult to bring misconduct charges against state judges.[57] And in a move viewed cynically by advocates for battered women, in 1989 the Quincy Bar Association awarded Judge Paul King "Man of the Year."[58]

1992: The "Rise in Domestic Violence" and the "Ineffectiveness of Restraining Orders" as Public Problems

Dissatisfaction with these official responses fueled new strategies for action in the community. Led by feminist activists and demonstrating a lack of faith in the judiciary, projects were established to train law students to work as volunteer advocates for battered women in the courts. These projects, operating in law schools and through the battered women's shelter network, created an alternate means of helping women to escape violence.

Recalling the weekly listing of "crimes against women" in the 1870s, advocates for battered women began to compile what could be called a "deathwatch." This was a continually revised listing of the names, dates, and circumstances of the killings of women by their partners, including a focus on whether restraining orders were in effect. This list was made available to the media and public officials. "We need to keep a record of what's happening," one activist said. "When people start hearing the names and how women die, they start to take notice. It's only when we start personalizing these murders that people stop being numbed by the violence."[59] Publicizing these killings, which seemed to increase in frequency between 1990 and 1992, succeeded in generating new action around woman battering.

In late 1991 the *Boston Globe* reported that domestic violence was increasing, based on a rise in calls to a battered women's shelter, an upturn in restraining order requests, and an increase in killings of women by their partners.[60] The deathwatch figures were cited in the story. By the end of 1991, it was further reported that complaints against batterers were now the most common type of complaints in the Massachusetts courts.[61] During 1992, the issue of domestic violence seemed to dominate the news in the Boston area, with deaths of women appearing regularly on the front page. As can be seen in Figure 3.1, the number of news articles on battering in 1992 tripled in number from the previous year. Readjusting the previous focus on judges, the dominant definitions of the problem in the *Globe* coverage centered on the "rise in domestic violence," especially femicide, and "the ineffectiveness of restraining orders" to stop this violence.

The "deathwatch" figures of how many women had been killed appeared consistently in news stories and were referred to regularly by politicians. The *Globe* reported that in 1990, a woman was killed by her abuser on the average of one every 22 days; in early 1992, the average figure was one woman dying every 16 days. By mid-1992, an average of one woman was being murdered every eight days.[62] Information on whether restraining orders were in effect became a leading issue. The list of front-page headlines in Table 3.2 reveals this rise in public action against domestic violence.

A review of the year's public events illustrates how this sense of a "rise in domestic violence" aroused political responses. On Valentine's Day, the Massachusetts coalition of battered women's shelters asked the public to wear red armbands to express concern for battered women: Boston Mayor Ray Flynn wore one and urged city employees to join him. In March, following a number of murders committed by men who had restraining orders against them, the Women's Legislative Caucus held a hearing at the State House addressing the ineffectiveness of restraining orders. In April, after a triple domestic homicide by a man under a restraining order, the Women's Caucus asked the lieutenant governor to declare a "public safety emergency" for battered women in Massachusetts, which he promptly did. A flurry of new legislation was proposed to increase funding for shelters and give judges more leeway to detain batterers.

Other public events followed. The Massachusetts Medical Society initiated a campaign to educate doctors on domestic vio-

TABLE 3.2

BOSTON GLOBE 1992 FRONT-PAGE HEADLINES
The "Rise in Domestic Violence" and the "Ineffectiveness of Restraining Orders" as Public Problems

"Restraining Orders Get New Review, Recent Domestic Violence Cases Focus Attention on Local Program" (2/16/92)

"Domestic Violence: No Easy Answers, Hearing Today at State House" (3/2/92)

"System Battered, Outrage Erupts on Domestic Abuse, Legislators Seek Protections for Women Victims" (4/7/92)

"Explosion of Violence Haunts Women, Families" (5/31/92)

"Thwarting the Killers Is Complex, Elusive Goal" (6/2/92)

"Domestic Violence: Roots Go Deep" (6/5/92)

"Restraining Orders Are at Record High" (9/23/92)

"Domestic Rampage: Police Say Estranged Boyfriend Killed Three, Then Self, in Chicopee" (9/30/92)

"Third of Court Orders Flouted, Officials Say" (9/30/92)

"Court's Shield Can Draw a Bullet" (10/7/92)

---

lence and raise money for shelters. A local television station held a telethon to raise money for services for battered women. In October the first annual "Walk for Women's Safety" was held to raise money for shelters, sponsored by prominent politicians and major Massachusetts corporations.

Along with this intense focus on femicide, news stories in the *Globe* informed women of their options for seeking help. The number of women seeking restraining orders continued to rise, and this increase in restraining orders then itself became news. But problems with the effectiveness of restraining orders were a consistent topic. Some speculated that serving men with restraining orders might actually be triggering increased violence, which generated the headline "Court's Shield Can Draw a Bullet."

Again, the *Globe* both reported on these events and weighed in with its own opinions. Seventeen editorials were devoted to the topic of woman battering in 1992. These editorials highlighted cases where a lack of coordination between judges and the police may have contributed to women's deaths. On the last day of the year, the *Globe* printed in its editorial the names and circumstances of all the domestic homicides, noting that 16 women, children, and bystanders were killed by men under active restraining orders in 1992. In a departure from the fleeting attention battering often receives in the news, this listing of deaths has become an annual year-end tradition in the *Globe*.

Consequences of the Rise in Public Attention

A pragmatic question can be asked about this rise of public concern: What has been the benefit for battered women? One thing seems clear: the glare of media attention began to change how the judiciary responded to women seeking protection.

In interviews, judges themselves made the case for how powerful the media can be as a force for institutional change. One judge said the intense news coverage of misconduct served to wake up the judiciary:

I think that when [the Pamela Nigro Dunn] case occurred . . . I think throughout the court system, it woke up the court because the criticism that came on as a result of that began, I think, to shake up some of the judges, making them far more conservative about . . . showing their frustrations.

This judge credited the media for shaking up the bench, but he said that advocates also helped create a situation "where the system became aware it had to do something."

For another judge, the press focus on the murders of women changed judicial responses:

I have just seen such a sea change in the three years that I've been on the bench in terms of attitudes, in terms of willingness to take these cases seriously. . . . [What has driven that change?] Media attention. And I say that as someone who really bemoans the scapegoating that they do. . . . I think the media, to the extent that it's made that clear that these people are dying. I mean, a Hispanic woman in Lowell who was killed by her children's father never made it to the front page of the paper before. She was lucky if she got an inch on the back of metro. And once it became part of a movement, it got reported. And I think that's important.

Of course, not all judges view the press or the influence of feminist organizing in a positive light. But even when stated reluctantly—or perhaps especially when stated reluctantly—judges reveal the impact of media attention. A grudging acknowledgment of this influence was offered by one judge:

The courts are focusing their time on the issue of domestic violence. And, I think obviously, part of it is as a result of a need to feel protected. . . . I think that the courts—and let's hope this is only a small part of the motivation to do a good job, but nonetheless it exists, and it would be unrealistic to suggest that it doesn't—our motivation is if we don't do a good job in this case, if we don't take the issue seriously, it'll come back to haunt us. And you only have to look back over a few years in the press to see what has happened to judges, to some of our brethren who have been accused of not being as sensitive as they should on these cases. . . . The most visible case for all of the judges was the Heffernan case. It seemed to go on forever. And that was the one that I suppose got all of us particularly sensitive to how this thing can come back and hurt you. . . . We just had a heightened awareness of the consequences of mishandling domestic violence cases. And I think that's continued, that heightened awareness has continued up to the present.

More than anything else, it seems, judges fear public humiliation in the news media. They don't fear feminists or other advocacy groups: indeed, refusing to bend to the pressure of such groups is a mark of judicial pride, perhaps especially in a state where judges are appointed rather than elected. One judge who trains other judges on domestic violence said that when she encounters antipathy for battered women or resistance to issuing restraining orders in her trainings, she responds with the question: "Why do you want your name on the front page of the *Boston Globe*?"

Other judicial reforms have followed in the wake of this media attention. Judges have been active in community round-table forums seeking to improve the operation of legal protections for abused women. Some judges have taken the lead in bringing advocates into their own courthouses to assist women seeking protection. Judges have also volunteered to provide around-the-clock assistance in emergencies and have found that 97 percent of the orders they issue after court hours are restraining orders in cases of domestic violence.[63] Drawing momentum from the study of gender bias, a commission on race and ethnic bias in the courts was established by the Supreme Judicial Court, and its final report identified pervasive bias in the court system.[64]

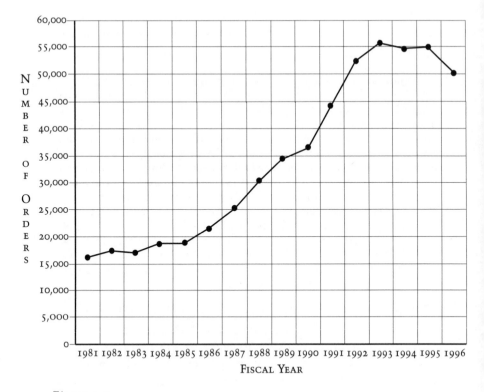

Figure 3.2

Restraining Order Requests in Massachusetts, 1981 to 1996

Source: "Annual Report of the Massachusetts Court System," Fiscal Years 1981–1996.[65]

Another consequence of the rise in media attention may have been the increase in women seeking restraining orders over this period. Figure 3.2 depicts the number of orders requested from 1981 to 1996. Restraining order requests nearly tripled in number between 1985 and 1993. News information on women's legal options, along with prominent stories on femicides, may have spurred women to seek protection from the courts. In Figure 3.2, sharp increases appear in the years following the 1986 scandal, and the number of orders sought peaks about the same time as the *Globe* news coverage depicted in Figure 3.1.

Whether this increase in restraining order requests is a good or a bad thing depends in part on what happens to women in the courtroom, which is examined in later chapters. But on its face, there is one way in which this increased court attention to battering may be an accomplishment. Judges, like others who provide help to abused women, come to fear violent men. Behind every kind of assistance that can be offered, whether legal assistance, emergency shelter, or medical care, there lurks a dilemma: Will providing this aid make a woman safer, or will it make her batterer more angry and therefore more violent? In this way, judges, advocates, social workers, and attorneys indirectly experience the double binds under which many women negotiate their daily lives. At times the threat becomes direct: batterers do threaten judges, and the staffs of a shelter or a hospital are sometimes harassed by abusers. But most often the threat is felt secondhand.

This dilemma might be described as "emotional blackmail": by empathizing with an abused woman, the judge indirectly feels the threat of the batterer's violence. This is not a fear of being personally victimized but a fear that providing a woman with assistance may further endanger her. This threat creates second-guessing, particularly given the limitations of legal interventions. One judge put it this way:

The cases that you really get nervous about are the cases where some alleged act of abuse has happened, and she is at home with very young children and has nowhere to go. . . . I just worry whether when a restraining order is issued, if the respondent isn't there, I wonder if she's going to be safe overnight.[66]

At the very least, the increase in restraining order requests means that more judges are sharing the burden of fear that characterizes battering. In the history of efforts to force the state to respond to battering, this may be no small achievement.

If this discussion indicates that media coverage can be beneficial to battered women, it is important to note that the local media, the *Boston Globe* included, have been sharply criticized for their reporting of other crimes against women. The Combahee River Collective, a black feminist organization started in Boston in the mid-1970s, publicly protested the indifference of both the police and the media concerning the deaths of 12 black women in a five-month period in 1979. When news reports finally began, these women were described in stigmatizing ways, as "runaways, prostitutes, or drug addicts," according to Barbara Smith, a member of the collective. Smith reports that a *New York Times* journalist from the Boston bureau refused to attend a press conference on the murders, saying, "Twelve black women murdered. That's not news. I could call any city in this country and get that statistic." A pamphlet entitled "Twelve Black Women: Why Did They Die?" was printed in English and Spanish, presenting an analysis of how racism and sexism lead to violence against women. Coverage by the *Boston Globe* was criticized in the pamphlet.[67]

The Boston news media, including the *Globe*, were also severely criticized for their coverage of the 1989 killing of Carol DiMaiti Stuart. In a story that received national attention, Carol Stuart, an upper-middle-class white woman, was shot in her car after leaving a prenatal class at a downtown Boston hospital. Her husband, Charles Stuart, who was also white, was driving; he claimed a black man was the murderer. Later implicated in the killing by his brother, Charles Stuart committed suicide. But in the months that elapsed before he was named as the prime suspect in the murder, Charles Stuart's lie managed to ignite a fury of white hostility against black men in Boston. The police publicly strip-searched black men in what one observer called an "occupation" of black neighborhoods in Boston.[68] Local news coverage was characterized as "racist, incompetent, and reckless."[69] The Boston media were criticized for printing and airing racist stereotypes about urban crime and for focusing prematurely on a black male suspect to the exclusion of more rigorous reporting.[70]

Biases and blindspots in news reporting will therefore greatly shape the process of collective definition, at times in disastrous ways. A recent study of newspaper coverage of the African American community in Boston found both class and racial biases in the kind of information considered "news." Examining the *Boston Globe* and the *Boston Herald*, the study concluded that "the press does not portray the black community as an integrated part of Boston."[71]

Dilemmas of Problem Construction

"News concerns the *event*, not the underlying condition; the *person*, not the group . . . the fact that '*advances the story*,' not the one that explains it in general," according to sociologist Todd Gitlin.[72] It is not surprising that the focus on femicide in the *Boston Globe* coverage of 1992 and 1993 rarely addressed underlying issues of poverty and racism. And where class and race were mentioned, the point was as often as not to discount their importance:

Domestic violence is in every neighborhood, every social class, every ethnic group.[73]

These women have varied profiles. They are young and middle-aged; they represent every race and social class.[74]

Battering crosses all racial and economic backgrounds.[75]

Domestic violence respects no social or economic boundaries.[76]

As I argued in the last chapter, these statements are only partially true: poverty and racism do indeed make women more vulnerable to violence, especially murder. Perhaps in the wake of the racial conflict inflamed by Charles Stuart, this is a kind of "political move"; the image of a classless and raceless victim of battering may mask a reluctance to talk seriously about poverty and racial divisions.

Many of those talking about woman battering in the press are white politicians, seeking to gain attention for themselves at a time when the issue is popular. At a time when "get tough on crime" campaigns are so common, Democrats and Republicans alike have come to sell themselves based on their ideas for responding to a crime so dramatically reported in the news. There is apparently much political gain in talking about the issue, even when no substantive action follows. Such "grandstanding" by state legislators on this issue is evidenced by the fact that of 60 domestic violence bills filed in the legislature in 1992 and 1993, only two were voted into law.[77]

This poses a dilemma: Framing woman battering in a classless and raceless way may have allowed politicians and major corporations to identify with the issue, but if poverty and racism contribute to femicide, how does ignoring this help stop the killings?

A second dilemma follows from such an intense focus on killings: How accurate a portrait of the problem of woman battering can be gained from looking chiefly at femicide? Although examining femicide has been an effective way to gain media attention, does it really address the daily experiences of battering that cause hundreds of women to seek court protection every week in Mas-

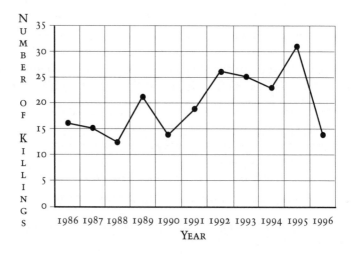

Figure 3.3

Intimate Femicides in Massachusetts, 1986 to 1996

Source: Executive Office of Public Safety cited in Lynda Gorov and John Ellement, "Most Women's Deaths Laid to Intimates," *Boston Globe*, January 3, 1993, 21, 25; and *Boston Globe* editorials, "Year of the Woman: In Memoriam," December 31, 1992, 14; "In Memoriam," December 31, 1993, 18; "In Memoriam," December 31, 1994, 14; "In Memoriam," December 31, 1995, 84; and "In Memoriam," December 31, 1996, A14.

sachusetts? Twenty-six women were reportedly killed by their partners in 1992. But over 52,000 restraining orders were sought statewide that year. If news coverage is driven by the most extreme cases, as was true in 1992, it sometimes seems as if nothing anyone does could ever stop a violent man from killing his partner. Relentless coverage of horrible violence may inspire action, but it may also produce feelings of numbness, indifference, and cynicism.

If murder drives attention to battering, news coverage and political attention may also rise and fall with dramatic changes in the murder rate. Figure 3.3 presents estimates of intimate femicides in Massachusetts from 1986 through 1996. These are estimates in at least two senses: the numbers, which appeared in the *Boston Globe*, include deaths where the identity of the assailant was alleged but not proven; and the numbers do not include the large percentage of deaths where the relationship between victim and assailant is simply unknown. This "unknown" category in Massachusetts is upward of 40 percent of homicides.[78] With these limitations in mind, there does appear to have been an increase in documented killings of women by intimates between 1990 and 1992 and a sharp decrease from 1995 to 1996. This roughly corresponds with the increase in *Globe* coverage of battering in 1992 and also with the falloff in coverage after 1995, as displayed in Figure 3.1. But while femicides have driven media attention to battering in recent years and exposed the ambivalence and incompetence of judicial responses, how well do murder stories capture the complexity of battering? How well do they reveal the sense of entrapment that women report? And how well do they depict the quality of justice women experience in the courts? Given the conventions of news coverage—"if it bleeds, it leads" being an organizational mandate—stories of women successfully resisting violence are not front-page material. Extreme cases may not be the best means of understanding women's daily encounters with judges in a space—the restraining order hearing—essentially created by feminist social action. It is toward an examination of these everyday courtroom experiences that this investigation now turns.

Summary

The activism of the past 25 years has not been the first time that feminists responded publicly to violence against women and challenged the collusion of the state with men's coercive authority. Oddly enough, despite the invisibility of this history, events in Massachusetts over recent decades mirror some of the actions taken by Boston area feminists 100 years ago.

Herbert Blumer argues that "a social problem is always a focus point for the operation of divergent and conflicting interests, intentions, and objectives."[79] In this chapter, I have sought to demonstrate how this conflicted "process of collective definition," as played out in one newspaper, has been both beneficial and troubling for public action against battering. The rise of "judicial harassment of battered women" as a public problem examined in the *Boston Globe* created a crisis for the Massachusetts courts.

While the issue was initially raised and even documented by advocates, it was only after the *Globe* made it a front-page story that—as one judge put it—"the system became aware it had to do something." Ironically, some of the most compelling evidence of judicial misconduct came from the courts' own taperecordings. This scandal set the stage for public attention to "the ineffectiveness of restraining orders" several years later, when femicides appeared to increase in number.

This media spotlight contributed to public action against violence, and by informing women of their rights it encouraged abused women to seek restraining orders. Nonetheless, several dilemmas are posed by the collective definition of the problem as it developed in the *Globe* and in public campaigns. First, must issues of poverty and racism be ignored in order to mobilize public support against violence? Is this really a sufficient strategy, given the different needs of abused women in different circumstances? Will a rising tide really lift all boats? Second, is it possible to address femicides in a public campaign without losing sight of the ever-more common experiences of coercion and threats that drive women to the courts?

Commenting on this renewed public attention, Katherine Triantafillou reflected on the restraining order legislation that she helped write:

With all of its troubles, I'm very proud of the Abuse Prevention Act. It was truly a grassroots piece of legislation, and it opened the door to change. It was already spreading across the country [at the time], but it did open a door. It has framed the question. It may not have found the answer, but it framed the question in a feminist way. We would not be having this [public] discussion about the problem without it.[80]

The privilege, ancient though it be, to beat her with a stick, to pull her hair, choke her, spit in her face or kick her about the floor, or to inflict upon her like indignities, is not now acknowledged by our law.

JUDGE CHARLES PELHAM, Fulgham v. State (1871)[1]

AFFIDAVIT: Describe in detail the most recent incidents of abuse. State what happened, the dates, who did what to whom, and describe any injuries. Also describe any history of abuse.

Instructions for completing affidavit for a
restraining order in Massachusetts courts (1991)[2]

Why Women Seek Restraining Orders: The Tactics and Strategies of Men Who Batter

After twenty-five years of renewed feminist activism, men's violence against women is more public than ever before. The courts are hearing women's testimony about battering to an unprecedented degree. Indeed, court responses to intimate violence have become bureaucratized. The complaint forms for restraining or-

From James Ptacek, "Tactics and Strategies of Men Who Batter," in *Violence Between Intimate Partners*, ed. Albert P. Cardarelli. Copyright 1997 by Allyn & Bacon. Reprinted/adapted by permission.

ders now contain language that indicates that the widespread occurrence of woman battering is now openly conceded, even though men's "privilege" to abuse women is no longer acknowledged in the written law.

Yet there is already evidence of a backlash against the modest gains made by feminist organizers in creating new legal remedies for abused women. Ancient characterizations of women as liars and manipulators who exaggerate their suffering have assumed new forms in public discourse. As indicated in the previous chapter, some judges claim that women dishonestly seek restraining orders to gain advantage in divorce cases, win child-support settlements, or unfairly displace men from the marital home. At a forum on restraining orders sponsored by the Dorchester Bar Association, one defense attorney summed up this perspective bluntly:

Of the fifty to sixty thousand restraining orders issued, how many women get charged with perjury?

Given the continuing political conflict over legal remedies, it is important to understand the nature of the events that women report to the courts. Why do women seek restraining orders? If battering is understood as social entrapment, as domination rather than simply physical assault, then both the *acts* and the *intentions* of men's violence must be detailed. This chapter presents an analysis of men's tactics and strategies, as reported by women in restraining order complaint forms. *Tactics* refer to the types of violence and abuse men use against women. *Strategies* refer to the intentions behind this violence and abusiveness—that is, what these men were trying to accomplish with their assaults. This is an analysis of the motives of men who batter that is drawn from the perspectives of battered women.

What can we learn about the motives of battering men from women's testimony? If motives are understood as the reasons behind the violence, it is essential that we understand how women explain and describe their violent experiences. Both feminist and criminological theories of battering emphasize the "social control" aspect of violence. "Battering is the sum of all past acts of violence, and the promise of future violence, that achieves enhanced power and control for the batterer," according to Barbara

Hart.[3] In analyzing crime as social control, Donald Black discusses how battering is often a means of punishing or violently enforcing a man's expectations of a woman.[4] Battering is, therefore, a brutal form of communication; to the extent that a batterer is sending a message, an abused woman's perspective on the meaning of this violence is crucial.

There is also evidence from studies of battering men that their own accounts of the violence cannot be taken at face value. The treatment literature on batterers has emphasized the tendency of men to minimize or deny the intentionality of their violence.[5] In my own interviews with men who batter, I found that individuals often shift back and forth between denying responsibility for their violent assaults and arguing that women deserved it.[6] Clearly, research on men who batter is needed to understand men's self-perceptions, the meanings that violence has for them, the social learning of violence, and the ways that battering can be stopped. In terms of the impact of violence on the social control of women, however, the perspectives of abused women will be more telling. Only women who have been battered can testify to both the internal suffering and the social consequences the abuse has wreaked on their lives.

In Massachusetts, court records on restraining orders are officially open to the public, in recognition of "the public's general right to examine and evaluate the quality of justice done in its courts."[7] Women's affidavits are also part of the court files. These affidavits are the written statements, signed under penalty of perjury, that women file as part of the restraining order request. In their own words, written in longhand, women detail in these statements the range of violence and abuse that prompted them to seek court protection. This examination of the motives of violent men is based on these sworn statements. While court documents are notoriously incomplete, what these affidavits lack in depth and completeness is balanced by the immediacy of the accounts, the descriptions of the objectives behind men's violence, and the portrait of the dilemmas of separation they reveal.

This chapter is divided into three main sections. The first reviews the research methods and discusses the status of the relationships between women seeking protection and the men accused of violence. Then these reports of men's violent and abusive tactics are examined for the types of abuse they depict, the levels of criminality they contain, and the injuries and other consequences of the violence they describe. The final section presents and interprets the strategies that women report.

Background Characteristics of the Women Seeking Orders

A random sample of 100 restraining order cases filed in 1992 was selected for this analysis—50 cases from Dorchester District Court and 50 from Quincy District Court. Dorchester District Court serves a working-class and poor, predominantly African American and Latino and Latina population; the court in Quincy serves a middle- and working-class, largely Anglo-American population. Since racial identity is not indicated on restraining order forms, however, the comparisons in this chapter are strictly between the courts where women sought restraining orders.

These are two of the busiest lower criminal courts in Massachusetts. In 1992, 2,251 restraining orders were filed in Dorchester; 1,695 restraining orders were filed in Quincy.[8] This made Dorchester the second-highest court statewide in restraining order filings for 1992; Quincy was the sixth-highest court. A record high of over 53,000 requests for restraining orders were filed in Massachusetts in 1992.

What kinds of relationships do these women describe? Just under half (47 percent) of the women in the sample who sought orders at both courts were married to the men named as defendants, as is indicated in Table 4.1. This is similar to figures from studies of restraining orders in Pennsylvania[9] and Colorado.[10] Surprisingly, only 35 percent of the women were living with the defendant when they applied for the restraining order. Most of the women in the Pennsylvania and Colorado studies were also living apart from the defendant when they sought restraining orders. Thus the evidence is that many women either had separated or had ended their relationships by the time they sought restraining orders. Women who were separated, divorced, had formerly cohabited, or identified their defendants as former boyfriends constitute 44 percent of the cases. Since some women did not provide a detailed history, this must be seen as a low estimate; at least

TABLE 4.1

**Relationship Status of Women
in Random Sample of One Hundred Restraining Order Files**

	District Court		
Status of Relationship	Dorchester	Quincy	Combined
Married, living together	26%	24%	25%
Married, separated	24	20	22
Divorced	2	4	3
Cohabiting	6	14	10
Previously cohabited	16	10	13
Dating, no children in common	4	8	6
Formerly dating, no children in common	6	6	6
Children, unmarried, not cohabiting, residence history unclear	16	14	13
	100%	100%	100%

half of the relationships likely had ended or at least had been drastically changed in status by the time women reached the court.

Stereotypical images of battered women as passive or helpless are undermined by this evidence of a refusal to tolerate abuse. This resistance is all the more remarkable when it becomes clear that these women are, for the most part, mothers of young children. In Dorchester, 82 percent of the women seeking orders were mothers; in Quincy, the figure was 70 percent. This is consistent with other studies of restraining orders.[11] In the overwhelming majority of these cases, the men named by these women are the fathers of their children. This complicates everything women do. Children increase women's economic dependency on men; children make leaving, even for short periods, extremely difficult; and fleeing with children makes it harder to keep a new location secret from a vengeful batterer.

It is interesting to note that most of the women who had children did not ask for child support as part of the restraining order, which they are entitled to do. In Dorchester, 39 percent of the mothers requested child support, but only 12.5 percent of these women were awarded child support by the judge. In Quincy, 49 percent of the mothers asked for child support, and 41 percent were granted support. This difference may reflect contrasting court policies toward battered mothers; Quincy District Court has developed policies to empower battered women that have received national recognition.[12]

The Tactics of Men Who Batter

As might be expected, women described a range of violence and abuse in their written testimony. When the kinds of abuse disclosed in these documents are compared with the criminal law in Massachusetts, it becomes evident that the majority of these offenses are crimes. Of course, saying that these acts fulfill the legal definition of crimes does not mean that they are *treated* as crimes by the police and the courts. Feminists have maintained that battering must be understood within the larger context of women's oppression. Physical violence against women is part of a continuum of coercive control that includes sexual abuse, psychological abuse, and economic abuse.[13] In terms of these four categories, what types of violence and abuse are women reporting to the courts?

"The privilege, ancient though it be, to beat her with a stick, to pull her hair, choke her, spit in her face or kick her about the floor, or to inflict upon her like indignities, is not now acknowledged by our law," Judge Pelham wrote in 1871.[14] All the tactics described by Judge Pelham appear in the sample of affidavits filed in Dorchester and Quincy District Courts. Table 4.2 presents the categories of physical violence reported by women in the sample. Women were threatened with objects, had their hair pulled, were choked, spit at, and kicked. Seventy percent of the affidavits allege acts that constitute assault and battery, according to Massachusetts law. Nine percent of the women said that men either had threatened them with or had used knives or guns. Eighteen percent of the women gave evidence of injuries, ranging from bruises and black eyes to broken bones, facial cuts and swelling, a miscarriage, and damaged eardrums.

Table 4.3 details the kinds of sexual violence and abuse, psychological abuse, and economic or resource abuse identified in the court documents. Six percent of the women said they had been raped or had suffered attempted rape. There are additionally

TABLE 4.2

**Physical Abuse Reported by Women
in Random Sample of One Hundred Restraining Order Files**

Type of Physical Abuse	*Number of Women Reporting*[a]
ASSAULT OR ASSAULT AND BATTERY WITH A DANGEROUS WEAPON	
Threatened with or used knife	7
Threatened with hard objects (screwdriver, scissors, wooden board, beer bottle, ashtray, clock)	7
Kicked	5
Threatened with, hit with, fired gun	2
SIMPLE ASSAULT AND BATTERY	
Punched	22
Pushed, thrown, dragged (including pushed into furniture, wall, and car and onto floor)	19
Slapped, hit	14
"Physically abused" or "physically assaulted" or "caused me physical harm," no other description given	12
Strangled, choked, grabbed throat	11
Pulled hair, dragged by hair	8
Grabbed	4
Bit	2
Spit at	2

a. This column represents the number of women reporting the different types of physical abuse but not the number of occurrences of these types of threats. The types of threats are not mutually exclusive. Because many women reported several different threats, the total of this column exceeds 100, the number of women's files examined.

a number of descriptions that seem to represent other forms of sexualized violence. Five percent of the women described being punched in the thighs, kneed between the legs, assaulted in a spanking fashion, or being shoved onto the bed; several of the women reporting forced sex also describe being punched or slapped.

Table 4.3 also lists the kinds of psychological and economic or resource abuse recounted in women's affidavits. Threats to kill appear to be common. Twenty-four percent of the women stated

TABLE 4.3

Sexual, Psychological, and Economic Abuse Reported by Women in Random Sample of One Hundred Restraining Order Files

Type of Abuse	Number of Women Reporting[a]
SEXUAL VIOLENCE, SEXUALIZED VIOLENCE	
Rape or attempted rape	6
Punched in thighs, kneed between legs, hit in spanking manner, shoved on bed	5
PSYCHOLOGICAL ABUSE: THREATS	
Threatened to kill woman	24
Threatened suicide	5
Threatened to kill child, boyfriend, neighbors	3
Threatened to harm woman physically	5
Threatened to harm daughter's boyfriend	1
Threatened to kidnap woman	1
Threatened to harm children	3
Threatened to take children	5
Made unspecified threats or threatening phone calls	11
PSYCHOLOGICAL ABUSE: INTIMIDATION	
Yelled, screamed, shouted obscenities, was verbally abusive	39
Destroyed property (television, bed, pictures, lights, doors, window, car windshield, car tires; disabled car engine or phone)	14
ECONOMIC OR RESOURCE ABUSE	
Stole money or property	5
Threatened to make her lose job or make her mother lose job	3
Threw her out of home, locked her out of home, threatened to throw her out of home	3
Prevented her from access to transportation	3
Refused to pay rent or child support	2
Prevented her use of joint bank account	1

a. This column represents the number of women reporting the different types of abuse but does not include the number of occurrences of these types of abuse. The types of threats are not mutually exclusive. Because many women reported several different threats, the total of this column exceeds 100, the number of women's files examined.

TABLE 4.4

**Criminal Behavior Reported by Women
in Random Sample of One Hundred Restraining Order Files**

Type of Criminal Behavior	*Number of Women Reporting*[a]
Assault and battery	70
Threat to do bodily harm	44
Unwanted phone calls	16
Malicious destruction of property	14
Breaking and entering	4
Stalking	3
Violation of restraining order	3
No clear evidence of above criminal acts	8

a. This column represents the number of women reporting the different types of crimes but does not include the number of occurrences of these types of criminal behavior. The types of crimes are not mutually exclusive. Because many women reported several types of criminal behavior, the total of this column exceeds 100, the number of women's files examined.

the defendants had threatened to kill them. In a Colorado study of 355 restraining order complaint forms, 31 percent of the women reported a threat to kill.[15] In Angela Browne's study of 205 self-selected physically abused women, 59 percent said their partners had threatened to kill them.[16]

Thirty-nine percent of women in the sample reported that their partners or former partners screamed, yelled, or otherwise abused them verbally. Intimidation through the destruction of property was apparent in 14 percent of the complaint forms. The kinds of property destroyed were often symbols of women's privacy and protective boundaries, as in the case of doors that were broken and windows that were smashed. In a number of other cases, men targeted women's mobility by slashing car tires, breaking the windshield, and disabling the car engine. Men's efforts to isolate women by cutting the phone cord or ripping the phone out of the wall also appear in women's statements.

Finally, Table 4.4 presents a breakdown of the violence and abuse that can be categorized as assault and battery, threat to commit bodily harm, unwanted phone calls, malicious destruction of property, breaking and entering, stalking, and violations of an existing restraining order. Ninety-two percent of the complaint forms described a recent or past action falling into one of these seven categories of criminal behavior. This level of criminality is consistent with other research done at Quincy District Court. One study of 663 restraining orders issued in 1990 found that 64 percent of the petitioners gave evidence of physical assault.[17] Another study of 500 restraining orders issued in 1992 at Quincy found that 78 percent of the women who were granted orders presented facts sufficient to support criminal complaints for assault and battery, threats to do bodily harm, unwanted phone calls, stalking, or breaking and entering.[18]

In summary, then, women's testimony about their abuse incorporates much more than physical violence. Even in affidavits written hastily before their initial court appearances, many women felt it important to name threats, intimidation, economic abuse, and sexual violence as important to why they came to court.

The Strategies of Men Who Batter

How do women seeking restraining orders describe the logic of men's violence and abuse? By interpreting men's violence in terms of *strategies*, this study draws from the sociology of emotions, as developed by Arlie Russell Hochschild.[19] Two of her concepts are useful here: gender ideology and gender strategy. A gender *ideology* is a set of beliefs about men, women, and relationships—beliefs that have deep emotional anchors. As individuals emerge from adolescence, Hochschild claims, they come to embrace or identify with a set of cultural ideals about manhood and womanhood. A gender *strategy* is the attempt to implement this ideology in daily life. Included in this strategy are the emotional preparations necessary to follow this plan of action.[20]

In their affidavits, women are often eloquent in their descriptions of the strategic goals of men's abusiveness. While it would be necessary to talk with the men named as defendants to fully explore their gender ideologies, nevertheless these affidavits suggest the outlines of men's deeply held beliefs about what they are entitled to as husbands, fathers, boyfriends, and even as former partners.

Out of the 100 affidavits, 50 gave some indication of the objectives behind men's violence and abuse. Four main types of strategies are described in these 50 affidavits. These can be characterized as (1) separation assault; (2) punishment, coercion, and retaliation against women's actions concerning children; (3) retaliation or coercion against women's pursuit of court or police remedies; and (4) retaliation in response to other perceived challenges to men's authority.

Separation Assault

In a feminist critique of legal discourse on battered women, Martha R. Mahoney argues that we need a new name for the kinds of assaults directed against women for leaving or attempting to leave violent men. Discussions of "why does she stay?" focus more on the failures of battered women than on the coercive actions of batterers, Mahoney states. What is needed is a way to refocus public attention on the struggle for power and control that is implicated in battering, a struggle that is only intensified by women's attempts to separate. Mahoney offers a new term, "separation assault."[21]

There is a significant difference, Mahoney insists, between stating that a woman's attempt to separate *triggered* a man's violence and saying that his violence represents an assault *"upon separation itself."*[22] Only the latter highlights the strategy behind the assault: denying women their autonomy. Separation assault names the violence and abuse that keeps women in destructive relationships and terrorizes them after they leave. Mahoney's analysis parallels that of other researchers who have found that men are often violent when women attempt to leave the relationship.[23] As Liz Kelly states it, "Male violence arises out of men's power and women's resistance to it."[24]

Desmond Ellis and Walter S. DeKeseredy have given particular attention to violence against separated and divorced women.[25] Using a different term, "postseparation woman abuse," Ellis associates an increased risk of violence with women's assertions of independence. Mahoney is concerned, however, that this term neglects attacks on the very *decision* to leave; she argues that these attacks on women's autonomy occur while women are still in relationships with their batterers.

In the above sketch of the relationship status of the women seeking restraining orders at Dorchester and Quincy District Courts, close to half of these relationships either have ended or have changed status dramatically. Mahoney's concept of "separation assault" finds substantial support here. Fully 48 percent of the affidavits that indicate a motive describe separation assault.

Violence and abuse aimed at *preventing women from separating* were reported in 18 percent of these affidavits. Women described being assaulted for their attempts to get a divorce, being physically prevented from leaving an abusive situation, and suffering violence and abuse for their efforts to get men to leave. These statements are illustrative of women's testimony:

He has repeatedly threatened to kill me threatened to burn down my home threatened to wreck my car pushed shoved me thrown things at me broken furniture and household items every time I have tried to discuss divorce/separation. He said he would not leave voluntarily. I would have to get a restraining order and if I did I wouldn't live to get to probate court.

I have asked him many times to leave but every time I do he will punch me and physically abuse me.

We are like a prisoner in the home. . . . My husband told the kids that I can't get him out of there. . . . By breaking the door he is proving to me that I can't do anything.

Violence and abuse are part of a plan of action on the part of these men; in each case, they repeatedly attack women's movements toward independence. This stifling of women's autonomy is also reported by women who have left. Eight percent of the women indicated that their former partners made threats or attempts at physically *forcing them to return to the relationship*:

When we got to his car he choked me when I asked him to please leave. He also said, "If you don't stay with me I will kill you."

The defendant has said in a telephone conversation, and in person, that he would be coming to my wedding. . . . He said he would like to kidnap me and take me away.

[My estranged husband] offered me a ride home in his car. After I got into the car he tried [to force] me to have sex with him.

In 22 percent of the cases, women reported violence and abuse in *retaliation for leaving*:

I have tried to end the relationship, but fearful, intimidated. . . . [Once he] came to my office, cried and threatened suicide if I left him. Finally, I ended it . . . and since [then he makes] . . . threats to use any means. . . . He has a gun permit.

He called me at my place of employment and threatened me. He told me that if he couldn't have me, no one will and also that he wanted to "cut my heart out."

[My former partner] found some jewelry from my male friend. He began questioning me then started calling me dirty names. Then I asked him to leave my home—he didn't. He argued with me and threatened me then he started choking me pushing me on the bed.

These attempts to maintain a coercive connection with women were reported as occurring even years after the relationship had ended. The following incidents involved men from whom these women had been separated for a year or more:

[He] called my house three times saying things like he was going to beat me up and also my boyfriend.

[He] came to the window and started to threaten [my male] companion. I went out of the building to try to intervene. . . . [He] threatened bodily harm with a [piece of lumber]. . . . police . . . arrived and arrested the defendant. I am now in fear of my life.

The sense that not only marriage, but even a past dating relationship, entitles men to possess or control women is apparent in these accounts. Adrienne Rich describes this kind of gender ideology:

It would seem that a man experiences the violation of some profound "right" when a woman leaves him: the "right" to her services, however lacking in mutuality the relationship. Through patriarchal socialization, men learn to think in terms of their "rights" where rights are not actually the issue: in areas like sexual behavior, maternal behavior, which are seen, not as springing from a woman's choice and affections but as behavior to which a man is entitled *as a male*.[26]

Rich identifies "husband-right" and "father-right" as forms of this kind of entitlement. In the violent relationships encountered through these restraining order documents, this entitlement appears to have been modernized to extend to men's rights in cohabiting and dating relationships; there seems to be a belief in "boyfriend-right," even "former-boyfriend-" and "former-husband-right."

Women who demonstrate independence or are no longer willing to remain with these men are verbally degraded: according
to women's affidavits, they are called "whore," "fuckin' bitch,"
"cunt," and other misogynistic names. These words serve to
transform and dehumanize women in men's minds. Such "trans-
formations" are a common practice among men to avoid dealing
with women as peers.[27] These verbal assaults may also serve as
emotional preparation for further attacks on women, just as use
of the dehumanizing term "gook" by American troops in Vietnam facilitated violence against Vietnamese soldiers and civil-
ians.[28]

Martha Mahoney states that separation violence represents
"the main reason women seek protective orders."[29] Taken together, attacks and abuse aimed at preventing women's separation, forcing women to return, or retaliating for their leaving are
described in nearly half (48 percent) of the women's affidavits
where a goal is identified. The evidence from this investigation
thus supports her observation.

Punishment, Coercion, and Retaliation Concerning Children

Motherhood profoundly affects women's experiences of violence and abuse, Mahoney argues. Yet both the law and even
much feminist legal theory, she claims, assume "that women
with children are individual actors." Mothers' connections with
their children are "existential, social and extremely practical,"
Mahoney states; "in many significant ways—our 'selves' simply
are not single."[30] Of the 100 randomly selected cases in this sample, 76 percent of the women were mothers. Underscoring the
relevance of motherhood to women's victimization, 7 percent of
the affidavits describe violence and abuse during pregnancy. One
woman reported being assaulted while holding her baby in her
arms. Eleven percent of the forms indicated physical abuse, sexual abuse, or threats directed against children. Men's threats to
take the children from their mothers were noted in 5 percent of
the affidavits. In 9 percent of the cases, women reported violence
or abuse occurring during the dropping off or picking up of their
children.

According to women's affidavits, the goals of men's violence
frequently centered on parental authority. In the 50 cases where

a motive was indicated, 22 percent fell into this category. Eight percent of the women presented their abuse as *punishment for questioning men's authority over the children*, as in these accounts:

He then became extremely abusive after I told him that I didn't like his language and how he was treating my daughter—with his language. . . . He then kicked her. . . . I was also physically abused.

[He] called our [daughter] names. . . . I asked him to stop because she started to cry and got scared. . . . He then went into our bedroom and started to smash things. All our pictures of the children, lights. . . . When he was doing this all he was screaming. Terrible dirty dirty words to me.

From women's descriptions, there seems to be an expectation on the part of these men that their authority as fathers should not be questioned, regardless of how abusive they are. Whether they are wives or unmarried partners, women ought to defer to men's rights as fathers, these men seem to be saying, even men's rights as stepfathers.

Threats and violence aimed at *coercing custody and child care decisions* were reported in another 8 percent of the women's affidavits:

He said he would get someone to kill me and make it look like an accident so he could get custody of our son.

Threatened to kill me if I was going to try to take his daughter away from him. He also stated that if he was to go and take her from where ever she is, no one will be able to stop him even if he has to hurt them.

He got furious and threatened to kill me if I send her to a day care [instead of having him baby-sit the child]. . . . He said if I got a restraining order, the police won't be here all the time, and he can kill me then.

These threats against women and their children represent another kind of assault on women's autonomy. From the perspectives of these three men, father-right is not incompatible with criminal threats and cruelty toward mothers and their own children.

Another dimension of father-right is expressed in men's violence and threats in *retaliation for women seeking child support*. This strategy was detailed in 6 percent of women's statements:

The defendant . . . and myself engaged in a very heated argument about financial support for our child. . . . As a result, he became very violent striking me in the head with his closed fist, also attempting to strangle me.

[He] called to tell me he was sending court papers to _____ court regarding child support. [He] does not want to pay child support because he doesn't see my [child]. Then . . . he called back and told me I would be hurt very soon. . . . He then called [a third time] and told me he would be at my house [within minutes]. I called the police.

If unquestioned authority over children is one dimension of father-right, another expression of it is a refusal to accept material obligations toward one's children. This is a common means of expressing hostility toward women for separation. The severity of the threats and violence in these cases indicates the level of some men's bitterness and desperation at losing their relationships. Here again, separation is not really a solution for these women but rather shifts the ground in a continuing power struggle to matters involving their children. Batterers' counseling programs have long understood that estranged fathers will often use children as weapons against their former wives or partners. This is a central theme of the Duluth Domestic Abuse Intervention Project's work with batterers.[31] Emerge, the Boston area batterers' counseling and education program, has developed a checklist for their work with men that identifies 34 violent and controlling behaviors toward children.[32]

Retaliation and Coercion Concerning Court and Police Actions

In 12 percent of the accounts of motives, women testified that the violence or abuse was related to legal actions they took beyond those involving custody and child support. These actions against which men retaliated included calling the police; being somehow responsible, in his eyes, for his conviction and sentencing for raping her; and taking out a restraining order, leading to his conviction and sentencing for violating it:

Kicked me in my back. Hit me in the back of my head. Threatening to get a gun and shoot because I called the police.

He thought I called the police (I have called them in the past) and he grabbed me, dragged me by my hair into the kitchen and threatened to kill me. He has repeatedly threatened to kill me and threatened me with kitchen knives.

He was released [from prison four days ago] since then I have been receiving crank calls all times of the night. . . . stating that I will not get away with this he will pay me back.

[He] came into my home and physically abused me. . . . [He] just got out of jail [three days before] for violating a restraining order. . . . [He] told me several times [that night] that he's going to kill me.

These accounts frame the dilemma of intervention in the starkest terms: they represent the terror that the legal system will only make matters worse. These are nightmare stories. Among other goals of their violence, these men are seeking *vengeance against women for being held accountable to the law.* It is as if the privacy of the home ought to protect men's privileges, which include a right to abuse women, and any breach of this protective cloak represents a betrayal that merits retaliation.

Two other affidavits identified *retaliation and coercion regarding divorce* as strategies:

[He] has put me in fear and is behaving aggressively with abusive language over the phone [and] when he returns children to me. He is especially angry over the recent court orders for me to have exclusive use and occupancy of our marital home.

[He] told me he wants a divorce but he wasn't going to move out and if I don't get it . . . he'll make me wish I had. . . . My husband has threatened me and threatened to destroy my property and my job. . . . My husband believes in payback. Please help me.

This kind of disregard for the law and the courts produces extraordinary fear and despair in women. Judge Albert Kramer, former presiding justice at Quincy District Court, testified at a public hearing about the defiance of the law he observed in batterers:

When we are dealing with batterers and perpetrators of domestic violence, more than any other violent offender, they are the most dangerous and with them you have the most potential for harm. . . . There is no other group of perpetrators of violence that is more tenaciously resistant to court orders and court efforts to curb their violence and prevent their almost relentless pursuit of their victims.[33]

The "ancient privileges" of husband-right and father-right— along with their modern equivalents as boyfriend-right and former-partner-right—represent for many men a more compelling moral order than that symbolized by the courts.

Retaliation for Other Perceived Challenges
to Men's Authority

For some of the men named in the restraining orders, the goals
of violence and abuse clustered around two matters pivotal to the
accomplishment of masculinity in the United States: drinking
and sexuality. In one-quarter of all the restraining order affidavits,
women described their abusers as drinking, drunk, or involved
with drugs and alcohol. But alcohol or drugs do not supply strategies in themselves. Drinking figures into the goals of men's violence when their drinking behavior meets intolerance. Of the
affidavits indicating motives, 6 percent of the women wrote that
they were abused after raising the issue of drinking behavior with
their partners. The goal of this violence and abuse appears to be,
at least in part, a *defense of their prerogative to get drunk at will*,
regardless of the consequences:

When I was five months pregnant we had an argument over how he's an
alcoholic and how he's treated me. I was trying to tell him that he needs
help. He got real angry and started pushing me. . . . He grabbed me and
pushed me down hard into the [furniture]. . . . I spent the night in the
hospital. . . . he knows he hurts me, he knows I suffer. He does it deliberately.

[I] questioned the defendant about his drinking because he's not supposed to be drinking, he's on probation. The defendant got angry and
gestured with a beer bottle. . . . The police came because someone had
called—he had been yelling and punching.

The guiding premises of the violence presented here would seem
to be that both men's rights to drink and the license drinking
provides to act irresponsibly are inviolable. Notions that battering is mostly drunken, "impulsive" violence do not account for
the routinized, repetitious nature of men's drinking behavior or
for men's defense of this behavior despite knowing its consequences for others.

Men's sexual entitlement and possessiveness have already
been addressed with respect to separation assault. Beyond assaults on women's attempts to separate, however, there are additional strategies relating to nonreciprocal sexual "rights." Two
affidavits recount *assaults on women's questioning of men's af-*
fairs:

[My husband] was drunk and I caught him talking on the phone with his girlfriend that he has. And I started yelling at him so he hit me and I left. . . . I'm afraid he'll kill me.

[My husband] is and has been having extra marital affairs with another woman. This morning he threatened to hit me when I notified him that I knew about his affair.

The familiar double standard appears to be operating in these cases: not only are men entitled to nonreciprocated sexual latitude, but women are not even allowed to bring it up.

Another woman reported her husband's *jealous verbal attacks and extreme possessiveness*:

He accused me of sleeping with my daughter's boyfriend. . . . I was called a whore and a bitch and the angry hurtful words just kept on [for the past five months]. . . . I am a grown woman and I am not allowed to speak to a male or even say hello unless its someone he associates with.

Accusations that women are secretly sleeping around represent more than a feeling of jealousy; such accusations represent a man's strategy, based on deeply felt entitlement, to circumscribe a woman's social life and make her negotiate the world outside the family household only through him.

Lastly, there is a residual group of 6 percent of affidavits where women named revenge as a goal without further specification:

[He called and said] he is sick of the way things are going and that he was going to meet me on my job and take care of me. . . . [Later] he grabbed me and, putting his hand on his gun, told me that he would "blow my goddamn brains out." . . . [I] phoned the police.

[He] began calling my home making threats against my life "I will kill you." . . . [The next day] he came to my door. I did not open it, he started screaming that he would get me one way or the other. He also screamed many vulgar statements and then drove away.

Neither of these were isolated incidents, according to women's accounts, but were part of a pattern of similarly threatening acts by these men.

Threats to kill a woman, made repeatedly over a period of weeks or months, are a form of psychological torture.[34] The parallels between the tactics used against battered women and the means of torture used against political prisoners have prompted feminist researchers and activists to name woman battering as a violation of international human rights.[35]

TABLE 4.5

**Men's Strategies Reported in Affidavits
of Fifty Women**

Type of Strategy	Number	Percentage
Separation assault	24	48%
Punishment, coercion, and retaliation concerning children	11	22
Retaliation or coercion regarding women's legal action	6	12
Retaliation against other challenges to men's authority		
Against challenges to his drinking behavior	3	6
Against questioning of his relationship with other women	2	4
Against actions arousing his jealousy	1	2
Unspecified vengeance	3	6
	50	100%

Table 4.5 summarizes the types of strategies described in the sworn statements by women. The gender ideologies of many of the men depicted in these accounts appear to be held with extraordinary tenaciousness, self-righteousness, and depth of feeling. This is similar to the beliefs and feelings of gendered entitlement I encountered in my previous research with men who batter. Most of the men I interviewed in an earlier study justified their violence as righteous punishment: they believed women deserved abuse for failing to fulfill the obligations of a "good wife." One man reported that he said to his partner, "I should just smack you for the lousy wife you've been." These men reported that they assaulted their wives and woman partners for a variety of perceived "failures," including not being a good cook, not being sexually available, not being sufficiently deferential, not knowing when to be silent, and for not being faithful. Their violence was thus an attempt to enforce women's compliance with a man's patriarchal "rights."[36]

Research on men named as defendants in restraining orders offers evidence that as a group these men have histories of being violent and of being charged with both violent and nonviolent crimes. While criminal records of the men named as defendants in these 100 orders were not obtained, a recent study of 644 restraining orders at Quincy District Court found that 78 percent of the men named as defendants had a previous record of criminal complaints and 43 percent of the men had records of violent crimes against persons. The average number of prior criminal complaints was 13.[37] A statewide study done by the Commissioner of Probation found that nearly 80 percent of the first 8,500 men identified in restraining orders had prior criminal records.[38]

There are two important implications of these findings. First, a large number of these men have what Albert Cardarelli calls a "proficiency" at being violent.[39] In comparison to the women who are or were their wives or partners, violence is a well-rehearsed tactic of control, rehearsed both physically and in terms of the emotional preparation for acting violently. If a man has been arrested for assault and battery on another man, his partner likely knows this. This colors the negotiations between them, whether or not they live together. A threat by this man that he will kill her has credibility. While the incompleteness of these court documents must be kept in mind, based on women's testimony and other research on restraining orders in Massachusetts, there appears to be ample reason for women's fear of these men. After weeks of reading and rereading women's descriptions of the violence, even I awoke several times from nightmares of being physically attacked.

Summary

The disorder that violence wreaks on women's lives is now being named in the courtroom by record numbers of women. An examination of affidavits filed with restraining order requests reveals a variety of physical, sexual, psychological, and economic tactics used by men who batter. But the accounts of abuse that women write reveal more than the types of abuse they suffered: they also indicate the strategies motivating men's violence.

Four main themes arise from women's testimony concerning men's strategies. Many of the abusive incidents match Martha Mahoney's definition of "separation assault," meaning they were aimed at preventing women from leaving, coercing women into returning, or retaliating for their departure. Women's affidavits also offer other evidence of the domination that violence constructs. Much of the violence appeared to be retaliation against women's legal actions or against other perceived challenges to men's authority as fathers, husbands, boyfriends, or even as former partners, absurd as this patriarchal logic may sound. Linda Gordon claims that battering arises "not just from subordination but also from contesting it."[40] Women coming to the courts to seek restraining orders are resisting men's coercive authority, and their affidavits testify that this has been an ongoing effort.

The consequences of battering identified in these documents include not only physical injuries to both women and their children but also the terror of living under threats of being killed, the destruction of property and other economic losses, and the disruption of being forced to leave home. Violence also colors what Dobash and Dobash call the "negotiation of daily life"—the discussion and allocation of money, time, and other resources in family households.[41] These are resources over which men generally have greater control. Given women's inferior position in the paid labor force and their deeper feelings of responsibility for their children, women must negotiate for these resources from a subordinate position. What these affidavits indicate is that after they separate or even divorce, women are often still forced to negotiate child support, child custody decisions, and visitation under the threat of violence. The term *domestic violence* therefore loses meaning when the web of fear and terror is spread this far.

The evidence from these 100 restraining order files challenges claims that the increase in restraining orders is the result of women's attempts to gain leverage in divorce settlements, win battles over child support, or claim the marital home. Half of the women seeking restraining orders, both in Dorchester and in Quincy, have never been married to their defendants and thus couldn't be seeking an advantage in a divorce. The majority of women with children at both courts don't request child support as part of the restraining order, and most that do don't receive it. Advocates for battered women report that women with children are often too afraid to ask for child support. And since most women seeking orders aren't living with the defendants, most aren't even seeking to have a man removed from their home.

What women are asking for is an end to violence, terror, and harassment aimed at limiting their autonomy. Some 120 years after Judge Pelham condemned the practice of men beating women with objects, pulling women by the hair, choking them, spitting in their faces, and kicking them, these identical practices were found in a random sample of 100 restraining order files. The question framed by women's testimony is, what are the best ways to support women's moves toward independence and break the ancient, yet modern control that batterers exercise over women's lives?

The finding of the Gender Bias Study that sex discrimination haunts the trial courtrooms of the Commonwealth is important and troubling. . . . Authority and leadership are diffused throughout the system. . . . Day to day, however, in courtrooms from Nantucket to Pittsfield, clients, counsel, jurors, witnesses, and our fellow workers understand and expect that judges are responsible for what takes place. . . . The judge's behavior and demeanor matter greatly. Much more by example than by precept does he or she communicate expectations of gender-neutral professionalism in and out of the courtroom.

JUDGE HAROLD FLANNERY[1]

Ma'am, I'm sorry, I won't be able to hear this case, not the way you're dressed. This is a courtroom. You don't come in shorts to a courtroom. This was not an emergency. You need to go and change and come back in the appropriate attire.

Judge to a woman seeking a restraining order

[To defendant] Did you kick her in the stomach when she was pregnant last year? . . . I am going to extend the order. . . . Did he surrender his keys? Do you have your keys to [address], sir? Give it to me. . . . Mr. _____ , how much money do you make a week, sir? . . . I am going to order you to pay $125 a week in child support.

Judge to a woman seeking a restraining order

5

Judging as Emotional Labor: Courtroom Observations of Restraining Order Hearings

What do judges do with their authority in restraining order hearings, after reading and hearing women's testimony about violence? From court to court and judge to judge, dramatic differences exist in the way that abused women are treated. These differences are so well understood by volunteer advocates that women are at times told to avoid certain courts and particular judges or even to come back another day in the hopes that someone else will be hearing restraining orders.

Consider the judge who ordered a woman seeking a restraining order out of the courtroom for wearing shorts. The woman appeared for her 10-day hearing, but before even examining her case the male judge determined that she was inadequately deferential to the court in her appearance. Other District Court judges who often heard restraining order cases would not have sent her out of the court: women and men appeared before them in shorts and casual summer attire. But on the morning of July 9, one judge was holding the abuse prevention act hearings, and decisions in these cases are virtually unappealable.[2] According to the newspaper, the temperature in Boston reached a high of 96 degrees on that day in July.

The judge who required the defendant to surrender his house keys offers a different face of authority. She asked the defendant to respond to allegations contained in a woman's affidavit that he kicked her in the stomach while pregnant the previous year and that he attempted to strangle her two weeks previous to the court date. The order was issued, and since it requires the defendant to leave and remain away from the residence, the judge asked the defendant to surrender his house keys on the spot. The symbolic message of the judge's extended hand, waiting for the defendant's keys, was that the court had authority to intervene into the privacy of the defendant's home and deprive him of access to it. This defendant was one of two men observed handing over house or apartment keys to the judge that morning. Demanding that he respond to his paternal obligations, the judge also ordered the defendant to pay temporary child support.

Based on courtroom observations such as these at Dorchester District Court and Quincy District Court, this chapter examines the different types of demeanor that judges display in restraining order hearings. Three main questions guide the investigation of these courtroom encounters: From a sociological perspective, how can we best understand judicial demeanor? Why is it important? And what forms does it take in courtroom interactions?

"Doing Authority" in the Courtroom: Judging as Emotional Labor

In his instructive essay "The Nature of Deference and Demeanor," Erving Goffman distinguishes what he calls "ceremony" from "substance" in social interactions. Ceremonial aspects of behavior are those that have implications for the character of the actor and for the character of the observer: a polite smile from a judge may express a particular image of judicial authority and at the same time convey respect for the intended recipient. Theoretically, ceremonial aspects can be differentiated from the substantive or instrumental purpose of behavior. Signing a restraining order, issuing an arrest warrant, or ordering child support are substantive acts, for which there is an official record; whether the judge communicates empathy or indifference while doing this represents the ceremonial dimension of behavior. Although ceremony and substance are distinct concepts, however, they are present in the same behavior; the ceremonial aspect is not fully separate or self-contained. This symbolic communication is rather an *element* or *gesture* contained in social behavior; nothing is *only* ceremonial, in Goffman's analysis.

According to Goffman, *demeanor* refers to "that element of the individual's ceremonial behavior typically conveyed through deportment, dress, and bearing, which serves to express to those in his immediate presence that he is a person of certain desirable or undesirable qualities."[3] Rather than a fixed aspect of an individual's character, demeanor is an *image* produced in interaction. In Goffman's approach, demeanor is best assessed from the eye of the beholder:

Demeanor involves attributes derived *from interpretations others make* of the way in which the individual handles himself during social intercourse. *The individual cannot establish these attributes for his own* by verbally avowing that he possesses them, though sometimes he may rashly do this. . . . through demeanor the individual creates an image of himself, but properly speaking this is not an image that is meant for his own eyes.[4] (Emphasis added)

The most accurate assessment of judicial demeanor, according to Goffman's interpretation, would therefore be that of those standing before the judge; for this reason, women's perspectives on judicial demeanor will conclude the investigation in Chapter 7.

Applying Goffman's analysis to judicial behavior, there is both a "what" and a "how" to judge's actions in restraining order hearings: issuing or not issuing the order may be considered the "what," and demeanor represents the "how." Chapter 4 discusses official actions that were taken in restraining order hearings. But this doesn't fully indicate *how* women were treated. And as is described in Chapter 3, the question of judicial demeanor was the crux of the public scandal involving judges Heffernan, King, and Tempone in 1986. Do judges express irritation, impatience, and even hostility toward women seeking orders? Or do judges use their authority to express concern for women's safety and connect women with resources that can empower them?

I propose that judicial demeanor is best understood as the *emotional presentation of authority* by judges. The focus on demeanor as *emotional* presentation frames judging as "emotional labor."[5] Judges *intend* to have an emotional impact on plaintiffs and defendants, and the Judicial Code of Conduct addresses this responsibility. The kind of emotional impact that judges have and the way that they accomplish this are the central questions of demeanor. Judging as emotional labor is explained more fully below. The emphasis on *authority* derives from the fact that in the courtroom judges are always "doing authority," even when smiling or joking with other court officers. The weight of their institutionalized power imbalances every interaction. Judicial demeanor names the manner in which judges "do authority" in the courtroom; it requires an emotional kind of impression management.

It is necessary to identify the range of behaviors that express demeanor in the courtroom. Goffman identifies five ways that ceremonial aspects of interactions are expressed: linguistically, gesturally, spatially, embedded in a task, and as part of the communication structure.[6] Following Goffman's analysis, Robert M. Emerson identified how juvenile court judges may change their tone of voice, physical distance from juvenile defendants, and level of formality in order to impress defendants with their willingness to listen and offer help.[7] How judges speak, the kinds of questions they ask, their facial expressions, how close to the bench they allow women to stand, how diligent they are at assisting women—all of these behaviors symbolically express an image of authority in the person of the judge.

The work of Arlie Russell Hochschild offers a way of theorizing the emotional dimensions of demeanor in even greater depth.

In Hochschild's sociology of emotions, judicial demeanor would be interpreted as "emotional labor." Jobs that involve emotional labor have three characteristics in common, according to Hochschild:

First, they require face-to-face or voice-to-voice contact with the public. Second, they require the worker to produce an emotional state in another person—gratitude or fear, for example. Third, they allow the employer to exercise a degree of control over the emotional activities of employees.[8]

Judges (and lawyers) fall into this category, in Hochschild's analysis. The responsibilities of judges certainly involve contact with the public, and the work by Emerson already illustrates the kinds of emotional states that judges attempt to produce in criminal defendants. Furthermore, the existence of state standards of judicial practice, the Judicial Conduct Commission, and the offices of first justices within each court represent the control that the system exercises (however minimally) over the conduct of judges.

This supervision of the Supreme Judicial Court over the conduct of Judge Paul Heffernan in the case of Pamela Nigro Dunn illustrates how important demeanor is to the appearance of justice. At the same time, the ruling of the state's highest court raises a controversy over whose perception of demeanor matters most. When the Supreme Judicial Court reprimanded Judge Paul Heffernan for "rudeness, discourtesy, sarcasm, and hostility,"[9] they found that he had violated the following section of the Code of Judicial Conduct:

A judge should be patient, dignified, and courteous to litigants, jurors, witnesses, lawyers, and others with whom he deals in his official capacity, and he should require similar conduct of lawyers, and of his staff, court officials and others subject to his direction and control.[10]

Whether judges are aware of the effects they have on plaintiffs, defendants, and other court officers became a matter of controversy with this case. In the ruling by the Massachusetts Supreme Judicial Court that reprimanded Judge Heffernan for his treatment of Pamela Nigro Dunn, the Court concluded that he was simply not conscious of the emotional impact of his behavior:

It seems reasonably clear that part of Judge Heffernan's problem comes from his loud, deep voice, physically imposing manner, and his *apparent unawareness* of the intimidating effect he might have on people who appear before him. We also conclude, however, from our review of Judge Heffernan's testimony in this proceeding that his level of sensitivity may need to be raised. The judge was unwilling in his testimony to recognize the obvious fact that many of his remarks in the Dunn case were sarcastic, rude, and undignified. He was also unwilling or unable to appreciate the negative effect of many of his remarks on Pamela Dunn and her witness/victim advocates. The judge's testimony that, in context, substantially all his remarks were proper is troubling. (Emphasis added)[11]

A "private" reprimand was the sum total of the sanctions imposed on the judge. Advocates for battered women were harshly critical of this decision and the lack of accountability for judicial misconduct they felt it represented.[12]

Judicial Demeanor Toward Women: Five Types of Authority Presented in Restraining Order Hearings

In the wake of this public attention to judicial demeanor, what kinds of authority are judges in Massachusetts presenting in restraining order hearings? Eighteen different judges were observed over a nine-month period between December 1992 and August 1993—nine at Dorchester District Court and nine at Quincy District Court. Twelve judges were white men, four were white women, and two were African American men. This sample is actually more balanced in terms of gender and race than the Massachusetts judiciary. At the time these observations were done, district court judges were 86 percent male, and 94 percent white,[13] in a state where people of color constitute 12 percent of the population.[14]

With such a small sample it becomes impossible to offer a meaningful comparison of male versus female judges or white versus African American judges. Nonetheless, a few observations are in order. Hochschild sees gendered patterns in the emotional labor required of workers. Are men or women more likely to be supportive of survivors of violence? Surely, this is the kind of emotional labor characteristically expected of workers who are women or who work at positions that are designed for women to fill. But while three of the four judges who happened to be women did indeed seem very supportive in their interactions with abused women, one seemed less supportive than many of the judges who were men. Furthermore, the two African American judges who happened to be men also appeared supportive in their exchanges with battered women. White male judges cannot easily be categorized; they represented some of the most and some of the least supportive judges. A more descriptive way of comparing judges is needed.

The work of Maureen Mileski was used to create a typology of demeanor. Mileski studied what she calls "courtroom encounters" between judges and defendants in a lower criminal court. She developed four categories to describe the demeanor of judges toward criminal defendants: good-natured (courteous, welcoming, supportive), bureaucratic (routine, businesslike, impersonal), firm or formal (conveys moral authority), and harsh (nasty, abrasive, contemptuous). Distinguishing between the material sanctions meted out in criminal cases (fines, prison time, or probation) and "situational sanctions" (warnings, verbal reprimands, or lecturing), Mileski found that the milder the material sanctions, the more likely the judge was to lecture or admonish the defendant in courtroom encounters.[15]

But judicial authority does not simply punish and constrain; following Michel Foucault, one could say that authority also facilitates and empowers.[16] Judicial authority is no less observable in the mobilization of resources for plaintiffs than in the disciplining of defendants (or plaintiffs). While Mileski's categories were developed to describe the varieties of judges' manner in dealing with defendants, they can also be used to distinguish the varieties of judges' behavior toward women appearing as plaintiffs. To these four categories, I added a fifth type of authority observed particularly (although not exclusively) in interactions between male judges and women: condescending or patronizing authority. As judicial demeanor is conceived here as the emotional presentation of authority, these categories of demeanor could be seen as different "faces" of authority presented in courtroom interactions.

Good-Natured Demeanor Toward Women

Restraining order hearings have no set formal structure in Massachusetts.[17] Unlike judges in criminal cases, judges hearing requests for restraining orders have no standard list of things that must be said about the right to counsel, the right to trial by jury, or other rights. In these hearings, judges write their own scripts. They may choose to ask a number of questions or no questions at all. They may take one minute, five minutes, or 15 minutes to issue a temporary order. If the defendant appears, which occurs in perhaps one-fourth to one-third of the hearings, they may choose to warn him of the consequences of violating the order, or they may say nothing at all about this.

"Good-natured" judicial demeanor is described by Mileski as "courteous, affable, even subservient."[18] The judges who exhibited this kind of demeanor used their authority to make women feel welcome in the court, to express concern for their suffering, and to mobilize resources on their behalf. Judges presenting this kind of demeanor greeted women in a friendly manner, perhaps gesturing to indicate that they could stand very close, acknowledging the difficulty of speaking publicly about their victimization. After taking the time to read their affidavits, these judges would then ask a few questions or explain how the restraining order worked. As if to counter the fear, confusion, and anxiety that many women display in these hearings, good-natured judges spoke in a pleasant tone of voice and maintained continuous eye contact, establishing a human connection in a frequently noisy and chaotic courtroom. There is an attempt to deemphasize the social distance that authority can impose in these interactions. These are the kinds of statements judges made that communicated a welcoming and inviting tone:

Anything you want to tell me that you didn't put in your affidavit?

Are you confused by anything I have said?

[To a woman who wants to drop the restraining order:] Has he threatened you in any way? . . . If the situation gets bad again, you should feel free to come back to the court. . . . Do you have any other questions?

You have to come back into court [to have the order extended]. . . . What time of day is better for you, morning or afternoon?

A willingness to listen and an attentiveness to women's feelings of confusion or intimidation are expressed in these remarks. These judges are well aware of the emotional dimensions of their impact. But perhaps more important than these deferential gestures are what Goffman calls "task-embedded" messages.[19]

In their diligence at mobilizing resources for women, the following judges indicate that a request for protection is taken seriously. A good-natured image of authority is expressed in their attention to issues of safety and their concern that women understand their options under the law, both civil and criminal:

Have you been to court before? I'm not saying that to make you feel bad. . . . Would you like to talk to someone from the district attorney's office to process criminal charges? . . . Are you sure? . . . Is Monday, _____ okay? . . . If that's bad, another time for you is okay. . . . This order is in effect now. If you have any problem you should call the police. . . . Do you have a minute to talk to [advocate]? She could give you numbers for other resources. . . . If you wait just a second, I can give you a card [containing information on battered women's shelters and resources].

My name is Judge _____ . . . . [After reading affidavit] There's no reason why you should have to tolerate this. . . . I'll put down on this restraining order that the issue of support is going to be raised at the next hearing. . . . If he so much as calls you, call the police. . . . I'm saying here that the defendant is to return only with police escort. . . . [mentions the option of seeking a criminal complaint].

You understand that if I vacate this order . . . you still have that right [to call police].

I'll give you this order. I just want to emphasize that the order isn't enough. . . . The criminal process takes a different track [explains criminal process].

In these negotiations between women and the state, judges used their authority to underscore the gravity of women's danger and make criminal justice remedies accessible. While not all requests for restraining orders allege criminal offenses, it bears repeating that 70 percent of randomly selected affidavits presented in the previous chapter alleged crimes of assault and battery and that 92 percent of the affidavits reported some kind of criminal act. The judges quoted above routinely mentioned criminal options to women seeking protection. They also made women aware of other resources in the courthouse, such as advocates, in the cases where women appeared alone. One judge above handed out cards with phone numbers of local shelters and other services for women, using the restraining order request as an opportunity to counter battered women's isolation.

Of the 18 judges observed, 10 (56 percent) conveyed good-natured demeanor in most of their negotiations with women; the

other eight did not offer this support. Even these 10 "good-natured" or supportive judges did not display this kind of authority
in every hearing. There was some inconsistency observed in several of these judges; one judge who appeared good-natured in most
of the hearings was condescending toward a woman in one case.
The kind of demeanor displayed toward men who were defendants was also different with most of these judges; this is taken
up further below.

Bureaucratic Demeanor Toward Women

In contrast to the active presence and emotional engagement
of the judges described above, bureaucratic judges were passive
and detached. Mileski describes bureaucratic demeanor as "a
manner that at least bordered on the impersonal. . . . the personal
involvement of the judge remains minimal. He is routine and affectively neutral in his outward behavior."[20] In their interactions
with women requesting orders, these judges were minimally
courteous but emotionally flat. Sometimes they also seemed impatient, rushed, or bored. While they might smile occasionally, in
most of their interactions they displayed little empathy. Two of
the judges categorized as bureaucratic spent more time looking at
the documents than looking at the women standing before them;
in both cases, they seemed to rely on court clerks to do the emotional labor. One clerk, sitting at a desk in front of the bench,
spoke to the women seeking orders more than did the judge.

There was a difference in task-oriented displays of concern as
well. Good-natured judges asked a number of questions to make
sure the order they issued was enforceable: they might ask for a
second address of the defendant to make sure he gets the order,
or they might want a woman to indicate how many yards away
from her she wanted the defendant to stay. Bureaucratic judges
asked fewer questions, did not generally explain the restraining
order process, and seemed not as concerned with the enforceabil-
ity of the orders. They were also less likely to ask women why
they wanted to drop orders and less willing to inform women of
their option to bring criminal charges. Hearings were often very
brief before these judges and lasted just a few minutes unless attorneys were present. (In a court other than Dorchester and
Quincy, one bureaucratic judge disposed of eight consecutive re-

straining order cases in less than 18 minutes. In comparison, a good-natured judge at Quincy took an hour and 45 minutes to dispose of eight restraining order requests. These represent the extremes in terms of time spent; most good-natured judges averaged around five minutes for each hearing.) The emotional distance between a "bureaucratic" judge and a woman seeking help can be startling:

You filled out a new form today? . . . What is your relationship to the defendant? . . . Will you tell me what happened? [After listening to the woman, the judge looks down, signs the order, says nothing to the woman, and hands the order to the clerk, without even looking at the woman again.]

This judge did not greet the women who came before him and did not indicate with any gesture that the hearing was over. Even most bureaucratic judges would say "good morning" and nod a good-bye.

Routine or bureaucratic demeanor was the most common type that Mileski observed in her study; 78 percent of her cases fit this description.[21] Six out of 18, or one-third, of the judges studied in Dorchester and Quincy presented a bureaucratic demeanor in their interactions with women.

Firm or Formal Demeanor Toward Women

Firm or formal demeanor was identified by Mileski as a tone of moral authority that judges assume with defendants. This kind of demeanor was observed much more frequently in judges' interactions with men accused of violence than with women seeking help. But one of the 18 judges exhibited this tone in most of his interactions with women, and several other judges did so occasionally. While firm or formal judges may be courteous in greeting women or nodding good-bye, there is a lack of supportiveness, a limitation of patience, a strictness, or an expectation of deference from women that is expressed. Unlike the passivity of bureaucratic demeanor, judges assuming a firm or formal tone take an active stance and accentuate their power:

[In a skeptical tone] Okay, I've read your affidavit. . . . You said he assaulted you in the past? . . . How is he authorized to carry a weapon? . . . [In a frustrated, impatient tone to plaintiff's attorney] I am perplexed because she has no concern for her personal safety. . . . Okay, what has he

done to put you in fear? . . . How long has he been abusive? . . . Well, that
certainly is a lot clearer than your affidavit.

While this tone of legal or moral authority seems cold and unhelpful to women seeking restraining orders, many of the same
judges who were good-natured to women adopted a firm or formal
tone when they spoke to the men accused of battering them, as
is discussed further below.

Condescending Demeanor Toward Women

This category, which is not part of Mileski's typology, was
added to account for patronizing and trivializing displays of judicial authority. These kinds of gestures from men, of course, are
common to women's experience of sexism. Condescending demeanor encompasses both judgmental expressions of authority,
as when the judge sent a woman out of the courtroom for wearing
shorts, as well as "joking" or other paternalistic remarks:

[Judge to a woman who is in court with the defendant to drop the restraining order] Are you reconciled? Are you sure? Let's see a smile there.

What is the message when a male judge, before granting a woman's request to drop a restraining order, asks her to smile? Is the
smile the judge wants to see a symbol of forgiving and forgetting,
a way of displacing the image of an angry or distressed woman?
Does the judge want the smile for himself, or is this meant to
reassure the defendant as well? This seems to be a case of simultaneously being supportive or good-natured toward the defendant
while acting in a patronizing manner toward the woman who
filed the order.

Another male judge displayed a trivializing and patronizing demeanor repeatedly toward women seeking orders from him. One
woman requested an extension of her restraining order; she alleged physical abuse by her husband, who was present. The judge
reluctantly granted an extension but only for six weeks. He suggested that they work out their differences, saying, "It might be
easier to talk about it."

To another woman, who was in tears and shaking throughout
her restraining order hearing, this same judge said:

Any chance of getting back together? . . . You took this out on Valentine's
Day.

The defendant was present in this case as well. From the perspective of this observer, the judge seemed to publicly shame this woman for seeking a restraining order, as if her action violated the rules governing intimate relationships. This was how he responded to her obvious distress. The message here for the defendant seemed to be that the judge was on his side.

Harsh Demeanor Toward Women

Mileski defines harsh demeanor as "nasty" and "abrasive."[22] This is a manner going well beyond firm or condescending demeanor. Mileski found this only rarely in her courtroom observations. In the present study, harsh demeanor was not consistently observed in any judge, but it was witnessed on one occasion. The harsh demeanor was directed not against a defendant for his criminal behavior but against a battered woman for violating the rules of courtroom deference. Mileski concluded that "a minor disruption in the courtroom or a show of disrespect for its personnel is more likely to give rise to situational sanctioning than is the allegation of a serious criminal offense."[23] While this study found substantial evidence of situational sanctioning of violent men, in terms of harsh demeanor Mileski's insight is relevant.

A woman sought to extend her restraining order and obtain child support. She alleged that the defendant, who was present, had attacked her with a knife and had threatened to kill her. The defendant denied this. Both individuals were African Americans. As the judge, a white man, began asking first her and then him what amount of child support would be reasonable, the plaintiff and defendant started to argue. Angry at this breach of decorum and the unwillingness of either party to stop instantly, the judge interrupted this argument. He directed his anger to the woman seeking to extend the order. While the judge's tone cannot be adequately represented in words, this is what he said:

[Judge interrupting the argument] Mrs. _____, Mrs. _____, I just told you to stop. [Loudly, angrily] *I am not going to say it twice.*

The tone of this judge's voice was intimidating and arrogant. Following a break shortly after this remark to allow the defendant to fill out a financial disclosure form, the hearing resumed for another 10 minutes. During this time the judge said little to the woman seeking an extension of the order and spent the bulk of his time talking to the defendant in a solicitous tone; at one point the judge suggested to the defendant that he may wish to see an attorney before the next hearing on child support. The judge told the defendant he wanted to set a modest amount for child support and that he had no interest in sending the defendant to jail. Another hearing was arranged two months hence, at the convenience of the defendant.

Although neither this observer nor the volunteer advocate assisting the woman heard the defendant ask for visitation, the judge struck out the part of the order barring the defendant from contacting the children and stated that visitation should be set up through an intermediary. According to the Supreme Judicial Court,[24] district court judges have no jurisdiction to order visitation in restraining order hearings.

The judge conveyed a punishing and intolerant demeanor to the woman seeking help, both with his anger and unwillingness to talk with her and through his conciliatory gestures to the defendant. Both she and her advocate left the hearing feeling enraged. It is unclear how this hearing affected the other battered women waiting in the courtroom for their cases to be called.

These five types of demeanor are summarized in Table 5.1. For each of the 18 judges observed, this table indicates the most characteristic demeanor presented toward women and toward men appearing as defendants.

Judicial Demeanor Toward Men Appearing as Defendants

Most judges were consistent in their minor gestures of courtesy toward plaintiffs and defendants, such as in how they greeted them or made eye contact. But most judges displayed a different demeanor toward men than toward women in terms of empathy, supportive actions, and remarks about the meaning of the restraining order. In the 43 hearings where men were present as defendants, judges presented three types of demeanor when interacting with these men. The most frequently observed demeanor was firm or formal, followed by bureaucratic and good-natured.

Firm or Formal Demeanor Toward Men

Judges assuming a firm or formal demeanor take an active presence in their interactions with men, emphasizing the power of

TABLE 5.1

Courtroom Observations of Judicial Demeanor Toward Women Seeking Orders and Men Named as Defendants

Dorchester Judges	Demeanor Toward Women	Demeanor Toward Men[a]
1	Good-natured	Firm
2	Good-natured	Firm
3	Good-natured	Firm
4	Good-natured	
5	Good-natured (condescending)[b]	Firm
6	Good-natured (condescending)[b]	Firm
7	Bureaucratic	Bureaucratic
8	Bureaucratic	Bureaucratic
9	Firm (condescending/harsh)[b]	Good-natured
Quincy Judges		
1	Good-natured	Firm
2	Good-natured	Firm
3	Good-natured	Good-natured
4	Good-natured	
5	Bureaucratic	Bureaucratic
6	Bureaucratic	Bureaucratic
7	Bureaucratic	Bureaucratic
8	Bureaucratic	Bureaucratic
9	Condescending	Good-natured

a. Not all judges were observed in hearings where defendants were present.

b. Parentheses indicate this demeanor was observed on occasion, but not consistently.

their office in the process. They appeared to be self-conscious and deliberate about how they presented their authority. While they greet the defendants and use polite terms of address, they insist that defendants acknowledge the seriousness of the restraining order and the authority of the court. Sixteen judges were observed in hearings with defendants present; seven of these judges displayed a firm demeanor to the defendants. Most of the judges who consistently conveyed a good-natured demeanor to women presented a firm demeanor to men when they appeared in the hearings.

Sometimes this type of demeanor was seen in the judge's insis-

tence on preventing defendants from engaging in arguments with
the women seeking orders. The judge in the following case sought
to make it clear that he was in charge of the hearing:

[Judge addressing the defendant] Mr. _____ , Mrs. _____ wishes to extend
   this for a year. Do you object?
[Defendant] Yes. [Defendant turns to the plaintiff and begins to challenge
   her statements.]
[The judge interrupts] You talk to me.

By interrupting in this way, the judge seemed to indicate that the
court was entitled and willing to intervene in his relationship and
that this authority must be acknowledged by the defendant.

   Firm judges warned or gave brief lectures to defendants to underscore the consequences of violating restraining orders:

Okay, sir, I am going to drop the part of the order that says [you are to
vacate the premises and stay away from her]. It still says you are not to
abuse her in any way. You will be in no trouble being near her unless you
threaten or hurt her. Threaten or hurt her and you are in trouble.

[Judge to a defendant at a hearing where he was found guilty of violating
a restraining order, and is given a sentence of one year probation, at the
prosecutor's request] Let's be very clear. . . . if at any other time . . . if
there is any incident of abuse . . . you have got two and a half years
hanging over your head. . . . Today is the last chance for you. The restraining order is going to order you not to abuse.

You were in violation of that order for calling her. . . . As a contempt of
court, I could put you in jail. This order is a serious order, do you understand that? . . . There are warrants outstanding for you in this court.
Threatening, malicious destruction of property. . . . There are also
charges in [another court]. Assault and battery . . . operating after license
is suspended. . . . [After reading this from the defendant's criminal record,
the judge asks the bailiff to take the defendant into custody; he is placed
in handcuffs and led out of the courtroom.]

[Judge] I do find that Ms. _____ is in fear of her life. . . . I am going to
   continue this in effect for one year.
[Defendant] I haven't been in contact with her whatsoever. . . . I haven't
   done anything wrong.
[Judge] If what you say is true, then you will not come before me on a
   violation. . . . This judge will treat this very seriously. Violating this
   will be a very serious criminal matter.
[Defendant] By you giving this woman power over me . . .
[Judge] No, no, Mr. _____ , I am giving her the power of the court. If you
   have no intention of going near her, then there won't be a problem.

These are deliberate and assertive displays of judicial authority. While not disrespectful, these judges emphasize their institutional power in these interactions. The last judge above states that the court, not the plaintiff, is wielding power over the defendant through the restraining order. These are examples of the kind of "situational sanctioning" that Mileski concluded was often imposed by judges as a substitute for more material sanctions such as jail sentences.

In the context of a hearing where battered women are present, however, there is a point to these lectures beyond their direct effect—or lack of effect—on the defendants. These expressions of judicial authority toward men are carefully observed by battered women. This is surely one lesson learned from the public furor over the death of Pamela Nigro Dunn. If judicial demeanor is defined as the presentation of authority in these interactions, in other words, then judges' treatment of accused batterers is a dimension of judicial demeanor toward battered women.

Similarly, how judges treat women communicates messages to defendants who are present. Firm demeanor toward men can be conveyed both directly and indirectly, as in the following interactions:

[Judge to defendant] If you appear before this judge again, I will deal with you very harshly, do you understand? . . . [To the woman who is granted the order] No one has a right to abuse you in any way. Do you understand that?

First of all, Mr. _____ , I will issue a restraining order today. . . .
Mr. _____ , you are not to abuse Ms. _____ , you are to stay 100 yards away from her, stay away from her house, and that order is in effect for a year. [To the woman seeking the order] You have had to put up with a pattern of abuse over a period of time. Are you sure you want to drop the criminal charges? . . . Do you want to keep the case open for a month, just to make sure? . . . I would suggest we keep the case open for a month, and if there are no further problems at that time, you can drop the [criminal] charges. . . . [To the defendant] Bear in mind, sir, that the restraining order is in full effect. . . . You see her coming down the street, you go the other way.

The judges above seem well aware of the symbolic dimensions of their tone and how it might be understood by both plaintiffs and defendants. In each case, the defendant is reminded of his responsibility by the judge's words to both parties. Both judges want the defendants to hear their remarks to the women seeking protection; both emphasize in several different ways their willingness to enforce the criminal penalties contained in the restraining order.

Bureaucratic Demeanor Toward Men

Judges who consistently displayed a bureaucratic demeanor toward women generally acted in a bureaucratic manner toward defendants as well. Six of the 16 judges observed in hearings where men appeared exhibited bureaucratic demeanor. As in the case with women, bureaucratic demeanor is best described as absence of feeling, passivity, boredom, and lack of engagement in dealings with defendants. It is better defined by what isn't said than by what is said at these hearings. Bureaucratic judges did not assert themselves in interactions with men and for the most part did not impose situational sanctions on defendants. When they said anything at all to defendants, it was affectively neutral or mild in tone.

For example, men were present in two of five restraining order hearings before a bureaucratic judge one morning. The judge extended one order for three weeks; he extended the other order for one year. The judge's tone was very detached: other than smiling slightly to the woman in each case, he expressed little emotion. The judge said very little to either of the men: there were few questions asked of the defendant, no reading out loud of what he was granting in the order, no explanation of the consequences for violating the order, no request for the keys to the apartment or house, no reviewing of the defendant's criminal record for outstanding warrants, no discussion of child support. This bureaucratic presentation of authority was characteristic of all the hearings involving defendants observed with this judge and four other judges.

Good-Natured Demeanor Toward Men

Three judges at times exhibited a manner toward defendants that went beyond courtesy and reached deference, supportiveness, or joviality. On these occasions, this manner toward defendants was paired with a less respectful demeanor toward the women who sought protection. In the case of one of these judges, this demeanor toward some defendants was interspersed with a firm demeanor toward other men accused of battering. Illustrations of good-natured demeanor toward men have already been provided: in a hearing described above, a judge's harsh demeanor toward a woman was combined with a solicitous manner toward the defendant. Further, the judges who expressed a patronizing or trivializing demeanor with women were simultaneously acting in a supportive manner toward defendants. One of these judges even joked and bonded with a defendant when the plaintiff did not appear for the hearing:

[Judge to a defendant at a 10-day hearing, where the plaintiff is not present] You have no idea where she is? . .
[Defendant] I made a mistake going out with a young girl. . . .
[Judge identifies with the defendant and jokes about what he did "before you were born"; judge dismisses the restraining order and suggests to the defendant] You might want to talk to a lawyer.

This judge used his authority to make the defendant laugh and to encourage him to protect himself legally from the plaintiff. The judge was friendly and engaging, but this manner seemed extremely inappropriate in a hearing involving allegations of abuse, before a courtroom filled with other women seeking protection.

Summary

Judges do many different things with their authority in restraining order hearings. Good-natured presentations of authority were the most common type observed in interactions with women. Judges who were good-natured with women were firm in their encounters with male defendants, often warning or lecturing men about the consequences of violating the restraining orders. Bureaucratic demeanor toward women was also frequently observed in these hearings; these judges assumed a detached and affectively neutral stance toward defendants as well. Condescending and harsh demeanor were observed in a smaller number of cases.

It is also clear that while judicial demeanor directed toward women may be distinguished from demeanor expressed toward men, there is a significant overlap in indirect messages. When men appear in these hearings, judicial demeanor toward the woman requesting help contains messages for the defendant, and presentations of authority toward defendants are witnessed and remembered by the plaintiffs. This has implications for the meanings of situational sanctions imposed on defendants.

Demeanor is described in this chapter as the emotional presentation of authority in courtroom encounters. There are two aspects of what is emotional about demeanor. The first point is that there is a quality to the courtroom atmosphere that the judge produces with his or her emotional expressiveness or inexpressiveness. The second point is that this demeanor, which is best assessed from the perspective of its recipients, has consequences of an emotional nature for the women seeking help and for the men identified as violent and abusive. How important is demeanor, from judges' perspectives? What kinds of demeanor do judges want to portray toward women and men in these hearings? And what do they do to accomplish this? These questions are the focus of the next chapter.

Its specific nature, which is welcomed by capitalism, develops the more perfectly the more bureaucracy is "dehumanized," the more completely it succeeds in eliminating from official business love, hatred, and all purely personal, irrational, and emotional elements which escape calculation. This is the specific nature of bureaucracy and it is appraised as its special virtue.

MAX WEBER[1]

Judges primarily function in purist jurisprudential theory to adjudicate facts and apply the law to those facts. . . . These procedures are inoperable as they relate to the area of domestic violence. Judges and lawyers disserve both themselves and the legal system unless they understand that the judge's function consists of more than adjudicating facts. Judges are expected to understand and empathize with the parties. The judge, in many instances, must serve to readjust the power balance between the parties.

JUDGE AUSTIN T. PHILBIN[2]

Judges' Perspectives on Restraining Order Hearings

Writing at the beginning of the twentieth century, Max Weber posited the impersonal nature of bureaucracy as "its special virtue," describing it in the passage above as "dehumanized" and elsewhere as operating "without regard for persons."[3] Maureen Mileski, describing the mass processing of defendants in the courtroom as a type of "business," found bureaucratic demeanor to be the standard procedure in courtroom encounters with judges.[4]

However, as was noted in the previous chapter, bureaucratic demeanor was actually not the most common type of demeanor witnessed in the two Boston-area courts. While one-third of the judges presented a bureaucratic demeanor, over half of the judges offered a "good-natured" face of authority, a more supportive type of demeanor. Amid the disorder and lack of consistency from judge to judge and court to court, new rules are being developed within the judiciary about how judges should intervene in violent relationships. Austin T. Philbin is a district court judge in Massachusetts. In the second passage quoted above, Judge Philbin indicates the ways that these reforms are challenging the tradition of bureaucratic kinds of responses to woman battering. Stating that these courtroom negotiations concern power imbalances between women and their abusive partners, Philbin states that judges must empathize with the parties if justice is to be served.

This chapter details the way that judges who see themselves as reformers think about and self-consciously display their authority. The judges whose thoughts are presented here represent that a segment of the judiciary that wants to adapt the traditional role of the judge to meet the relatively new circumstances posed by domestic violence restraining orders. Eight Massachusetts judges were interviewed about how they conducted themselves in restraining order hearings. Two were from Dorchester District Court, two were from Quincy District Court, and the others sat at various other Massachusetts courts. Four of the judges are white men, three are white women, and one is an African American man.

Seven of these judges have assumed a high profile on the issue of domestic violence, in either their work training other judges on the problem, their participation on committees, or their writing and public speaking on the subject. This means that they are not typical of the judiciary on the whole; they are not even representative of the other judges in their own courts. A number of other judges were asked for interviews, several of whom, from my observations, displayed more traditional types of authority in their interactions with battered women. Perhaps owing to judicial suspicions of researchers at a time when the courts were in the public spotlight, these judges declined to be interviewed.

All the judges who agreed to be interviewed underscored the

need for empathy in interactions with battered women and the importance of making a variety of resources available as part of the restraining order process. In descriptions of their own self-presentation in restraining order hearings, they all gave accounts of what could be called "good-natured" demeanor toward battered women and "firm" demeanor toward violent men. Significant inconsistencies and contradictions, however, were also apparent in their remarks.

How do these judges view the matter of judicial demeanor? How do they see themselves wielding authority in courtroom interactions? What do they want to convey to women and their defendants in the courtroom? What are the limits—even inconsistencies and contradictions—regarding how supportive this kind of authority is?

The Importance of Judicial Demeanor

> *Because of my imposing size, I tend to tone my voice down, lean over to the bench, look the individual directly in the eye, let them know that I've read the affidavit. I tell them. I take time to read the affidavit right here in front of them. . . . Then I might have some questions from the affidavit. I might inquire as to what the situation is: does the individual have keys, do you have a place to go, do you have any personal effects in the house? I think [the idea is]* not to let them feel rushed in any way.

> *I think demeanor is very, very important. And I actually think judges are now—I think with all the training that [the Chief Justice of the Trial Court] is providing to the court, our understanding is that* that's just as important as fashioning the remedy. (*Emphasis added*)

Offering his own presentation of self as an illustration, the above judge indicates that changes in judicial demeanor are now a focus of the upper hierarchy of the Massachusetts judiciary. The presentation of authority in courtroom interactions, he states, is seen to be as important as the official decisions made by judges during these hearings.

All eight judges emphasized the importance of judicial demeanor, but several different elements of authority were identified in their discussion of *why* demeanor was important to their work in the courtroom. According to one judge, a woman who had served on the Gender Bias Study of the Massachusetts Supreme Court, the emotional dimensions of her presence are highly symbolic. In her view, demeanor communicates to women seeking their rights whether the court, in the person of the judge, will use its authority for her or against her:

Demeanor is very important to the victim. It tells the victim whether—typically she—is welcome in the court, whether the court is there to serve them, whether the court is *trivializing* what's happened to her, or whether the court takes it *seriously.* Whether the court will be there for her, *sympathetically,* or will it be *hostile.* Also whether the court is sort of a *welcoming* place for her—that is, to offer services, as opposed to *something that she's terrified to come into.* (Emphasis added)

To this judge, demeanor is communicated by extending the resources of the court as well as by facial gestures, consistent with Goffman's identification of task-embedded symbolic expressions.

In a similar vein, another judge contrasted the new face of judicial authority with the old, regarding woman battering:

[There is] a long social history of the "wink and the nod." . . . We're not winking and nodding.

The phrase used by the above judge succinctly captures how patriarchal support for violent men can be communicated through demeanor, over and against the written law.

Several other judges described demeanor as important to the experience of justice in the courtroom, for both women seeking restraining orders and men appearing as defendants:

I think it's very important. . . . When the litigants are in the courtroom, I think it is very important that I *look formal, not stuffy, necessarily, or stiff, or icy, or impersonal, but formal, in the sense that everyone is treated with respect.* . . . I think the dignity of the courtroom communicates itself to the litigants and they feel—one, they behave in accordance with those expectations, or are likely to behave in accordance with those expectations, and two, it seems, what happens there seems fair. To a degree, not completely, but to a degree. (Emphasis added)

Authority seems to be a somewhat fragile form of currency, to this judge; her power to influence behavior depends on gestures of deference toward both women seeking orders and defendants.

She uses a number of adjectives to delineate a space between a faceless bureaucracy and undignified informality.

The impact that demeanor may have on the effectiveness of judicial remedies was amplified by another judge:

> You know, you can tell someone—and I've never done this in my life— that they are a no-good scum and I am going to send you to 30 days in jail. And you can tell someone that you really understand entirely how they got into this, but the law requires that they pay the price and pay the penalty for what they've done, and give them 90 days in jail, and the second one will feel they have justice, and the first one who got a very light sentence will feel that you, the court, and the justice system have denied them their integrity. . . . *Demeanor is not just—it is not just some form of image. It is substance.* (Emphasis added)

By "substance" this judge means that trust in the system of justice is at stake in courtroom interactions and that abusive demeanor on the part of judges can make even sanctions such as incarceration meaningless in terms of their long-term impact on individuals.

Judges also saw demeanor as a symbolic communication with more people than just the immediate parties. This was especially emphasized by one African American judge, who spoke of demeanor in restraining order hearings in this manner:

> What I want to convey to women, and also to the community, is that, you know, domestic violence is not to be tolerated. . . . They have a right to a relationship free of abuse. . . . They have a right to seek the protection of the court.

This judge was concerned with what he saw as the "tolerance" of violence in the communities served by his court.

Drawing these complementary perspectives together, they portray demeanor as an image of authority that can be expressed either for or against women's demands for justice. These judges were able to articulate many different kinds of behavior that carry symbolic messages, including facial expressions, mannerisms, posture, rules of conduct in the courtroom, and availability of additional resources. Demeanor is further seen as part of an interaction not just with women and violent men but with all observers in the courtroom, as witnesses for the wider community. These judges believe that demeanor has consequences both for the experience of justice in the courtroom and for the effectiveness of judicial remedies. In marked contrast to the "apparent unawareness" claimed for Judge Heffernan by the Supreme Judicial Court, these judges seemed acutely conscious of their emotional presentation in the courtroom.

The Means and Ends of Emotional Labor

One judge offered a Goffmanesque, even Hochschildian response to a question about demeanor, replete with dramaturgical metaphors:

> I think it's very important. I think there is a certain amount of theater involved in being a judge in a court—you know, the trappings, the liturgy of judging. I think it is very important for a judge to be controlled. The worst thing a judge can do is lose control of himself because if you can't control yourself, you can't control what's occurring in front of you. It is important to maintain control of what is happening in front of you. Judges who can't control themselves are usually very incapable of doing a very good job with that. Although, you know, from time to time a little display of anger or impatience is part of the theater as a way of conveying a message to people that this or that will not be tolerated.

This judge indicates a Goffman-like sense of his judicial self that is a product of ritual performance, aware of his audience, and self-conscious of the impressions he wants to convey. What is consistent with Hochschild's theory of emotions is the judge's awareness of working on himself—controlling his own feeling and emotional presentation—in order to affect the emotional state of the people in the courtroom. This is a portrait of judging as emotional labor. This concept was introduced in the previous chapter, but it is necessary to develop it further to fully appreciate how judges "do authority" in courtroom encounters with abused women and violent men.

Emotional labor is a double-sided concept: it names both the *means* and the *ends* of a type of work. The ends of judging as a type of emotional labor involve making an emotional impact on plaintiffs and defendants. There is also an emotional dimension to the means to this end, and to have this impact, judges will be most effective if they act on their own feeling and emotional expression. If the goal is making a woman feel welcome in the court, the means may involve controlling or suppressing inappropriate feeling, such as frustration; or it may require evoking a desired feeling, such as empathy, that may not readily be there at the end of a very long and draining day. Truly engaging with a woman seeking an order requires more than merely *pretending* empathy. To really reach someone who has been assaulted and who may be intimidated and upset, a judge is more effective if he or she *genuinely feels* empathetic. How do these judges think about and act on themselves, emotionally, in the performance of their work?

Techniques of Emotional Labor: Altering the Emotional Presentation of Self

Arlie Russell Hochschild identifies three ways that individuals consciously alter their own feeling. In the performance of emotional labor, individuals can act on themselves through cognitive, expressive, and bodily techniques.[5] Cognitive methods were mentioned most frequently by the judges.

The cognitive techniques involved reading the literature on woman battering and attending trainings to better understand the effects of trauma and the dilemmas that battered women face when they claim their rights. One judge had done considerable reading on woman battering, including feminist scholarship, and spoke of how he reminds himself of what he has learned when women come before him:

For people who have not been in abusive relationships, I think it's very difficult to understand why, or how, or what it is that causes the interplay between these two people. . . . And that can result in frustration. I mean, there are some people that we see here in this court, and I'm sure in others, on a weekly basis, who come in and out of the courtroom. The victim wants the order, the victim doesn't want the order. Wants the order again, doesn't want the order again. Well, that can be frustrating if you're dealing with other cases, too, that are pressing on you. *But what you have to keep in mind is that . . . all you can do is issue orders. The victim has to live outside with the individual, with the perpetrator. So there has to be some freedom for them, too.* (Emphasis added)

By thinking about the circumstances of women who suffer violence, this judge alters his feelings in the courtroom; he resists the feeling of frustration with women's demands for redress that characterizes the culture of the judiciary.

Another judge spoke of how her sense of what was "intuitively" true about battering, a sense she learned from other judges, shifted when she began reading about women's experiences of violence:

> Those judges who I *thought* were the most creative and the most sensitive were judges who would typically take the time and say, "Okay, let's work this out in the family." But, I mean, I think intuitively you would do that, *unless you read and started to realize that by doing that, you were enforcing precisely the wrong things in the situation.* That isn't what you want to do. You need to treat this as a crime. You can't perpetuate this as a family matter. Well, those are all really learned responses. I don't think they are intuitive. (Emphasis added)

What feels intuitive, what seems like common sense is really a product of institutional learning, this judge appears to say. With violence against women, this is especially problematic when the traumatic impact of abuse and the dynamics of men's intimidation are not readily apparent.

One judge who has taken a leading role in the drafting of new guidelines for the district courts spoke candidly about her own changes in thinking about violence against women:

> I heard [feminist activist and attorney] Sarah Buel speak in Albuquerque, at a nationwide conference on juvenile and family court justice . . . and she spoke about the effect of violence on children. And I had no idea. I was someone who was a rape and child abuse prosecutor 10 years ago, for six years. . . . *Thought I knew something about violence against women and children. And had no idea what the extent of the violence was.* (Emphasis added)

By learning about woman battering through feminist literature and workshop presentations by feminist activists, these three judges altered how they presented their authority in these cases. Feminist perspectives on woman battering challenge the prevailing "commonsense" understandings embodied in both written law and judicial practice that dismiss woman battering as "trivial" and enforce the barrier of "family privacy" on behalf of violent men.

Efforts to alter their feeling and demeanor through expressive techniques were also mentioned by the judges. One judge offered an unusually self-critical portrait of how he worked on himself to change his emotional presentation:

I have the good fortune here, in this particular court— . . . I think there is tremendous camaraderie here, and we've taken it upon ourselves to kind of, to observe one another, and to make suggestions about where they think that we could improve judicial demeanor. Now one of the judges told me—I happen to have a very stern face, you know, unfortunately God has blessed me with this face that can be—you're sitting up on the bench, you've got the black robe on, and you see this 250-pound guy [he gestures above his eyes] and these thick, thick eyebrows. He said, "You look very, very stern up there, and I think some of the women are intimidated." I was very appreciative of that. *I went back and I listened to the tapes, and I thought I was being instructive. Like I was, I kept saying, "Do you understand?" and the tone was like* [deepening his voice] *"Do you understand?" And it did sound, after evaluating it, it did sound threatening. So I've—hopefully, I have softened it up considerably. And just—*[softening his voice] *the tone of my voice is softer.* (Emphasis added)

This judge identifies how facial expressions, tone of voice, physical stature, and even costuming and architecture play a role in the presentation of authority. The monitoring of one another's demeanor among the judges at his court seems uncommon; two of the other interviewees had mentioned that they never see other judges at work in the courtroom.

If cognitive and expressive techniques are the *means* by which judges work on themselves, what are the *ends* of emotional labor that these judges intend? What emotional impact do they want to make on abused women who come to court to claim their rights?

The Intended Impact of Emotional Labor: How Judges Want Women and Violent Men to Feel in Court

The literature on the victimization and trauma as a result of woman abuse indicates that there are a variety of feelings that women experience at the point when they claim their legal rights or take other actions to stop the violence. Mary Ann Dutton identifies fear, terror, anxiety, anger, depression, shame, and betrayal as some of the feelings that battered women experience. She insists, however, that understanding the "racial, cultural, ethnic, political, and economic context" in which women live is essential to understanding women's experience of violence. Dutton argues that institutional responses mediate the psychological effects of abuse and influence women's strategies to protect themselves.[6] Kathleen J. Ferraro and John M. Johnson describe how battered women's feelings about themselves, their abusive partners, and their situations are part of a dynamic interactional process. They have found that the response of institutions to women's help-seeking has a great impact on women's emotional and cognitive responses to violence.[7] Based on interviews with battered women in Scotland, Rebecca Emerson Dobash and Russell Dobash describe a pattern of staying, leaving, and returning on the part of women. This process reflects a number of social and material circumstances that affect women, in their analysis; indifferent responses by the courts and police heighten feelings of isolation and desperation, narrowing women's ability to escape.[8]

All eight judges spoke about the emotional impact of the restraining order hearings on women. Since "separation assault" is a major type of violence found in the affidavits submitted to these two courts, women's court appearances—as dramatic acts of separation—intensify their feelings of vulnerability. Asked how they assessed women's fear, this is how two judges responded:

You can tell to some degree by the affidavit, *by the expression on the woman, by the condition that she's in.* Some women will express that fear, or you might ask them. Or by the—by way of observation, checking a defendant's record. I see more of that at arraignment, when the defendant is there, and the victim is present. That's when there is the two parties in the room, that those issues tend to become more readily apparent. (Emphasis added)

Well, it's hard to articulate. The first thing is what she says. But that's not all. I mean, obviously, if she relates that there's a lot going on, that there's a long history of abuse. . . . The things they talk about, lethality . . . extreme jealousness and possessiveness, stalking behavior. *Once I get my antenna up I might ask if there is suicide threats . . . or threats to hurt the children . . . weapons and all that stuff. And then the nonverbal cues, you know? I mean, somebody who's rocking, you know, or crying, or shaking.* You know, those kind of things. (Emphasis added)

The first judge is a man, the second is a woman. Both judges are aware that many of the effects of violence are unobservable. The second judge is particularly adept at naming the variety of acts by batterers that produce fear and the ways women may express fear indirectly.

Given this awareness of women's fears and of the intimidating character of the court, what did these judges want to convey to women seeking help?

First, the first thing I think that we want to convey is that *we care about their plight*—that the whole process should be designed to indicate that we, we are concerned for their well-being and that we care.

My experience as a district court judge is that it is very important to have the victim understand *that the court is a place where she can come, where the court will*, to the extent possible, protect her. . . . Obviously, we can't protect her. We can make her understand *that we'll be there for her*—that if she changes her mind, we'll still be there for her. (Emphasis added)

The thing I want everybody most to feel is *that they were heard, that they got a fair shot to be heard. And that their case was decided on the merits.* That's true of plaintiffs and defendants in 209A cases. I do also believe, particularly at the ex parte sessions, that it's not inappropriate to convey *concern for somebody's safety*, to reinforce the idea that the court is available insofar as we are able to provide protection, that it will make referrals. That that's *not a hostile place to be*, certainly. (Emphasis added)

You have to give them the sense *that you're going to listen and that they don't really feel like they're overpowered* by the court. Because most people coming in in those cases or sexual abuse cases . . . they feel very disempowered when they come in. Very nervous and very concerned about discussing a very personal issue. So what you attempt to do is to do what you can to *get them to relax* so you can hear what they are going to express. (Emphasis added)

I want to convey to her *that we take seriously credible charges made.* We will enforce the law. . . . One wants to convey the sense of empowerment, that you can do something. (Emphasis added)

If demeanor is an image of authority, the image these judges wanted to communicate is one of empathy and support. They want to use their power to make women feel welcome in the court and to facilitate their requests for judicial remedies. There is an awareness by these judges that this demeanor is communicated by the design of court processes, by their patience, by open expressions of concern, through their listening to both parties, and by serious attention to the criminal nature of violence and abuse.

Such statements by judges indicate that a segment of the judiciary has traveled quite a distance from traditional responses to battered women. Of course, these comments must be interpreted within the context of the public scandal over judges reportedly harassing women seeking orders. These judges appear aware of the continuing skepticism about judicial authority. Through their remarks about caring, concern for safety, and women's fear of hostile treatment, they are attempting to counter the public images of an indifferent or even harsh demeanor toward women.

All these judges adopt a different emotional stance toward men appearing as defendants than toward women claiming their rights. But here, the gender of the judge seems relevant to the intensity of indignation or compassion expressed toward men accused of violence. Here is how two female judges talked about their judicial demeanor toward men:

With the men it is a control issue. I try to make it clear that it is no longer a problem between them and the woman. It is now a problem between them and the Commonwealth . . . with penalties including going to jail. . . . "It simply isn't an excuse. What you have done is a crime." *The point is to dramatize that the man is no longer in control in the relationship.* . . . [As a result of this challenge to a man's control] the worst violence occurs after we issue the restraining order. (Emphasis added)

If the judge takes it seriously, then [the defendant] is more apt to take it seriously. . . . If it is kind of like "wink, wink"—you know, "Don't do this again"—then that's the message that he gets. I think you see it typically when the man will come in and say, "Well, judge, I didn't mean to hit her, but she did this, this," and if the judge stops that immediately and says, "Listen, I don't care what she did, I don't care that she—the coffee was too hot, or she didn't come home after work. . . . I don't care about any of that because that's not what we're here for. We're here because you hit her, and that's what's not being tolerated, and that's a crime." . . . It's a message to the victim that this isn't your problem, it's his problem, but *it's a clear message to him that this is a crime, and you can do time. And you are gonna do time if you violate my order.* So I think the judge's demeanor is critical, for both persons involved. (Emphasis added)

While there is certainly much similarity in the remarks by all these judges concerning the seriousness of men's violence, there is an insistence and a sense of deep outrage communicated above that contrasts with the judicial empathy for offenders expressed by the following two male judges:

Lot of times [the defendant will] say, "I want to go back." You know, "I want to be with her." And she's already expressed that she wants him out. And then you have to say, pretty much, it's not their decision. . . . Therefore, as long as she's taken that position in the court, and now backed that position, "I've got to tell you what will happen here. I want you to listen to what my orders are and what will happen if you don't abide them." Then, I will tell them, "Look, you want to prove something to her? I don't know if she'll ever buy it, but you're drunk all the time. I would be glad to provide a program and monitor the program, and maybe with sobriety, maybe there's a chance later on. No guarantees." . . . You attempt to steer them or get them into a batterer's treatment program. . . . So what you want to convey is, "This is serious. These are the restrictions. You've got to be very clear if something happens in violating them that you'll be accountable." *And at the same time, offer to provide them some assistance if you can.* (Emphasis added)

I'd like them to feel that it's a serious matter—that the court takes it serious, that we care about what's happened to this woman that he's been accused of, that we intend to take it seriously, that there'll be consequences for this kind of action, that it shouldn't have happened. *I also would like him to feel that we are concerned about some of his interests as well.* That principally occurs in the area of visitation. As you know, probably, we don't have jurisdiction over visitation. People are forced to go to probate court. There are real barriers to getting into probate court. And if they can't get visitation in the district court, they will not get it at all. I try to at least address the issue of "You wanted to see the kids." Most women want them to see the kids. . . . From the man's point of view, I suppose, that's something that usually is in the back of my mind—that I try to consider that the court's figuring that both parties—. My tendency is to extend the restraining order, almost invariably, and I don't want to get into him accusing her, or her accusing. . . . I know that most relationships, there is wrong on both sides from time to time. I want to clarify the situation and if possible address visitation, so that he has at least some opportunity to be in a relationship with the children. (Emphasis added)

The compassion for violent men is of two different kinds in these statements. The first judge believes in rehabilitation; he wants to offer violent men a chance to change their behavior, mentioning alcohol treatment (which in and of itself does not address violence) and batterer's counseling, which is provided at his court. The second judge seems to stand in the defendant's shoes, so to speak, and as he talks, he expresses concern for men's visitation rights—something that he admits defendants are not entitled to at a hearing on a complaint initiated by a woman. This empathy for defendants, which may arise from sharing "the man's point of view," as he puts it, seems to conflict with his initial remarks about the seriousness of the violence.

Bureaucracy and the Costs of Emotional Labor

> *It appears that the main mechanism of the power of the state in sustaining men's interests, in resisting or limiting feminist demands, has not been the direct assertion of men's privilege—naked patriarchy so to speak—but* rather the character of the state's procedures as impersonal processes. Patriarchy resides in the "objectivity" of the state's structures.
> *(Emphasis added)*

SUZANNE FRANZWAY, DIANNE COURT, AND R. W. CONNELL[9]

There are a number of reasons that the institutional processes of the court favor bureaucratic procedures, particularly with cases involving woman battering. The interviews with judges revealed aspects of the gendered division of labor and the gendered patterning of emotionality in the courts that cast light on some of these reasons. These reasons are important to identify because there is powerful institutional resistance to the kind of supportive or "good-natured" demeanor observed in the two courts.

There is a relationship between the "objectivity" of the judiciary and its support staff. Arlie Russell Hochschild uses the term coined by Ivan Illich, "shadow labor," to identify the kind of unacknowledged emotional labor that women perform to ensure that institutions run smoothly.[10] In the courts, the clerical staff and advocates do this kind of emotional labor, offering a human face to plaintiffs and defendants. One judge admitted how his "objectivity" depended on the work of advocates:

A lot of people are illiterate, you know. You can't read the affidavits. You know, they just don't make sense. I mean, you can't read it. You have to kind of pull it out of them. And sometimes, you know, that bothers me. I wonder if I am becoming more of an advocate. *I am very grateful when they come in with domestic relations advocates, and I can sit back and play a more objective role* because they'll articulate what their concern is. (Emphasis added)

Note the metaphor of physical distance in the judge's statement—"sit back"—denoting greater emotional distance. Other judges also indicated they are more comfortable and less frustrated when advocates are present to inform women of their options and supportive services. Yet only one-third of courthouses in Massachusetts have full-time, trained advocates on staff.

Often, the courts rely on battered women's shelters and law students to provide this emotional labor. There is, then, a dependence of the courts on advocates and simultaneously a denial of this dependence and a lack of acknowledgment of, or responsibility for, providing this emotional service.[11] It is left to the largely female clerical staff of the courts to facilitate this process, not as part of their job descriptions but out of the gendered expectations that both the institution and the individuals seeking redress from it make on these workers.

Beyond threats to judicial "objectivity," there is also a personal cost to judges who present a "good-natured" demeanor. Empathetic engagement with women who are suffering from terrorizing violence can be exhausting. "Trauma is contagious," according to Judith Lewis Herman. Speaking about therapists working with trauma survivors, Herman states that in the role of witness to a violent crime, the therapist "experiences, to a lesser degree, the same terror, rage, and despair" as the survivor.[12] This is called "vicarious traumatization." Judges who are willing to recognize women's experience of victimization will also feel this, as will advocates, shelter workers, and other feminist activists. With the volume of battering cases on court dockets, a district court judge in Massachusetts will meet several hundred women who have been abused and hear several hundred accounts of violence every year. One judge spoke of how she dealt with the personal strain of working with women who had been abused. She described the restraining order hearings as a "terrible emotional burden":

I think that two things help me with the stress. One, I talk about it. A lot of people say, "Don't do that. You put it out of your mind." I don't do that. . . . I try not to make it identifiable, and I'm careful about confidences. But the things that are most traumatic, I do talk about. Both with friends and in terms of public speaking, as examples. And I do a lot of committee work. And I know that people who say that that's not a good idea either. But I find that that gives me a sense of contributing in a way that dealing with the case by minuscule case—as much as I enjoy that, and I take each case very seriously. I think that if you feel like you are having some long effect, or short-term effect, anyway, on the system as a whole, it's easier to deal with the grind.

By talking about traumatic events, and engaging in work on battering that is less isolating and individualized than sitting on criminal cases, this judge seeks to create a social environment that will strengthen her ability to stand as witness to such violence. Herman argues that "the perpetrator's arguments prove irresistible when the bystander faces them in isolation."[13] Given the patriarchal structure of the state and the threat to the gender order that a campaign against sexual violence represents, it becomes tempting for judges to abandon the burden of vicarious trauma and turn against women who have been victimized. The current social environment for hearing and affirming women's testimony about violence was created by the feminist movement. Herman insists that the ability for our culture to sustain this recognition and support depends on the continued strength of this movement.

When one judge retired from his position after 20 years at the Dorchester District Court, press accounts reported he "is simply tired and wants to do something new after hearing thousands of heartbreaking and sometimes heinous cases involving the very poor."[14] On a personal level, then, a more human way of relating to women who are claiming their rights in restraining order hearings may be costlier than a passive, detached, bureaucratic response.

Inconsistencies in Judicial Demeanor: Race, Class, and Women's Invisibility

> *Although violence is a common issue among women, such violence usually occurs within a specific context that often varies considerably depending on the race, class, and other social characteristics of the woman. . . . These characteristics can be better understood and addressed through a framework that links them to broader structures of subordination which intersect sometimes in fairly predictable ways. These intersections limit the utility of interventions that are not constructed with them in mind.*
>
> KIMBERLÉ CRENSHAW[15]

Having addressed the institutional logic of bureaucratic demeanor, it is now important to detail the contradictory and inconsistent responses of even those judges who see themselves as reformers. The limitations most apparent in the judges' discussions of the restraining order hearings concern a failure to treat battering as a phenomenon that is rooted in class and racial domination as well as gender domination. Woman battering is primarily treated as a problem of violence and, to some extent, housing; the economic dimensions of battered women's suffering and attempts at separation, especially as they relate to children, are less visible to the courts. Kimberlé Crenshaw argues above that interventions for women that ignore the complex structural circumstances of violence will have limited effect. Racism and class intersect with violence, particularly in the lives of the women appearing in Dorchester District Court.

In the interviews, judges were quick to emphasize the importance of providing women with access to resources in restraining order hearings. Consistent with Goffman's identification of task orientation as a means of communicating demeanor, the judges spoke of how important it was to make women aware of their legal options, including the right to seek temporary child support as part of the restraining order. Here is how two judges—the first an African American man, the second an Anglo woman—state the importance of addressing the material dimensions of women's situations:

Well, as you know, that's part of the temporary order. . . . I always check the box and instruct the individual. I say, "Listen. I'm going to check off the box for child support and alimony for you and the child. Now you should think about what your needs are, so when you come back to court, you can help the judge fashion a remedy that makes sense." . . . This is all part of the package. I mean, it's—you know, *it's an illusory kind of a Pyrrhic victory to kind of just tell him to stay away and not worry about child support.* (Emphasis added)

It's an area that we don't do often enough. We don't raise the issue, we don't pursue it. . . . But for a lot of women, economics are what sends a woman back. . . . You can't allow a man to use this leverage. *Even if she doesn't ask, when she tells me she has children, I ask her if she needs support.* (Emphasis added)

Despite the acknowledgment of the material dimensions of women's victimization by most of the judges interviewed, however, in the case of Dorchester District Court, where the women seeking orders are mostly African American or Afro-Caribbean, women's requests for child support and compensation were generally ignored. Chapter 4 presented an examination of 100 randomly selected restraining orders that found that women requesting child support were three times more likely to receive it in Quincy than Dorchester. What are the institutional processes that produce such disparities between these courts?

I presented two judges in Dorchester with these findings, drawn from their own court records. Several themes can be identified in their responses to these data on child support that shed light on how race, class, and motherhood are misperceived in the courtroom.

Each judge responded in a different way. The first judge, a white man, believes that it is important to communicate concern to women seeking restraining orders. "I want to express a concern for what they are having to contend with," he said. "I think the way the judge talks to the victim, the whole court expression of concern—'What do you want?' 'What can we do?'—I think all of that contributes to it." Nonetheless, this judge acknowledged that women are discouraged from seeking child support in his court. He admitted that there is a new concern to make child support a regular part of the orders, but he said he is willing to go along with this only reluctantly:

Well, let me tell you, Dorchester Court used to do child support cases almost to the exclusion of everything else. . . . In my view, there was a terrific imbalance given a court where we have violence, drugs, guns. We were putting a really disproportionate effort into child support enforcement. . . . You've got to be able to get back into doing more serious court business in this community. So I think there is a tendency here to encourage women who come in for child support as part of a 209A—many of whom are on public assistance; you know, you are not going to get the money anyway—to go over to the Department of Revenue. They'll start the process. We're passing it off to the Department of Revenue and to a lot of the probate courts. . . . We perhaps don't focus as much on support as somebody might say we should. . . . I would admit that it's not something we have looked for. . . . It's been kind of forced upon us.

In the authority of this judge, this court has deliberately discouraged women from seeking the material remedies available through restraining orders. He points to the poverty of the women who appear before him. And the law does indicate that women who are on Aid to Families with Dependent Children (AFDC) are not entitled to collect child support but must instead seek support through the Department of Revenue. But this recognition of the class position of many of the women in Dorchester apparently makes him discourage petitions for child support across the board. To the extent that he acknowledges the poverty of women claiming their rights in the court, this acknowledgment serves to stigmatize them. There seems to be an assumption that poor and working-class women of color seeking legal redress are not "honorable citizens."[16] Their class and racial characteristics seem to mark them as untrustworthy and as wasting the court's time with their concern for material relief. It would seem that material suffering is unrelated to battering, in his account.

What message is symbolically conveyed to women who request child support, as the law allows, only to be "passed off" to probate court or otherwise discouraged from pursuing it? And if the actions of judges communicate symbolic messages to the other women and men in the courtroom and even to the local community, what image of authority is expressed through this type of institutional indifference?

The second judge, a white woman, offers a contrast to such frustration with women's requests. She believes that nothing is more important than responding to domestic violence. "I believe it is the most important thing that district courts do. I think it is the thing that more people get hurt at. It is the thing that has the most long-range implications for society," she stated. And when presented with the findings on child support in Dorchester, she was surprised, in contrast to the first judge. Indeed, she accepted personal responsibility for the court's failure to respond. However, what is revealed in her explanation is the invisibility of women's material circumstances. This is how she responded to the evidence that the majority of women's requests for child support were ignored in her court:

We just dropped the ball. And it was probably me because I was in that session most of the time. . . . Last year, that's probably me. . . . I think that, um, what I have noticed, and have started—and I've been out of it for about a month; I took a break to go to the jury session, frankly, and a big part of the reason I wanted the break was the restraining orders—but *what I was noticing this year, in the last couple of months, was that I was seeing it on the application more. And I think it was because I was looking. I think that it may be that before that they were checking the box, and I wasn't doing it. I wasn't bringing it up. And if nobody brought it up, I didn't do anything. I mean, I think I wasn't—I was reading, going straight to the affidavit, asking her what she wanted, if she didn't say anything—I was ordering it and not reading the application. And I bet that's when most of them fell through the cracks.* (Emphasis added)

Rather than a deliberate policy of ignoring women's needs, this judge states it was unintentional. She hadn't seen the requests on their complaint forms. And when women—without lawyers, without advocates—fell silent in the courtroom and didn't restate what they had checked off on the forms, the forms were ignored. Their requests for support weren't even considered. Focusing mostly on their affidavits, this judge assumed that women would repeat everything they indicated on the restraining order forms when standing before her. But even the most welcoming and patient demeanor of the individual judge does not overcome the intimidating power of the office.

Told about the difference between Dorchester and Quincy in attention to child support requests, this second judge saw advocates as making the difference:

A good part of that difference, I think, is advocates—which is not to take anything at all away from [the judges in Quincy], who are very good about this—but I also think it's a way that those things don't slip through the cracks. Which does not at all diminish my responsibility for not looking at the applications.

I also asked this judge about why no woman at Dorchester was granted compensation for losses suffered due to the abuse, which is another option offered as part of the restraining order. Of the 20 requests by women for compensation in a sample of 250 consecutive cases examined, none received it at Dorchester; the issue of compensation was made a part of the 10-day hearing in only one case. Asked about these figures, the judge's answer was the same. "Well, this is sobering," she said. Again, she had failed to read women's applications carefully.

Quincy's record was only somewhat better. Of 250 consecutive order requests filed by women in Quincy, seven women sought compensation, and two received it. Spousal support, another part of the restraining order petition, was requested by 12 percent of the sample of 250 women at Dorchester, and 8 percent of the sample of 250 women at Quincy; in both courts, it appears that these requests are also routinely ignored. The right to have compensation and spousal support included in a restraining order is therefore an "empty right" in two of the courts with the highest public profiles on these issues.[17]

What image of authority is communicated by this type of institutional neglect? If judicial demeanor is communicated through the clarification of legal options, it is also conveyed by a refusal to consider them. There is then a limit to the responses of even judges who assume a high profile on these issues.

In the literature on both racism and sexism—the intersection of which is at issue here—the theme of invisibility has a long history. In *Invisible Man*, Ralph Ellison describes the problem of racism not as one of complete invisibility but rather as the lack of recognition of the full humanity of black Americans, a "feigned moral blindness" on the part of white Americans.[18] Patricia Hill Collins names the ways that black women are denied status "as fully human subjects" by being objectified by a variety of controlling images, including that of the "welfare mother."[19] Shulamit Reinharz offers a new term, *gynopia*, to name not the overtly brutal practices of misogyny but "the inability to perceive the very existence of women as fully human actors."[20] After thinking about the above judge's interview later that same day, I became extremely disillusioned at how poor and working-class women of color remained so invisible.

These two judges, then, sitting at the same court, describe different institutional processes that have the same result. Both through deliberate action and unintentional neglect, through stigma, trivialization, and invisibility, the material dimensions of women's requests were ignored in Dorchester District Court. Only selective dimensions of women's experiences were perceived through the legal process.

Judges at Quincy District Court took these requests for child support much more seriously. It is a court that has many more services for women, including advocacy, and a much longer history of prioritizing these orders, so its response is not surprising. Even at Quincy, wide disparities exist between different judges on these matters, with some routinely scheduling hearings on support and others routinely refusing to do so. But most women claiming their rights in Quincy are not burdened by the powerful racist image of the black "welfare mother," an image that may cause court officials to prejudge their credibility and the importance of their requests.

Among some judges, there may be a profile of an ideal victim operating in restraining order hearings, similar to one observed by Gary D. LaFree in rape trials. In his study, LaFree found that white middle-class jurors were less likely to believe a woman's account of rape if she was black. The extent of a woman's adherence to traditional feminine behavior was also related to jurors' empathy for her.[21] The Massachusetts judiciary is largely composed of white men.[22] The "ideal victim profile" of a woman seeking protection from battering would describe a white woman who speaks English and has no material needs or who has the means to hire an attorney to seek financial support through probate court. Women whose identity and circumstances fit this profile may have their needs more clearly recognized and may find greater support in restraining order hearings. But women of color, poor women, and non-English-speaking women who suffer battering in the context of racial and class entrapment may be only partially visible and may have the economic dimensions of their requests neglected, either deliberately or through institutional blindness.

Token Displays of Judicial Authority

Both in the previous chapter and in this chapter's analysis of judges' accounts, an important distinction has been made between superficial displays and substantive actions that express demeanor. Consistent with Goffman, task embeddedness is one means by which demeanor is conveyed. Concern for women's safety and conscientiousness in mobilizing resources characterize supportive or "good-natured" demeanor, not empty gestures of "niceness." One judge articulated this difference between the superficial and more substantive presentations of judicial authority:

When . . . you are in a very busy court, where there are—. It's late in the afternoon, and there are 10 or 15 209A petitioners, plus hearings, and you're the only judge, and there's no victim-witness advocate, and if there's a language barrier besides. *You realize that you are just going through the motions. And then that order is just a piece of paper. . . . If* something happens, if the inevitable happens, you're covered. That's it. *You're covered because you've issued the order, and you've dotted the i's. But you know in your heart that you have not done anything that is going to protect that woman.* Because what you have given her is that piece of paper. But you have not made her aware, really, of how frightening the situation should be for her, where she can go, what her options are, what she should do in an emergency. I mean, you've just not done any of that. And you know that you've really been ineffective. (Emphasis added)

In her account, she contrasts not just effective and ineffective judges but also effective and ineffective institutions. Judges are ineffective when they are tired and overworked and ignorant of the local community; but courts also limit judicial effectiveness when they don't have advocates, translation services, or relationships with shelters. She offers a contrast between the same judge working under two different sets of circumstances. While further illustrating the dependence of the system on advocates, she also makes an argument for the limits of what individual judges can accomplish without an institutional commitment to mobilize resources for abused women.

Summary

This chapter has examined judicial demeanor through interviews with judges who assert its importance. These judges are articulate and reflective about the images of authority they present in the courtroom. They receive training on demeanor, and they talk about it with other judges. They use a variety of techniques to make their self-presentations more effective in conveying empathy and support to women who report abuse.

These judges also indicate that the emotional labor of judging is draining, and they acknowledge a dependence on advocates to assist with this burden. Indeed, the emotional cost to judges who genuinely engage with women seeking protection may be one reason that other judges sit so passively in restraining order hearings. The logic of court processes may encourage male judges in particular to present a bureaucratic face of authority.

The judges interviewed here resisted both the record of judicial hostility and the indifference of bureaucratic court processes in their attempts to deliver justice to abused women. They sought to alter courtroom rules of deference and demeanor to create a more supportive environment for women seeking protection. But this chapter also demonstrates that even among judges who see themselves as reformers, there are limits to empathy, support, and acknowledgment of women's legal rights. Empathy and support may not extend to a full recognition of the ways that racism and economic deprivation undermine women's ability to escape violence.

The judge was terrible and not concerned. . . . I could have dropped dead in front of her. She was more concerned about visitation on Christmas. . . . She said it was a "lovers' quarrel." I said, "We're not lovers. There's a history here." She said, "It's just a lovers' spat."

Woman who was denied a restraining order
at Quincy District Court

I was surprised that so many people were concerned and supporting me. I have to tell you that the courts are more responsive to women than they used to be. . . . I've been to court many times over the years, and I notice a difference. . . . They used to send you before a judge who would say, "Here you go. Here's your restraining order and good-bye." Now it's more of a process to get a restraining order, and the system seems to be catching up with the times. . . . I felt people took their time and explained things to me and really informed me about what was available to me.

Woman who obtained a restraining order at
Dorchester District Court

7

It sounded good in the courthouse. But when you leave, that's it. Like I said, I'd have to hide if anything happens.

Woman who obtained a restraining order at
Dorchester District Court

Women's Experiences Seeking Restraining Orders

What role do judges play in the ongoing process of women's victimization? How well do judges help women to resist and escape violence? Abused women appear in court generally a day or so after being assaulted or otherwise terrorized by the defendants. Only police officers, shelter workers, and emergency room medics see as many women so soon after the abuse occurs. Photographs taken by the district attorney's office are included in the restraining order files at Dorchester District Court. There are color photos of flesh wounds made by cigarette burns, bruises covering many parts of the body, slashed clothing, black eyes, and facial swelling so severe that it closes the eyes.

Staged so soon after the most recent violence, judges' interactions with abused women have tremendous importance. To make sense of women's experiences, the idea of judging as "emotional labor" needs to be advanced one step further. Up to this point, I have developed the insights of Erving Goffman and Arlie Russell Hochschild to address the staging of courtroom encounters and the intent of judges to have an emotional impact on women and men standing before them. The previous chapter detailed the efforts of judges to alter both their emotions and their self-presentation to accomplish this goal. But Goffman and Hochschild focus more on the people doing the emotional labor than on its intended recipients. It is important to examine these courtroom encounters from women's perspectives. How do women seeking restraining orders perceive their court experiences? How are they affected by the different faces of judicial authority? And what impact do restraining orders have on their lives? To address these questions, telephone interviews were conducted with 40 women who sought restraining orders in 1992 in either Dorchester or Quincy District Court.[1]

This chapter begins by placing women's courtroom experiences within the context of victimization and trauma. Only then can the impact of judicial authority on abused women be appraised. For the power of men's violence is present in these courtroom encounters, even when the abusive men are absent.

Fear, Disempowerment, and Disconnection

It is not only the physical wounds that are raw when many women enter the courtroom. Battering leaves psychic wounds that affect not only the self but also the relationship of the self to others. In her recent work on psychological trauma, Judith Lewis Herman identifies damage to women's social relationships as a primary consequence of violence:

The damage to relational life is not a secondary effect of trauma, as originally thought. Traumatic events have primary effects not only on the

psychological structures of the self but also on the systems of attach-
ment and meaning that link individual and community.

Because traumatic life events invariably cause damage to relationships,
people in the survivor's social world have the power to influence the
eventual outcome of the trauma. A supportive response from other people may mitigate the impact of the event, while a hostile or negative
response may compound the damage.[2]

Physical wounds heal in accordance with timetables set by
natural processes. The psychic trauma produced by violence,
however, must follow a social process for recovery. Human relationships are required for healing of this kind. This social timeta-
ble can exceed a lifetime; an inability to heal from psychic
wounds can even lead to suicide. Evan Stark and Anne H. Flitcraft
report that battering may be "the single most important context
yet identified for female suicide attempts."[3] In a study of hospital
records, they found that 26 percent of the suicide attempts reported to hospitals were associated with battering; 50 percent of
black women who attempted suicide were abused. If recovery
from psychic trauma is a social process, this process will be more
difficult for women in communities that are already suffering
from economic and political isolation.

According to Herman, the prolonged and repeated traumatic
events experienced by battered women produce fear, terror, disconnection, and disempowerment. "The response of the community," Herman concludes, "has a powerful influence on the
ultimate resolution of the trauma."[4]

Judith Lewis Herman draws a parallel between battering and
the means of coercion used against political prisoners. The same
coercive techniques identified by Amnesty International as common to the experiences of political prisoners are found in the testimony of battered women, Herman argues. In both cases, she
states, "Methods of psychological control are designed to instill
terror and helplessness and to destroy the victim's sense of self in
relation to others."[5]

Terror is the fear of lethal violence.[6] In the telephone interviews, women spoke of fear and terror. Of the 40 women, 65 percent indicated the defendant had threatened to kill them. This
figure was the same for women in Dorchester and Quincy. Fully
45 percent of the women stated they were threatened by the de-

fendants with a knife or a gun. Hospital visits due to injuries from the violence were reported by 35 percent of the women interviewed. Injuries included a concussion, broken noses, kidney damage, cuts requiring stitches on the hands and face, black eyes, and bruises on the leg, shoulder, and internal organs. Several women suffered physically in other ways that they attributed to men's violence against them. One woman, who had three miscarriages, believes they were caused by the violence; another was hospitalized for three months for treatment of depression.

Thirty percent of the women reported they had suffered sexual abuse. This is a substantial percentage, especially given the fact that only one question was asked concerning sexual abuse. Other researchers have found that to gather information from women about sexual assault, elaborate interview guides are necessary.[7] Catharine A. MacKinnon has argued that beyond rape, physical assaults on women have sexual dimensions: battering frequently occurs in the bedroom, it is often precipitated by men's sexual jealousy, and it is eroticized in popular culture.[8] In Liz Kelly's qualitative research with women, 24 of 25 women who had experienced domestic violence "defined aspects of the abuse as sexual."[9] They described the physical assaults either as accompanied by rape, as part of attempts to coerce sex, or as motivated by a man's sexual possessiveness. Kelly claims that "physical" and "sexual" forms of violence cannot be clearly distinguished from one another. While the telephone interview guide did not offer an opportunity for women to go into great detail about sexual violence and abuse, a figure of 30 percent offers some support for the points made by MacKinnon and Kelly.

Table 7.1 indicates that in addition to physical and sexual abuse, fully 98 percent of the women reported psychological abuse. "Yes, that was the worst," one woman said; she had been threatened with a knife. "Bruises heal; mental abuse stays with you for a long time." These women described a number of other intimidating actions by men, such as vague threats ("In more ways than one, I'll make your life miserable"), attacks on pets, destroying property, and punching holes in the wall. Telephones were pulled out, and doors were broken down in several cases, serving to literally disconnect women from their social resources and to warn them of their vulnerability.

TABLE 7.1

Types of Abuse Reported in Telephone Interviews with Women Who Sought Restraining Orders

Type of Abuse	District Court		
	Dorchester (n = 20)	Quincy (n = 20)	Combined[a]
Physical abuse	80%	85%	83%
Sexual abuse	30	30	30
Psychological abuse (threats, destruction of property, stalking, harassment, humiliation)	95	100	98
Economic or resource abuse (taking her money and property, refusing to support children)	75	75	75

a. This column represents the percentage of women reporting the different types of abuse. These types of abuse are not mutually exclusive. Because most women reported several different types of abuse, the total number exceeds 100 percent.

Several forms of monitoring or surveillance were also identified. Herman states that perpetrators often seek to destroy the autonomy of victims through "scrutiny and control of the victim's body and bodily functions."[10] One woman who was interviewed said, "He used to watch me go to the bathroom and stand there. . . . He was either too nice to me, it'd make me sick, or he'd be all over me." Other women said they were stalked; one said she was locked in her room.

Since most women seeking restraining orders in Dorchester and Quincy are mothers of young children, women were asked specifically about threats against children. Of the women who were mothers, 51 percent stated the defendant threatened either to take the children himself or to go to court or to call the Massachusetts Department of Social Services and report that the woman was an unfit mother. A number of the men threatened to kidnap the children and take them out of state, never to be seen again. Four men did attempt to deprive women of legal custody of their children; in one case, the defendant succeeded in doing so. Nearly a fourth of the mothers who sought restraining orders reported the defendants had abused or threatened to abuse the children, either physically or sexually.

Further evidence of damage to women's relational lives can be seen in responses to the question of who knew about the violence. Most of the women who were interviewed had talked about the violence they suffered with their friends and family. Seventy-three percent talked about the abuse with their friends, all of whom supported the women's decision to seek a restraining order. One woman said she didn't talk openly about it with her friends but only "dropped hints" that were apparently not picked up; she said she was isolated from everyone after awhile. But 20 percent of the women did not talk with their friends at all about the abuse before seeking a restraining order. This loss of closeness and trust with friends, along with the support this provides, is part of the social damage inflicted by batterers.

The same percentages hold concerning family members. Of the 40 women, 73 percent discussed the abuse with relatives. Most supported the women's decision to go to court:

My family was adamant about me protecting myself, especially one of my brothers, who didn't want me to let my daughter see [the defendant].

Two of the women had sisters who were in similar danger: "all of us were going through the same thing with men abusing us," one said. But three women indicated their relatives discouraged them from going to court. One woman, who had gone to the hospital for her injuries, was told by her mother-in-law not to get a restraining order because it would ruin a family event that week. Another woman stated her mother minimized the abuse and told her to be a "good wife." A different sort of advice was reported by another woman. She said her brothers discouraged her because they "wanted to take the matter into their own hands. They wanted to hurt him and didn't want me going to the courts."

One-fifth of the women said nothing at all to family members.[11] For these women, fear, beliefs about "family privacy," and shame or denial apparently isolated them from their kin networks:

I had to be quiet because he would beat me if I told anyone.

I kept it well hidden. I didn't want to believe it was going on.

Such remarks reveal the isolation with which batterers cloaked these women. When they came to court for help, both women spoke in public about violence they had still not disclosed to their families. Men exerted control in these relationships by forcing their partners to choose between either reducing their fears of re-taliation or getting support. The first woman hid the violence from others; the second tried to hide it from herself.

Economic forms of domination were reported by 75 percent of the women interviewed. The most common examples given were refusal to pay child support and theft of money and property. This produced chaos in women's lives, causing food deprivation, prob-lems with landlords, and dependence on public assistance. Given the poverty of many of the women in Dorchester and Quincy, these economic dimensions of battering must be addressed on more than an individual level.

Violence, Poverty, and Racism

The women in Dorchester, who were mostly African American, were poorer than the women in Quincy, who were mostly white. Sixty-five percent of the women interviewed from Dorchester were black, and 10 percent were Latina or Cape Verdean. Ninety-five percent of the women interviewed from Quincy were white. Forty-five percent of the women who sought orders at Dorchester District Court were receiving some form of public assistance, in most cases from Aid to Families with Dependent Children. Of those women who went to Quincy District Court, 25 percent were receiving public assistance. The different levels of poverty among the respondents in Dorchester and Quincy, therefore, have a rough correspondence with the racial character of poverty in the greater Boston area.[12]

It is important to expand Herman's themes of disempow-erment and disconnection to address the class and racial dimen-sions of women's lives. A study of over 1,000 poor households in Boston by the Persistent Poverty Project of the Boston Foundation found that poverty is characterized by social disconnection:

Many poor people experience a kind of social isolation or lack of connec-tion. The majority of those who responded to this survey say they have little knowledge of community organizations which exist to help people with problems. And many could sorely use official services which—for whatever reason—they do not seem to be receiving.[13]

This isolation is compounded by racism against communities of color in Boston. In a recent study of urban poverty, Douglas S. Massey and Nancy A. Denton have identified patterns of social, spatial, economic, and political isolation that result from the residential segregation imposed on black Americans. Residential segregation creates such social marginalization and concentrations of poverty that these authors entitled their study *American Apartheid*. They argue that segregation is as effective in perpetuating racial inequality as apartheid was in South Africa, and that "whites are no less culpable for the socioeconomic deprivation that results."[14] Massey and Denton identify Boston as a highly segregated city.[15]

In addition to the disconnection and disempowerment associated with poverty and racial segregation, women of color who seek protection from violence are further burdened by a racist criminal justice system. State actions such as the public strip-searching of young black and Latino men, discussed in Chapter 3, create dilemmas for women of color. A fear that the police or the courts will mistreat men of color may inhibit women from claiming their rights under the law. It may also affect the experience of those women who do seek justice in the courts. A Gallup Poll conducted in the wake of the Nicole Brown Simpson killing revealed sharply different expectations of justice among black Americans and white Americans. Pointing to the historical collusion of the law with racist oppression, one commentator referred to this rift as an "apartheid of perceptions."[16]

Women's Resistance and Previous Efforts to Obtain Help

To avoid misrepresenting women's resistance to the violence, it is important to review their efforts to leave and obtain institutional help prior to seeking court action. Of the women who had ever lived with the defendants, 68 percent left because of the violence on at least one occasion, and another 15 percent had made the abuser leave at least once.

Before they went to court to file for restraining orders, the majority of the women interviewed had already sought assistance from a range of other institutions. Table 7.2 indicates the kinds of institutional help that women had sought. The most common

TABLE 7.2

Types of Institutional Help Women Sought
Prior to Restraining Order, Reported in Telephone Interviews

Type of Help	District Court		
	Dorchester (n = 20)	Quincy (n = 20)	Combined[a]
Police	90%	65%	78%
Counseling center	15	45	30
Battered women's shelter or hotline	25	25	25
Social service agency	15	10	13
Church	15	10	13
Hospital (discussed abuse)	15	10	13

a. Categories are not mutually exclusive. Because most women sought more than one type of help, the total number exceeds 100 percent.

institutional resource sought was the police; 78 percent had called the police before seeking orders. In fact, 43 percent of the women said they learned about obtaining an order from the police. Mental health institutions were the next most common resource sought. This includes counseling obtained through community mental health centers, HMOs, self-help groups such as Alcoholics Anonymous (AA), Parents Anonymous (PA), and private therapists. Despite the history of racism by the Boston Police Department, women in Dorchester were more likely to contact the police than were women in Quincy; women in Quincy were more likely to seek counseling than women in Dorchester. This may reflect differences in both class and the range of resources available in these two communities. Although self-help groups such as AA and PA are free, most other kinds of counseling are prohibitively expensive for poor women, and as a group the women in Dorchester are poorer than those in Quincy.

Women's shelters or hotlines were contacted by only one-quarter of the women interviewed, with identical figures for Dorchester and Quincy, even though 65 percent of the women said they had heard of shelters. This is discouraging given the range of resources shelters offer to women. It may be that battered women's shelters are misunderstood as only offering a place of last

resort or that there is a reluctance on the part of women to identify themselves as "battered women." Staying in a shelter also
imposes a considerable sacrifice. To prevent violent men from
finding the shelter, women are generally required to suspend contact with family, friends, their workplace, and the children's
school while residing there. It is also recommended that women
stay in shelters some distance away from their own communities.
Often, women move with their children from one shelter to the
next while they seek to regain control over their lives. Despite
these severe impositions, over 3,000 women left home for shelters in 1993, with 4,700 children in tow.[17] The demand continues
to outstrip the supply of emergency housing. Two of the women
interviewed for this study had gone to shelters to escape violence.

Even before seeking restraining orders, these women made numerous efforts to resist and escape men's violence. This pattern of
attempts to leave, getting the man removed, and obtaining other
institutional assistance is consistent with studies of battered
women's help-seeking.[18]

Fear and Emotional Deference in the Courtroom

How did these women feel when they went to court for a restraining order? Most women reported feeling frightened and nervous,
especially the first time they appeared in court. Asked whether
they were afraid for any reason to take out a restraining order, 65
percent of the women said yes. They feared violent retaliation by
the batterer:

I was threatened if I took court action something would happen to me
and my son.

I was petrified and scared for my life. He physically abused me and tried
to strangle me.

I felt that getting a restraining order might stop it on the one hand, but I
felt it might make it worse at the same time. I worried that he might go
out and come back with a gun to kill us. . . . Afraid that he would burn
the house down.

Yes—afraid of what he would do, think, react, repercussions. It was an
unbelievable big deal. Was scared to death.

At first, yeah, because I was afraid of the consequences. . . . I mean it's
only a piece of paper, and he could kill me if he wants to.

I wasn't sure if the restraining order would be the best thing or whether it would make things worse. There had been so much in the news about women getting killed.

Yes—in an abusive relationship, you reach a "balance." It almost always escalated the situation to get a restraining order.

These women assumed considerable risk by taking this action. By claiming their rights under the law to be protected from violence, they were challenging men's control over their lives. The last woman quoted above said that the restraining order symbolized the retaking of power on her part and that for this reason she feared his response. The prevalence of "separation assault" in the random sample of affidavits discussed in Chapter 4 demonstrates that such fears are well grounded. Women's sense of danger is shaped by knowledge of her former partner and of how other men in the community act toward women. The murders of women in Massachusetts, a number of whom had restraining orders in effect, intensified the worries of at least one of the women above. The commonness of violence against women enters into the expectations that give rise to fear.

Not all women expressed this level of fear. Some women had gone to court many times before and said they weren't afraid. One woman said she was "a little bit" afraid, but said, "I had to get it because you feel safer." Another woman said she was more afraid of *not* having a restraining order.

Adding to their apprehensions, many women also felt intimidated by the institution itself. This is how they described what the first hearing felt like:

I was absolutely positively petrified. I was by myself too. . . . All these men and then there was me.

Real, real scary. I get scared in courts and in hospitals. . . . The [woman from the restraining order office] told them to give me a restraining order. I didn't understand everything they said. It went so fast. Judge talked to the lady. . . . I was crying.

Scary, shaky. . . . I've never been in front of a judge before, and I wanted to walk out. . . . It was very intimidating, and there were a lot of people there, which made it hard to talk.

I was very nervous, hands sweaty, and I was trying to talk clear, not so fast. . . . I took a deep breath and tried to calm. Once I got it out, I felt more eased.

I was so scared and so nervous just being in a courtroom because I had never been in a court before. . . . Going there and being judged. It's kind of hard to do that because there are no guarantees.

Such feelings mark the disclosure of personal suffering in a public space. Along with being frightened of the defendants and feeling distraught from the recent violence, the atmosphere of the courtroom produced its own intimidation. Uncertain of what would happen, these women stood before the judge, surrounded by the chaos of a crowded courthouse. It is no wonder one woman didn't understand everything being said.

Following Erving Goffman's analysis, Robert M. Emerson describes courtroom proceedings as "ceremonial confrontations" that are "consciously shaped" to induce intimidation, degradation, and humiliation.[19] In both Dorchester and Quincy, police officers wearing revolvers routinely walk in and out of the courtrooms; bailiffs wear handcuffs and enforce order by hushing spectators and even forbidding the reading of newspapers; and all are instructed to rise when the judge enters and departs. One day while I was sitting in a courtroom, I was asked by the judge who I was and what I was doing there. I responded that I was observing hearings as part of my research. As I was talking, the bailiff said, in a loud tone, "You will *stand* when you talk to the judge." Startled, I immediately jumped to my feet and prefaced my next statement with "your honor."

The emotional dimension of courtroom rules of deference have emotional impact. But Arlie Russell Hochschild emphasizes the depth at which these rules of deference guide feeling and how much *feeling itself* becomes a gesture as significant, in its own way, as a physical action. "We bow to each other not only from the waist, but from the heart," Hochschild states.[20] There are "feeling rules" among the expectations of deference in the courtroom. There was oblique acknowledgment of these rules by some women:

Intimidated—but maybe that was just me and I shouldn't have felt that way. I'd never been there before . . . kind of scared.

I was scared, but I knew I didn't have anything to be ashamed of.

The first woman questions whether she was *supposed* to feel intimidated in the courtroom, suggesting that maybe she was. The second woman states she had no reason to feel ashamed, again raising the issue of whether she somehow *should have* felt ashamed. Both statements offer evidence of feeling rules. For Hochschild, such rules are most easily noticed when they are violated—that is, when there is a "pinch" between what you *think* you should feel and what you *actually do* feel.[21] Perhaps these rules are primarily meant to oblige feelings of intimidation in criminal defendants, but they also affected many women on their first visits as plaintiffs, along with one courtroom observer.

And in fact, the courtroom produced other feelings along with intimidation. Ironically consistent with Emerson's findings on how juvenile defendants are supposed to feel in court, a number of women spoke of feeling embarrassed, humiliated, and degraded:

I found it embarrassing and humiliating to stand there with a bunch of strangers.

I felt really nervous and uncomfortable, wondering how loud he would talk. . . . There were about 10 people or maybe 15 in the courtroom, and I was aware that they could hear what I was there for.

I felt kind of funny, stupid because here it is the third time going through this with the same person. I wondered what they thought of me being back there.

Degrading—because I had to go through this with a person who I had been with for so long.

It was a little nerve wracking. It's a full courtroom, and it's a private matter. . . . I know that juvenile hearings are confidential, maybe restraining orders should be. . . . They always refer to you as a victim, and I don't like that. You can't really stand your back up straight. . . . You almost feel a little dumb.

Under such conditions of personal risk and exposure, these women felt vulnerable to judgment. Standing in a subordinate position before the judge, they felt themselves bowing from the heart, to use Hochschild's insightful expression. They also observed that this emotional deference came at a substantial personal cost. Some women felt "stupid" or "dumb" under the weight of the ceremonial staging. The label of "victim," for one woman, reduced and deformed her sense of self.

Several women worried they would not be believed and imagined the judge rejecting their testimony:

Very scary. Didn't know what to expect. Would the judge believe me or him? Would the judge blame me?

I feel like the court itself is another world. It's evil—like another planet. In a way, when going in I felt like I wasn't going to be believed because of what I was going through at home—the degradation and put-downs. And because I have stuck with him for so long. I wasn't sure if they would believe me.

This last woman reveals how the psychological abuse she was suffering came to affect her in the courtroom, undermining her confidence in herself. For some women, being in court was so overwhelming they felt numb or faint:

I don't really remember. . . . I was worried about my daughter and wanted to get her back. I was nervous and all. I don't really have any feelings— just like a daze or a dream. It didn't seem real. I have no feelings.

Sick—I felt sick. I was shaking so bad and felt like passing out. . . . I felt nervous. I have nerves, problems with my nerves.

These accounts reveal the extent of psychic strain women may experience while standing in the courtroom. Both estrangement from feeling and being flooded with feeling are common responses to violence, responses that, Herman states, can be revived by testifying in court.[22]

Some women also felt deeply conflicted about being in court, due to complex feelings about the defendants:

[Felt] like I was the criminal. . . . It's awful because you're scared the defendant is there. You're sad. You're alone. You feel guilty.

Painful. Not fearful. . . . I have this thing where I don't want to hurt other people, and I felt like I was hurting him. It wasn't scary. It was more painful. . . . I felt hate at the time.

A little shaky. . . . You just be a little shaky because of safety, because sometimes doing it you could get the man in trouble. I just worried about him and what would happen to him.

The whole time I was sitting on a bench and the asshole was sitting right beside me. I was there by myself, but he doesn't scare me. There was another black girl sitting behind me on the bench, and [the defendant] said to me, "I don't know why you black women want to lock up all the brothers." I told him, "If you are going to act stupid, I'm going to do this." He started getting loud, and so I moved to another bench. [He] kept saying, "Don't do this."

The legal options that abused black women have are burdened by the racist history of the courts and police. A belief that the police could seriously mistreat the defendant seems to worry the last two women above. Racist institutional responses undermine the credibility of the courts and the police in communities of color. In the last account, the defendant uses this history to his own advantage by trying to convince this woman—unsuccessfully—to drop the order.

Three dimensions of fear have been presented as important to women's court appearances—fear of the defendant, intimidation produced by the institutional setting, and fear of being treated unjustly by the judge. Given the risks that women took to testify and the emotional vulnerability that the courtroom produces, what kinds of experiences did these women have with judges?

Judicial Demeanor from Women's Perspectives

Judicial demeanor played an important role in women's experiences with restraining orders. It is already apparent that being in court in itself was for many women a memorable, even traumatic experience. One-quarter of the women said that their interactions with judges were the most helpful aspects of their court experience. A smaller number of women (8 percent) found their interactions with judges to be either harmful or the least helpful aspects of going to court.[23] On the whole, both the women who sought orders from Dorchester and those who went to Quincy rated the demeanor of the judges positively. These 40 women described 55 different interactions with judges. Since the restraining order is generally a two-step process, this means that a number of these women went to court twice attempting to get an order effective for one year. (In cases where the man has been arrested and is in custody, both parties may be in court for the initial hearing, making a 10-day hearing unnecessary.) Four women decided not to return to Dorchester District Court, and thus their temporary orders expired after 10 days. Two women were denied orders in Quincy District Court.

Of the 55 different hearings women attended, 67 percent of the judges were described as supportive in ways that correspond with "good-natured" demeanor. Women characterized 24 percent of the judges as presenting a bureaucratic, passive, or detached demeanor. In 9 percent of the hearings, women said the judge's demeanor toward them was condescending, harsh, or otherwise demeaning.

Judges attempt to produce particular emotive states in the individuals standing before the bench. The judges interviewed in the previous chapter, for example, spoke of wanting women to feel welcome and supported. But women's experience with judges is also mediated by what they are seeking from these interactions. Guided by Judith Lewis Herman's theory of trauma and recovery, this discussion is framed in terms of three underlying expectations that appeared in the interviews. According to the women's accounts, supportive judicial demeanor responded to their desire for recognition, their need for safety, and their appeal for justice. While the differences between bureaucratic, condescending, and harsh demeanor will be delineated, none of these types of demeanor were perceived by women as adequate responses to their help-seeking. Bureaucratic, condescending, and harsh presentations of authority failed to address—even betrayed—the recognition, safety, and justice they sought.

Indeed, in some cases judges' responses amounted to a secondary victimization. Evan Stark and Anne H. Flitcraft have argued that battering consists of a "dual trauma," the result of not just violence but social entrapment arising from institutional collusion and indifference:

The modal experience of battering is a dual trauma, fear and anger induced by violent subjugation combined with a sense of increasing entrapment. . . . Typically, [this] sense of entrapment is a reality-based response to a history of denial, minimization, and victim blaming by those from whom they have sought support and protection, including police, doctors, social workers, and therapists.[24]

Following from this analysis, when the consequences of violence are investigated, the contribution of social responses to trauma must be paramount, according to Stark and Flitcraft:

It is easier—and safer politically—to probe the childhood experiences and/or psychological motives of violent men and their victims than to ask whether the institutions to which women had gained access—such as the police or the court system—might not be undermining their formal entitlements to security, health, and safety.[25]

Judicial Demeanor and Women's Desire for Recognition

If social stigma represents the reduction of one's identity to a single discredited characteristic,[26] then the antithesis of a stigmatizing interaction is one that recognizes the full humanity of an individual. The terms *victim, battered woman,* and *welfare mother* have come to be seen as stigmatized identities. These terms are often applied to people to rob them of the full range of their humanness; the deployment of such labels against black women has its own political history.[27] In their descriptions of courtroom interactions, women who had supportive experiences spoke at length about judges' efforts to establish a human connection, one that transcended both stigmas and the bureaucratic character of the court:

He was very helpful and concerned not just for me, but for my son and my family. . . . Acted like I wasn't just another case to him. I was a person, a human being. . . . He showed that he cared. It wasn't just a judge to a victim. It seems like he reaches over the boundaries and shows caring and concern.

Talked to me like I was a teenager but a person. Didn't go overboard with the big words. . . . He let me know in plain English what I had to do and how the restraining order works.

Very kind. . . . He understood I was upset. . . . He had empathy . . . treat[ed] me like a person, not like a name and number and accepted my story and told me not to be afraid.

I felt that he was sensitive to the issue. You know you go in to a room, and you can't tell your family, but you have to go to a court, in a public place to talk with a judge. . . . And he was very sensitive and patient. . . . He looked attentive, let me talk. Said, "Take your time." . . . Asked questions but didn't direct or push me—gave me space to talk. . . . I felt comforted, just to be believed.

Such expressions of a desire for recognition run throughout the interviews. Women who felt supported talked of being understood, being believed, being listened to by judges. They sought a human connection to break through the isolation that both violence—and indifference to violence—impose on them. They described supportive judges as using a "sympathetic," "compassionate," "kind," or "comforting" tone of voice or as speaking in a soft voice that afforded some privacy in such an exposed setting. The fear of a dehumanizing interaction is the flip side of this desire, and a number of women could not articulate the experience of being supported without naming this underlying apprehension. In the accounts above, women feared being treated like a "victim," a "teenager," or merely a "name and number": these are ways of being made invisible. In fact, supportive encounters with judges were frequently described in terms of being seen:

[The judge was] calm, quiet . . . could tell I was scared . . . reassuring voice. . . . He looked me right in the eye.

Standing in front of the judge was kind of nerve wracking. He looked at me and could see it in my eyes that I wasn't lying. I think judges seem to know what I was going through.

I'm a fighter and I have always been. I look at myself as an abused woman. I'm not battered—what comes to mind is someone who is beaten to a pulp. . . . That judge, she was really concerned. I looked into her eyes, and I can tell when someone is bullshitting me. But she wasn't.

Making eye contact is a visceral way of communicating and receiving both support and honesty in these accounts. Women also indicated that supportive judges were patient and took sufficient time with them in the hearings, even when the court was crowded, as it often is in Dorchester and Quincy.

Judith Lewis Herman emphasizes that public recognition is essential both to recovery from violence and to social action against violence. She argues that this has been the experience of combat veterans, political prisoners, children who have been sexually abused, women who have been raped, and women who have been battered. Rather than looking away from the violence—Herman calls this the "ordinary response to atrocities"[28]—supportive judges acted as witnesses to their experience of fear and terror. This mattered greatly to the women who were interviewed. Of course, recognition and empathy alone do not stop the violence and abuse. But they are essential for any meaningful provision of protection by the courts.

Bureaucratic judges were viewed by women as distant and unconcerned and as less likely than good-natured judges to spend sufficient time with them. The human connection that women found so supportive with good-natured judges was absent from their experience with bureaucratic judges. Instead of recognition and compassion, women described feeling like just another case:

Not as kind. He seemed rushed, abrupt, businesslike. . . . It was just routine, and I felt more like a name and number, more impersonal.

He didn't really [talk]—just signed it, and I left. . . . Like it was routine for him. . . . That day I felt like it was paper-pushing. . . . It felt rushed—not just the judge but the whole procedure was boom, boom, boom.

This was how these judges responded to the crisis women reported, and the risks they endured to appear in court. Recognition or in these cases lack of recognition is again expressed in terms of feeling faceless and invisible. Judges in these hearings are "doing authority" as much as more supportive judges, and they make their own emotional impression on women with their presence and actions. But from women's perspectives, the image of authority they projected was one of indifference. Both of the women above said the defendants had threatened to kill them.

One woman described an interaction with a judge she found to be condescending:

He kind of made me feel intimidated, like I was on trial. Like he was belittling and didn't take it serious, like it wasn't a big deal. Seemed like he had a sense of humor, but it didn't seem appropriate to me. Very quick and rushed through. He didn't take much concern for me, didn't feel like he cared, cold. . . . Made me feel a bit jumpy, like I was smaller than him. . . . No eye contact with me. . . . I was trying to be formal and make eye contact so he knew I was telling the truth. . . . Thought he might not sign it. . . . Worried. . . . He never tried to see if I was telling the truth.

This judge responded in a patronizing and indifferent way to a woman who had been terrorized. This woman was driven out of state, against her will, by the man she was living with. He said he intended to strip her of her clothes, beat her, and leave her where no one could find her. She managed to escape from the car, found her way back home, and had this encounter with a judge over a restraining order three days later.

The descriptions of harsh encounters with judges also concerned recognition in the sense of feeling ignored and unseen. Highlighting the impact of institutional responses on the psychological consequences of abuse, one woman was hospitalized for several months for depression after being denied a restraining order against her husband. He had previously been arrested for violence against her; he had a history of shoving and grabbing her, of screaming at her, breaking objects, and punching walls. This is how she related her experience of misrecognition with the judge, who refused to even grant a temporary (10-day) order:

Felt like I did something wrong, embarrassing in front of all these people. . . . Totally awful experience. Had a friend with me, which was the only thing that got me through it. . . . [The judge] was a jerk. He wouldn't listen: "Answer yes or no." . . . Felt like I didn't matter, I wasn't a victim, my fault. . . . Harsh, nasty, unfeeling.

She reported that the judge didn't listen to her and wouldn't allow her to describe her experience. If she had seen the right judge, she believes, it may have prevented her hospitalization. "It was the beginning of my being sick, my breakdown," she said. She stated that members of his family made threats to kill her while still in the courtroom.

Judicial Demeanor and Women's Need for Safety

The restraining order hearing is premised on the need for protection. Obtaining an order is, of course, no guarantee of protection, as anyone reading the newspaper knows. At least seven of the 28 women who were killed by their partners or former partners in 1992 had obtained restraining orders against these men; five women had orders that were still in effect when they died. One woman had withdrawn the order; another had obtained an order, but it expired the previous week.[29] Most women were frightened of retaliation by the defendants for seeking restraining orders. In women's eyes, then, supportive demeanor was expressed through concern for the danger women face and institutional action to help provide safety:

I couldn't stop crying. . . . He said don't be afraid to tell him the truth. Because he could get someone to take me home and make me safe as possible.

He was prepared and looked at me and asked me what I wanted. He was fully informed. . . . Seemed like he cared personally about my safety and wanted to reassure me that he would give me whatever I wanted. . . . He asked me what I wanted, how long I needed it for. He told me that "Whatever you need to feel safe, we'll do it for you."

He talked more and asked me if there was anything I was fearful of. Did I need anything or any places to go? I think he was more understanding than the first judge.

There is a great variation in what judges do with their authority concerning safety. Under the scope of the restraining order, judges have the authority to demand that firearms in the possession of the defendant be surrendered to the local police station. Yet according to the interviews with women, most judges do not routinely ask about weapons, and those that do often don't seek to have them confiscated. Of the 40 women interviewed, 23 percent reported being threatened with a gun; one woman had her windows shot out with a rifle, and another was forced into the woods with a sawed-off shotgun. Judges who presented a supportive demeanor were more likely to ask if the defendant had weapons.

Concern for safety can be expressed by explaining the ways women can obtain protection under the restraining order, including such arrangements as getting a police escort to return home and pick up their belongings. The public scandal over the judicial treatment of Pamela Nigro Dunn, examined in Chapter 3, erupted in part because the judge was unwilling to provide protection for Dunn some months prior to her murder. Informing women of their right to press criminal charges is also a way of demonstrating task orientation around safety because criminal convictions give judges more leverage over violent men. It is worth repeating that of the 100 randomly selected restraining order affidavits examined in Chapter 4, 70 percent made allegations consistent with assault and battery. Supportive or "good-natured" judges were more likely than other judges to explain the order to women and more likely to inform women of their right to file criminal charges. Some judges also informed women of extralegal resources, such as by handing women phone numbers for shelters during the hearings.

According to women's accounts, bureaucratic judges were unlikely to ask about weapons, unlikely to inform women about their right to file criminal charges, and generally did not spend sufficient time with them:

I told my side of the story and wanted to get him some counseling and to leave me alone. . . . Felt the judge was on my side. But he didn't do much, just filled out the papers.

[The judge] allowed me to speak. I begged him not to let [the defendant] out of jail. He said to me, "You truly are a victim." Ha! Big deal. He still let him out. I said, not only has the system victimized me, but you are victimizing me. . . . He was out on the street before I got back to my house, and then the phone calls started. Didn't look at me; checked every box. Three minutes in and out.

This limited contact and lack of attention to safety is consistent with the impatience, passivity, and lack of engagement with women cited previously.

One woman had a condescending experience where she felt the judge ignored her fears of the defendant:

Didn't get to speak at all. . . . Not good at all. Totally dissatisfied. Didn't pay me much attention, nor my fears. [The defendant] acted like a hood and was disrespectful to me, and she didn't say anything to him. . . . She didn't ask me how I felt or what type of danger I feel. She seemed to say that I brought some of it on. . . . She asked how long it took me to get out of the situation, as if to say it was my fault.

This woman said she had gone to the hospital twice for injuries inflicted by her husband, including black eyes, bruises, and cuts that required stitches. The defendant, from whom she had separated, had also reportedly threatened her with a gun. Although the judge granted an extension of the order for one year, this woman felt so enraged by how she was treated that she stormed out of the hearing before it was concluded.

Judicial Demeanor and Women's Appeal for Justice

Judith Lewis Herman describes violence against women as a "physical, psychological, and moral violation."[30] The moral response of the community is critical to restoring a sense of justice to battered women. Yet as the history reviewed in Chapter 3 reveals, the law continues to be in disorder about whether battering represents injustice.

Justice involves many institutions within the criminal justice system. Here the focus is on women's perceptions of justice in the courtroom. Women's experience with the police, especially after receiving restraining orders, also has a great bearing on this issue; the connections between the courts and the police are addressed below.

Some of women's descriptions of supportive judicial demeanor addressed the issue of moral responsibility for the violence:

She was really nice. She told me I have nothing to worry about and it was not my fault.

He talked like he don't want these males to get away with anything. Like he was fed up with these restraining orders and he wanted to do something about these guys who were abusing women.

Very sympathetic, understanding. He asked why hasn't he been arrested.

Through these kinds of statements, judges define abuse as injustice. Such public acknowledgments, made to women who have

taken considerable risks to appear in court, offer support at a critical point in the process of victimization. Kathleen J. Ferraro and
John M. Johnson found that a change in the external definitions
of abuse is one of the catalysts that enable women to reject ratio-
nalizations for violence and move toward autonomy.[31]

How judges acted toward defendants who appeared for restraining order hearings also concerns justice. In the interviews,
women were asked how it felt to observe these interactions. Consistent with the courtroom observations presented in Chapter 5,
women reported that judges who were supportive of them generally displayed firm demeanor toward the defendants:

> [The defendant] went on and on and said he wanted the judge to let him
> write to his children. He said he wanted to be a father to his kids. The
> judge said, "You had that chance and blew it. Too bad." I liked that be-
> cause he gave him a chance to talk but didn't let him get away with that
> story about how much he wanted to be a father. . . . Happy about it
> because [the defendant] is so conniving and deceiving. He manages to
> pull the wool over everyone's eyes—but not that time. I felt good to see
> the judge see the truth and realize that he's so conniving.

> [The judge] held him accountable. He told him how his drinking was
> affecting his wife and that he needed treatment. He was like a father
> figure. He used his authority with him and took the situation seriously.
> Of the three times I got restraining orders, it was the only time a judge
> took it seriously and did something. He saw what the issue was.

> [The judge] was very firm and let him know . . . that he only had two
> choices—go to jail or go to drug treatment. He let him know in no uncer-
> tain terms that he wasn't going to play around. . . . He had a choice, and
> [the judge] told him that if he saw him in court again, he'd be going to
> jail. . . . I was pleased. I felt like someone was on my side, not just think-
> ing I was a lunatic housewife ranting and raving.

A firm judicial stance toward abusive men was very affirming of
these women. In these accounts, women indicate that their experience had previously been concealed by the misrepresentations
of the defendants and trivialized by the indifference of judges. The
last woman quoted above sketches some of the misogynistic images of battered women that she fears will be imposed on her for
speaking out about the violence. By presenting a firm demeanor,
judges both challenged men's entitlement and supported wom-
en's sense of justice.

Women attended closely to judges' interactions with the defendants. Even small gestures of judges are noted by women and interpreted against expectations of justice. One woman said, "He just had a 'look' when he talked to my husband that I knew meant he understood my situation." Another supplied words to a judge's expression: "He looked at him like, 'Who do you think you are? You have no right.'"

One bureaucratic judge was criticized for the disparity between his treatment of her and the defendant:

There wasn't much [interaction]. He didn't look at me. [The defendant] got to talk more than anyone. . . . Quick—it was late in the day. . . . Kind of neutral, distant. . . . [Felt] kind of like, where's the justice?

This woman felt intimidated and nervous standing before the judge. She described the judge's demeanor toward the defendant as "nice" and "patient" and said the judge listened to him. She sought a restraining order because she was being hit and kicked by the defendant while she was pregnant. While the judge did grant the restraining order for a year, she felt ignored during the hearing. "Even though he gave me the order, I didn't feel comfortable with it," she stated.

Most of the condescending and harsh experiences that women had with judges occurred when the defendants were present:

It seemed like she didn't want to listen. It was very frustrating at the second hearing. . . . Her behavior was—I would say she was in a bad mood. She wasn't all that pleasant, not nearly as nice as she was the first time. . . . Didn't talk to me—said she would sign off on it and said to go to probate court for a divorce. . . . I was afraid that she might not have extended the restraining order. . . . He was there with a lawyer and the way she was talking, "This is a family problem, and you guys go straighten it out yourselves in probate court." . . . Her tone of voice [toward the defendant] was soft. . . . She acted normal, no harsh feeling or nothing. It felt like she was saying, "It's your wife, you can abuse her." That's how I felt.

The judge was terrible and not concerned. . . . I could have dropped dead in front of her. She was more concerned about visitation on Christmas. . . . She said it was a "lovers' quarrel." I said, "We're not lovers; there's a history here." She said, "It's just a lovers' spat." . . . I thought things were in my favor. I felt like I had a case and I had done the right thing. . . . I felt so angry like I wanted to scream, and I did. . . . Like I was the criminal and the table was turned. . . . Very nice toward him. . . . [The judge] advised him about visitation. She offered her own opinion about it. She should not have done that. . . . I felt like she was in the wrong and she had no right. She didn't believe me. . . . If she was so concerned about me, why was she so nice to him?

In each of these interactions, good-natured demeanor toward the defendant was accompanied by condescending or harsh demeanor toward the woman seeking protection. Disorder in the courts is illustrated sharply in the last account of a denial of a restraining order at the second or 10-day hearing. The defendant had a history of criminal complaints of violence, including violence against this woman. At the first hearing, a different judge had asked this woman why the defendant had not been arrested, given his threats to kill her and his previous conviction for violence against her. Yet the judge at the second hearing denied the restraining order, dismissing the threats as a "lovers' quarrel" and pressing the woman to arrange visitation by the defendant with the children—which goes beyond a judge's legal authority, as established in a 1986 Supreme Court decision.[32] This woman was so enraged that she began yelling at the judge and was asked to leave the courtroom.

The gender of the two judges above requires some discussion. Both judges are women; this in itself indicates nothing about a pattern of demeanor. Both from the interviews with women and my own observations reported in Chapter 5, women and men are included among both the judges categorized as most supportive and those seen as least supportive. Reflecting their numbers on the bench, only four of the 19 judges described in the telephone interviews were women, making comparisons meaningless. Only one of the judges discussed was African American (a man), raising a similar limitation. Nevertheless, if negotiations with judges are colored by the expectations brought to them, it may be that at times women who seek orders anticipate greater support from women judges and feel a particularly sharp betrayal when met with indifference or harshness. As one woman put it, "Some women judges don't have any sympathy. Sometimes they are worse than the males."

To restore a sense of justice to women who have been brutalized and terrorized, more than a ceremonial encounter is necessary. Two women used very similar words to highlight what they viewed as the limits of judicial authority:

It sounded good in the courthouse. But when you leave, that's it. Like I said, I'd have to hide if anything happens. . . . They make you feel like you're hearing something good, but when you leave, it's not so good. . . . [The judge] really got on him, but when I left, I had a feeling it didn't matter.

At first, it sounded good, but then I realized it's just a piece of paper and men do break the orders, though he hasn't so far.

Since the power of judges depends on police enforcement of their orders, it is important to discuss women's experiences with the restraining order after they left the courthouse.

Police Responsiveness and Judicial Credibility

In the interviews women spoke of a dual promise about restraining orders made by judges and the police. Even before restraining orders had been sought, police had been called to the homes of 88 percent of the women interviewed because of the violence and abuse. The police often recommended that women seek a restraining order. Of the 40 women, 43 percent said they either learned about the restraining order from the police or were encouraged by the police to obtain one. In their hearings before the judge, women were routinely told that if there is any further abuse by the defendant, they should call the police. The credibility of the judge's authority therefore depends on the responsiveness of the police. Most women did call the police to enforce the order. Of the 34 women who obtained extended orders—that is, orders in effect for more than the initial 10-day period—59 percent called the police after obtaining orders. There is, then, a dual promise made to women in their negotiations with the state over their rights to be free from violence: the police tell women they must obtain an order to be protected, and after receiving it, judges tell women that the police will enforce the orders.

Women's experiences with the police ranged from very supportive to demeaning and even threatening encounters. Women in Dorchester reported as many negative interactions with the police as positive ones. In comparison, the women in Quincy had mostly positive experiences. When describing satisfactory interactions with the police, emotional support was the most common characteristic mentioned:

Very nice, supportive. The time I went to the shelter, they were over, giving emotional support. . . . The officers were great.

They were sympathetic and came when I called. . . . They listened to me.

Very satisfied. Very helpful . . . concerned for my safety.

Quick responses to their calls for help were also mentioned by a number of women who were satisfied with the police, along with providing resources such as assistance getting to the hospital or the court, information on shelters, emergency phone numbers, and help getting belongings out of the house. Recognition and safety again appeared as common expectations.

The most common reason for dissatisfaction with the police was their unwillingness to arrest. This unwillingness erodes the trust that the system represented by the judge and the police really means to stop the violence:

The court system isn't doing anything to him. When he was arrested, he had four warrants out on him because of complaints for violating the restraining order, and he didn't serve any time. They let him out in his grandmother's care and that was it. . . . And to get him arrested, I went down to the police station . . . every day for one week. I was constantly after them, and he was in jail for one night.

This is when I got really dissatisfied with the police. The judge even gave them permission to arrest him. But they didn't. . . . One time he called the house harassing, and the police were at my house and they talked to him. But they never picked him up.

I called about two months ago, recently, and told the police that he violated the restraining order. They took my name and said they would put a warrant out for his arrest, and he's still on the streets! . . . He keeps calling and threatening to get me. But the police said that unless he shows up at the house, they can't do anything. It's only phone calls. Do I have to wait until I'm dead before they do anything?

Along with frustration from this type of response from the police, victim blaming and minimization were also named as problems in the interviews:

The police saw it was a domestic thing, and he was a good talker. He said I was crying wolf. The police said that if it was so bad, leave him.

I'm not educated, and he is and uses fancy words. . . . He looked better than me, and police believed him and said if it was so bad [I] should get a restraining order.

I called 911, and the policeman said, "We're trying to look for the vehicle, but if we can't find it, we can't do anything." He was in a car. He said we have worse cases. What a waste of time.

One woman said the police threatened that if she didn't stand up to their story in court, they would not come if she called again to report violence.

Police recommendations to obtain restraining orders and their enforcement of those orders reveal two different aspects of the state's willingness to stop men's domination of women. On the one hand, police recommend the restraining order as a way of securing greater protection. When a restraining order is in effect, regardless of whether it is a temporary or extended order, police are mandated to arrest a defendant who violates the restraint from abuse, vacate, or no-contact provisions of the order. The order can therefore extend the powers of the police, since some of these actions by the defendant, such as showing up at the woman's residence, become crimes only because they are prohibited by the order. Most women who obtained orders in Quincy felt the police were applying the law in this fashion. But on the other hand, some women said the police told them that unless they get a restraining order, they couldn't do anything. This was more characteristic of the experience of women who obtained orders in Dorchester. Such a statement made by a police officer would be false; state law states that in cases where no restraining order is in effect, "arrest shall be the preferred response" where probable cause exists that a felony, misdemeanor, or assault and battery has been committed.[33] In these cases, the restraining order appears to serve as a new layer of bureaucracy, a credential proving that this is a bona fide "battered woman"; without an order she is not entitled to police action. Instead of extending police powers, police officers who make such a lawless interpretation are recommending the restraining order to "cool out" women who seek help. They are urging women to go to court to justify their own inaction.

The Authoritativeness of Restraining Orders

How much authority did the restraining orders have with violent men? In terms of the 34 women who were issued orders, 62 percent reported that the defendants violated the terms of the orders. This is consistent with research conducted on the statewide database of Massachusetts restraining orders.[34] Most of the violations, however, did not involve physical violence. In three cases, women gave accounts of physical assaults; in one of these cases, the defendant was arrested, tried, convicted, and sentenced to one year in jail. The other violations involved threats over the telephone, contact prohibited by the order, and other forms of psychological abuse.

Given this evidence of violations, it may seem surprising that 86 percent of the 34 women who obtained an extended order nonetheless said that the order either stopped or reduced the abuse. They offered a range of observations about the impact of the orders, but there is a pattern of the orders having a substantive effect:

Stopped physical [abuse]. We're back together, and he won't raise his hand to me. He hasn't. He knows it's serious.

Initially it made a difference, and we were able to work some things out. But then he went back to his old ways, and I'm tired of it. You can only give so many chances. I'm not sure he wants to change. . . . It got better for awhile.

I'm not going through the same mental anguish that I used to.

Physical abuse lessened, stopped, but mental abuse worse now than ever.

Overall it did [stop the abuse], right at the beginning. When I had a restraining order from probate court, he called and harassed, but after I got a restraining order at Quincy, he hasn't called, hasn't come around.

It stopped any further abuse.

He's afraid to get arrested, and I know a lot of men don't listen to it, but he does, and I'm lucky for that.

I think it helped because it made him afraid that he could get arrested.

To pursue this matter further, women were asked whether they made the right decision in seeking a restraining order. Even with their mixed experience with the police, and the pattern of violations, 88 percent of the women interviewed said yes. This includes two women who had decided not to appear at the second hearing and therefore didn't obtain extended orders. This also includes one woman who was denied an order; she said, "I would do it again and pray that I wouldn't get the same judge."

The most common reason that women believed the restraining order was a good idea is because, as one woman put it, "it shows him that the law's on my side." For a number of women, the restraining order process seems to have strengthened their sense that the violence was unjust and that the state was obligated to intervene:

Now I know he can't do anything and he can't come close to me or the children. So far he's not violated it, and I know if he does, all I need to do is report him.

He knew he could go to jail for it because I had the restraining order. That was the main reason I got it, to show him that this was no game. . . . If I felt afraid, I would get another one. I would go in a minute.

Some women emphasized the feeling of safety that the restraining order provided:

I wouldn't be sleeping at night if I didn't have it.

He's not coming and bothering me, and I feel safe. Otherwise I don't have anything to be safe. . . . I can't keep calling the police every day.

Even a woman who doubted that the order protected her nonetheless wanted to make courts and the police responsible for her safety:

Mainly I figured if I got the restraining order and he was out of the house, then he should know I meant business. And I assumed that he would get the message. It did get him mad, and I still fear him. But if he kills me, my sons will sue everyone. I know it helps because the police take things more seriously now.

Even with her doubt about the willingness of the state to protect her, this woman felt she made the right decision. The violence was now a problem shared with the state.

In their study of restraining orders in New Haven, Connecticut, Molly Chaudhuri and Kathleen Daly found that for many women the process was "its own reward."[35] Many of the women in Dorchester and Quincy also stressed that by taking action, they had forced a shift in the balance of power:

I would do it again if I had to because I proved something to him and proved something to myself. I could put my feelings aside after 14 years of being with him. Even if I love him, I know it's not right how he acts.

It has helped me a lot. Because my personal feeling is that if any woman who has been taken advantage of, been physically hurt, doesn't deserve it, she shouldn't put up with that kind of behavior. . . . It has supported me, and it has given us a chance to attempt to work things out with each other. We're still separated, but we can talk civilly and spend time together with our son.

If I hadn't, he would have continued to think I was helpless and not very resourceful. I know I tend to depend on him and not put my foot down and stick up for myself. I think it made him believe he had power over me. So it got him to back off and realize that he couldn't treat me like he did.

Just doing it, it puts you in touch with services you might not know about. You have to do something like this. . . . It makes you feel less powerless, like there's something to do. . . . Also, the restraining order makes you not have to wait to have something happen. He just needs to be there, and the police will come.

By creating a legal crisis, these women challenged the coercive control that men were exercising over them. Most women felt supported by the process and left the court with new resources that placed them in a better negotiating position with their partners or former partners. Further follow-up with these women would be necessary to judge the long-term consequences of asserting their rights; it is already clear that most of these men had already violated at least the no-contact provisions of the restraining orders. Some men also intensified the psychological coercion as their abilities to use physical force were circumscribed. Hochschild refers to this as the principle of "balancing": often when men lose power in one way, they compensate for this loss by exerting power in another way.[36] Even with these limitations in mind, however, most of the women who sought orders in both Dorchester and Quincy felt that they had benefited from the process. Asked whether they would recommend a restraining order to a woman friend if she were being abused, 90 percent said yes.

Summary

The psychic aftershocks of violence affect battered women's encounters with judges. Women reported that the effects of the violence were present in these hearings in the form of terror, fear, pain, nervousness, guilt, numbness, and rage. The aftermath of violence unnerves women in the courtroom, just as it disorders their lives everywhere else. This increases the asymmetry of the exchange between judges and women seeking orders, intensifying the consequences of the emotional labor that judges perform.

Along with the "internal injuries" that battering causes, the courtroom staging itself produces feelings of intimidation and shame in women claiming their rights, even before the judge speaks. Psychologically and physically battered by their partners or former partners and overwhelmed by the imposing courtroom surroundings, many women feared they would not be believed.

Three dimensions of fear were reported by women as particularly salient in affecting their interactions with judges: fear of retaliation by the defendants, the intimidation produced by courtroom rituals of deference, and fear that they would not be believed. Judges who were described as supportive presented a demeanor that addressed these fears. Supportive or "good-natured" judges responded to women's desire for recognition, safety, and justice. Bureaucratic, condescending, and harsh presentations of authority were perceived as indifferent or even hostile to women's needs.

According to the women interviewed, most men violated the restraining orders. Nonetheless, most of the women who obtained extended orders said that they were helpful in reducing, if not stopping, the abuse. Overall, the great majority of women felt they had made the right decision in going to court for restraining orders. The leverage they were able to gain through the threat of criminal sanctions was seen as beneficial; for many women, standing up for their rights also offered its own rewards.

For women seeking a confrontation between the coercive authority of violent men and the legal authority of judges, the emotional experience of judicial demeanor was important to their sense of whether justice was done.

When I began reporting two years ago on allegations of widespread harassment of battered women by judges in the lower courts, I was mystified to find that a unique set of rules governs the public's relationship with men and women whom I had been taught were public servants. These rules, I soon learned, were uniform and largely unspoken. They are enforced by a culture of deference that, I would argue, makes it all but impossible to hold a judge in the state accountable for the way he treats people in his courtroom. Correction: make that our courtroom. History, literature, even architecture conspire to enthrone the judge above those he is empowered to serve. . . . Institutional indifference to battered women can only contribute to the frightening statistics surrounding domestic violence.

EILEEN MCNAMARA[1]

8

Disorder in the Courts: Battering and Judicial Responses

In 1986 Eileen McNamara's news reporting in the *Boston Globe* made the "judicial harassment of battered women" a public issue in Massachusetts. As she describes it above, the scandal was not only that judges were routinely mistreating women who sought restraining orders. Among the findings of her investigation were that many judges knew of this misconduct and yet remained silent about it until the public spotlight began to glare. While this public attention forced changes in the judiciary, there is still disorder in the courts concerning battering.

To begin with, *disorder* describes the social impact of battering: batterers wreak havoc in women's lives. "In more ways than one, I'll make your life miserable," one man said to his partner. "He's shown up at my job, my apartment, my school and continues to harass me," a woman reported. Since leaving her abusive partner she has taken self-defense courses; carries mace; has told her workplace, school, and child's daycare provider about the abuse; and has her friends on alert.

Feminist social action brought this "disorder" into the courts, where judges now share—secondhand—some of these dilemmas. Like abused women, some judges now lose sleep worrying whether their action or inaction will inspire greater violence from an abusive man. One reason that advocates have been welcomed into the courts is that judges hope that advocates will bear this emotional labor for them.

Recognizing the injustice of battering "disorders" the courts in still more ways. Moving the judges away from their historic collusion with batterers creates disequilibrium in a patriarchal state. Resistance and backlash are a predictable result. Tension within the ranks of the judiciary has arisen as some have accepted responsibility for changing the courts, while others deride attention to battering as a "fad," as one judge put it during a restraining order hearing. It is no wonder that judicial reforms first began after women had achieved a critical mass in legal practice, in state legislatures, and on the bench.

These conflicting messages from the court have created a crisis of judicial authority around battering. Public skepticism about the worth of restraining orders is central to this crisis.

"Just a Piece of Paper": Restraining Orders and the Crisis of Judicial Authority

Over the course of this research, I encountered no single phrase regarding restraining orders more repeatedly than "it's just a piece of paper," a phrase that has disturbing implications. To interpret the significance of this expression, it must be related to the different perspectives of the people who use it.

This phrase is heard from violent men. As one woman reported, "He said, 'A restraining order to me is a piece of paper, and I'll rip it up.'" He is saying the order will not protect her, that it will not prevent him from harming her, and that he feared no sanctions for violating it. Such a remark by a batterer is a threat.

This same phrase is also heard from judges. Sometimes what a judge means is that without the time and interpreters and advocates and community referrals needed to make a difference, the restraining order "process" really consists of a token display of authority. One judge criticized the legislature for what he saw as its posturing on the issue of battering while offering no new funds to support the overburdened and understaffed court system. Without budgetary commitments from the state and without cooperation from the prosecutor's office and the local police, the institutional commitment behind the order is indeed illusory in many communities. Given the minimal penalties for violating restraining orders, one researcher stated that as it is currently implemented, the restraining order could be considered a case of "consumer fraud."[2]

Several women interviewed for this study said that the order is merely a "piece of paper," meaning that some batterers are incorrigible and will stop at nothing. As has been shown, fear of an abusive man's disregard for the law is well grounded: research on restraining order defendants in Massachusetts reveals that at least 75 percent have previous histories of criminal complaints, violent crime being the most common offense.[3]

Finally, for the public at large, the remark "it's only a piece of paper" often means that the legal system offers only "empty rights"[4] to women. The disordered response by the courts and police has created a sense of resignation about stopping violence. A fatalistic acknowledgment has grown that violent domination by men is not being seriously challenged by the system.

Many other meanings are given to this phrase. But the interpretations sketched above indicate a crisis of judicial authority. If abusive men violate restraining orders with impunity, if judges process them with only token gestures of authority, if women experience them as an empty promise of their civil rights, and if a community becomes resigned to a *de facto* judicial tolerance of battering, then the credibility of the courts is debased.

This is part of a broader problem that is confronting judges in major urban areas, a crisis of fear and distrust of both police and the courts. One Dorchester judge related a nightmare to a newspaper reporter that crystallizes this crisis of legitimacy:

Lately it occurs to Judge James W. Dolan . . . that he may be overseeing the collapse of the judicial system in the inner city. After 20 years of dealing first with simple robberies and burglaries, then with bloody spasms of violence, and finally mixing in vexing domestic abuse cases, Dolan has a recurring nightmare. In it, he arrives at his old-fashioned courtroom ready to hear the day's cases and no one is there: no defendants, no complainants, no witnesses, no police. "People will have come to the conclusion that the process is irrelevant," Dolan said.[5]

Why is the court process becoming increasingly irrelevant, according to this judge? What explains the failure of witnesses or victims to testify in the "inner city," which really means poor African American and Hispanic neighborhoods?

"You find victims of robbery charges, assault charges, owners of stolen cars—they won't often appear," Dolan said. . . . The primary reason for all the victims and witnesses disappearing, Dolan said, is fear—a sense the criminal justice system cannot protect people from gangs or stalkers. The second reason, he said, is more frightening. . . . They believe the system is their enemy.[6]

The crisis feared by this judge is driven, in part, by recent changes in patterns of urban poverty: the disappearance of jobs, the racialized concentration of poverty, cutbacks in social services, and the resulting alienation felt by citizens in poor communities. But fear and distrust are also generated by the criminal justice system itself, by racially discriminatory police practices and the misguided sentencing policies of the "war on drugs."

Yet despite all of this, it is the argument of this study that even with the inconsistent responses to battering by judges in Massachusetts, in two of the busiest courts the restraining order is more than merely a piece of paper. Of those women who sought restraining orders in Dorchester, which contains some of the poorest neighborhoods in Boston, 80 percent said they had made the right decision. Ninety-five percent of the women in Quincy said they had made the right decision in going to court. Most women in both courts said the order either stopped or reduced the abuse. For some, going to court was a way to break out of the isolation imposed on them and obtain resources to shift the balance of power in their struggles with violent men. Most of these women said they made the right decision and would even recommend the court process to a friend suffering abuse, which indicates that the process had relevance in their lives.

Against the background of this ongoing crisis in the courts, this chapter summarizes how judges affect women seeking restraining orders. The discussion begins with ways that judges, wittingly and unwittingly, reinforce the power of batterers and then moves to ways that judges empower battered women, drawing together insights from court documents, courtroom observations, interviews with judges, and interviews with abused women.

Judges and the Dynamic of Battering

What judges do in restraining order hearings becomes part of the ongoing dynamic of battering. These courtroom encounters with abused women take place in the shadow of men's violence. It is important to relate judicial responses to what women are experiencing from their batterers. A useful way to do this is to begin with a theoretical map of battering and insert the judiciary into it.

Figure 8.1 is the "power and control wheel" designed by the Domestic Abuse Intervention Project (DAIP) in Duluth, Minnesota. This diagram was developed in a series of educational sessions held with abused women by the Duluth battered women's shelter in 1984.[7] The shelter wanted a description of the behavior of batterers drawn from the perspectives of women who live with this abuse. In this diagram power and control, rather than physical injury, is made the central element of battering. Violence, which includes sexual violence, serves to hold together these other means of controlling an intimate partner. These various tactics of control, which occur in battering relationships more often than physical assaults, draw their power from violence and the threat of violence. The power and control wheel is used in the batterers' counseling curriculum developed by the DAIP. In their community discussions with battered women, members of the DAIP pose the question, "How do community institutions reinforce batterers' use of abusive tactics?"[8]

Following the outline of the Duluth model, I have shown in

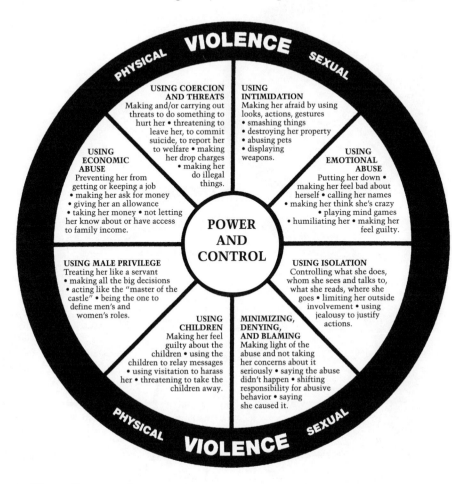

Figure 8.1

Power and Control Wheel

Source: Reprinted with permission from Minnesota Program Development, Inc., Domestic Abuse Intervention Project, 206 West 4th Street, MN 55806.

Figure 8.2 how judges, intentionally and unintentionally, may be reinforcing the power of men who batter, and thus furthering women's entrapment. The main elements of the Duluth wheel appear in the smaller wheel. The "judicial entrapment" wheel outlines the encounters between judges and abused women that take place in the aftermath of men's violence. The indifference and mistreatment women experience in the courts mirror, in a number of ways, the abuse women suffer from their partners.

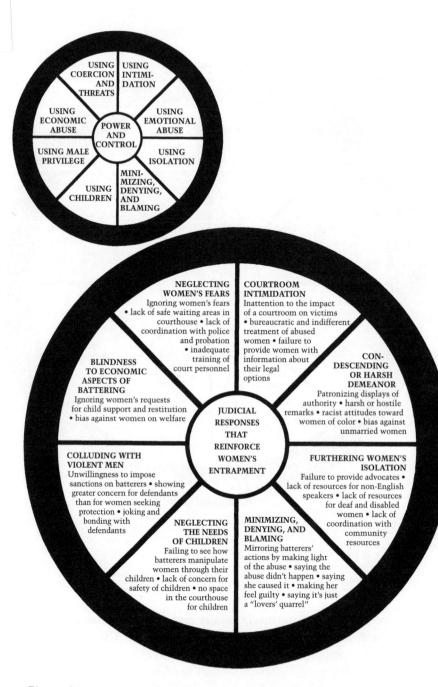

Figure 8.2

Judicial Responses That Reinforce Women's Entrapment

The power and control wheel, for example, identifies "using emotional abuse" as a common tactic of men who batter. Condescending and harsh judicial demeanor is a form of emotional abuse that parallels this tactic of batterers. This connection was made by one woman who feared the same emotional treatment in court that she experienced at home. "Going in I felt like I wasn't going to be believed because of what I was going through at home—the degradation and put-downs. . . . I wasn't sure if they would believe me," she said.

Awareness of isolation as a key tactic that men use to undermine women's resistance highlights the ways that courts may unwittingly further this isolation by failing to connect women with available resources, many of which are free. I visited a court where a volunteer advocate sat in an office, waiting for judges to send battered women to talk with her, only to discover that some judges fail to inform women about the office. The other elements in the judicial entrapment wheel similarly parallel the tactics of men who batter. If minimizing, denying, and blaming are common tactics of abusive partners, how must it feel to a battered woman to hear a judge say the violence was really only a "lovers' quarrel"?

According to the interviews with abused women, however, most judges in the Dorchester and Quincy District Courts presented a supportive demeanor toward them. In Figure 8.3 I have summarized these helpful judicial responses and placed them in a "judicial empowerment" wheel. Judicial demeanor is an important part of this diagram, but a range of responses can indicate support, including the creation of safe spaces in the courthouse for abused women and children to wait for hearings. Judicial attention to the economic dimensions of battering are included in this diagram, as are relationships with community programs that offer assistance to abused women. Connections to resources for batterers are also important: most men in batterers' counseling in Massachusetts are court mandated, meaning that judges, more than anyone else, determine whether men enter treatment.

These diagrams illustrate the worst and the best of women's encounters with the courts. But this necessarily simplifies these interactions and their impact on women's lives. Even when a judge does the "right thing," what a court offers may be meaning-

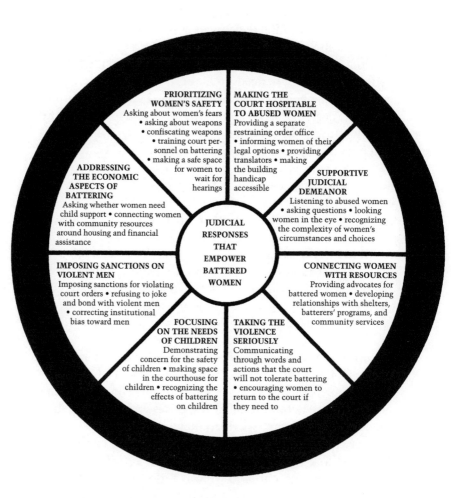

Figure 8.3

Judicial Responses That Empower Battered Women

less to a woman. The dilemmas created by violence in a woman's life cannot be revealed in a five-minute hearing. For this reason the role of the advocate in the courtroom is important.

Every currently existing or potential remedy for battering can have multiple outcomes for victims. The formal remedies offered by the criminal justice system are rather crude—restraining orders, arrest of batterers, jail or prison time, batterers' counseling. They can backfire or lead to unanticipated results. In their important new model of "woman-defined" advocacy, Jill Davies, Eleanor Lyon, and Diane Monti-Catania urge that the complexity of battered women's choices must be acknowledged:

As the search for solutions to end domestic violence continues, battered women must cope with each experiment. . . . For individual battered women, each option presented and each service provided has a consequence. Arrest could stop the attack, but end privacy or result in the woman's arrest as well. Custody orders may lead to some stability for the children, but could also result in visitation that places them in danger. Leaving might reduce the violence, but could lead to homelessness and loneliness. The pursuit of any option could bring on an escalation of the violence. Advocates are the key to helping women assess the consequences of available options and choose among them.[9]

Although women's encounters with judges were the focus of this investigation, a number of the women studied also had contact with advocates, through either a district attorney's office, a shelter, or volunteer advocates provided by law schools or colleges. At Quincy, court staff working in a separate restraining order office also functioned as advocates. Roughly a third of the women in Dorchester had contact with advocates; twice as many women in Quincy saw advocates. Fully 70 percent of the women in Quincy mentioned advocates or the staff in the restraining order office as the most helpful aspects of the restraining order process. These are the kinds of things women said about these experiences:

Emotionally, I was pretty much of a wreck. I don't think I could have done it without the help of the advocates.

The women in the restraining order office, the advocates, were very good. They answered my questions and were very helpful and gave me a lot of info and numbers of shelters and groups for women. . . . They had someone in the courtroom who sat beside me the whole time.

The first time I went [13 years ago], there was a woman advocate there who was offering information about alcoholism. It was through that referral I got involved in treatment. It really changed my life. I got sober and then into recovery.

Advocates humanized the bureaucracy, providing compassion and support. They gave information about criminal justice processes and community resources. They helped women develop strategies to keep themselves and their children safe.

There are different perspectives from which to define what advocacy is. According to Davies and her colleagues, *woman-defined advocacy* "builds a partnership between advocates and battered women, and ultimately has each battered woman defining the advocacy and help she needs."[10] This kind of support acknowledges how truly difficult the choices can be concerning safety and survival. They distinguish this from another kind of advocacy: "When advocates focus exclusively on providing a service, whether or not it fits into a battered woman's risk analysis or safety plans, they are providing what we call *service-defined advocacy*."[11] Insisting that a woman take out a restraining order, regardless of her circumstances or her own judgment, is an example of service-defined advocacy.

Judges largely determine whether advocates are available for battered women in the courts and what kinds of roles advocates can play in the courtroom. Every year more courthouses across the state are being staffed by advocates to support women seeking orders and inform them of community resources. Shelters have provided advocacy for years, but increasingly district attorneys are hiring domestic violence advocates. Law students and undergraduates are providing volunteer labor; there seems to be no shortage of women students willing to assist abused women in the courts. As a result, more women are taking out orders, and more women who appear for initial hearings return to obtain extended orders.[12] Judges who are attempting to restore credibility to the bench are ironically depending on feminist organizing to humanize the bureaucracy.

Battering as Social Entrapment

Interactions between abused women and judges must be seen in a broader social context. Battering, I have argued, is most practically understood as social entrapment. Men who batter are attempting to control women and the social world around them, often including their children and their ties to extended family, friends, and the larger community.

I have outlined the elements of social entrapment in Figure 8.4. The diagram begins with the strategies of men who batter—that is, what batterers intend to accomplish with their violence. Abusive men target women's autonomy. According to restraining order affidavits in two courts, preventing or retaliating against women leaving is the most common motive for battering. Violence in defense of men's authority over their children is also common, as is retribution for calls to the police or court actions.

Women's losses further reveal the social character of battering. Along with immediate physical and psychic consequences, battered mothers fear losing their children. Women routinely lose friendships and relationships to other family members. They lose their jobs and their housing. Even ties to their communities are damaged by fear of violence and fear of social stigma. Through threats and manipulation of economic resources, batterers create bitter dilemmas for women, especially when small children are involved.

In the social entrapment diagram, women's ability "to resist or escape" violence, to use Linda Gordon's phrase, is determined by a host of factors.[13] These can be summarized under community networks, institutional responses, and structural inequalities. Informal networks such as ties to family, friends, and neighbors play an important role in women's ability to resist violence, as these are often the first places abused women turn. The responses women receive from family and kin networks may be supportive, as seemed true for most women in this study, or they may be unhelpful or blaming. Perhaps because of the support that family and friends can provide to women, men who batter are frequently suspicious and threatening about these relationships. Recall that 20 percent of the women interviewed about their court experiences talked to the judge before discussing the violence with either their families or friends. The effect of this social disconnection may be that women's encounters with judges (or police or doctors) have greater emotional significance in the light of this isolation.

As with community networks, the responses of major institutions may be supportive, unhelpful, or punitive, as the previous diagrams of judicial authority illustrate. Along with criminal justice institutions, social services, medicine, mental health, and re-

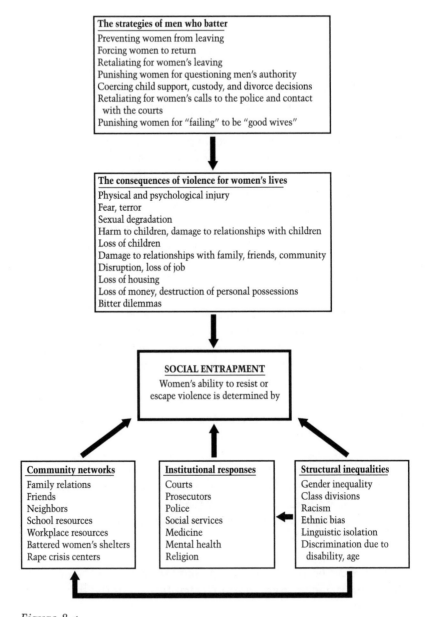

Figure 8.4

Battering as Social Entrapment

ligion form the web of institutional responses to battering. The Domestic Violence Project in Kenosha, Wisconsin, has outlined a "Medical Power and Control Wheel" and an "Advocacy Wheel" that address ways that doctors and nurses can use their authority to either increase women's entrapment or empower women.[14]

In the social entrapment diagram, structural inequalities create women's entrapment in a number of ways. Institutionalized male supremacy historically blocked the courts from treating intimate violence seriously. Attention to violence against women is one measure of the current challenges to gender inequality. But gender names only one dimension of inequality. Poverty and racism further construct women's vulnerability to violence. The elements that make a woman feel "like a prisoner" in her own home will be different depending on their position within these intersecting inequalities.

Michelle Fine and Lois Weis suggest there are class and racial dimensions to the shame women fear and thus the secrets women keep about battering. In their study, white working-class women reported greater taboos around speaking about violence in their communities than did African American working-class women.[15] Ethnic bias, linguistic isolation, and discrimination based on disability and age also affect women's efforts at resistance. Together, these structural inequalities corrupt the responses of major institutions to abused women, as gender bias and race and ethnic bias studies of the courts have indicated.

These structural inequalities further determine women's options through their effects on community networks. Sexism often divides families into those who blame abused women and those who support them. Poverty subverts the ability of community networks to respond: one Boston study found that 27 percent of African American and Hispanic families earning less than $10,000 had no telephones, and 10 percent of white families making less than $10,000 were without phones.[16] Fear of the stigma of poverty may also prevent some women from seeking battered women's shelters. Patterns of racial segregation in finance, insurance, and real estate practices concentrate poverty in African American and Hispanic communities. Linguistic inaccessibility further affects access to resources.

Seeing battering as social entrapment highlights the interaction of these elements with women's struggles with violent men. At the same time, this offers a map of what must be done to reverse this fearful isolation. In Quincy, the district attorney's office routinely calls women who take out restraining orders to inform them of support groups and ask whether they need other resources. The court also sends women letters when their restraining orders are about to expire, telling them a hearing time has been set should they need to extend the order.

Katherine Triantafillou, who helped write the law on restraining orders in Massachusetts, has developed a new citywide initiative around battering. Triantafillou, who is a member of the Cambridge City Council, calls her initiative "Cambridge as a Domestic Violence-Free Zone." Around the city there are signs that say, "Cambridge Is a Domestic Violence-Free Zone: Abuse Prevention Laws Will Be Enforced." Her idea is to arrange meetings where all Cambridge institutions and agencies involved in domestic violence can coordinate training, public education, and prevention strategies. This would include shelters, batterers' counseling, criminal justice, hospitals, and mental health and social service agencies. But it also includes city officials and businesses, which have a role to play in educating and providing assistance to their employees.

Visions of justice for battered women continue to evolve in the work of feminists around the world today. In a time of unprecedented changes in rates of imprisonment, there is a need for feminist revisioning of all the institutions of criminal justice. This is especially urgent because feminist-led legal reforms are currently colliding with the racial injustice of the "war on drugs." This "war" is damaging poor communities of color in ways that are antithetical to stopping violence against women.[17] And with numerous reports of sexual violence in U.S. prisons, involving the rape of both female prisoners[18] and male prisoners,[19] there is a need for greater feminist insights here as well. Such brutality serves no one's futures, least of all those who wish to live in peaceful communities. A vision of social justice cannot stop at the doors of our prisons and jails. Is it possible to link activism around battering with efforts to hold the state accountable for such institutional violence? These are thoughts that emerge from drawing issues of poverty and racism "from the margins to the center" of an analysis of violence against women.[20]

Possibilities

Feminist efforts are helping to make the judicial process relevant to more and more women. As a result of feminist legal scholarship, feminist research on battering, and trainings by activists from the battered women's movement, judges in Massachusetts are changing what they are doing with their authority. A number of judges are now taking responsibility for reforming court responses to abused women. Through their work on the Gender Bias Study,[21] development of resources within their own courts, and participation in community roundtables with shelters and other service providers, judges are helping to bring about institutional change.

But despite this activity, the structure of accountability within the Massachusetts courts continues unchanged. The rules governing the Judicial Conduct Commission remain the same. This is the commission that deliberated for over two years before reprimanding one judge for expressing "hostility" toward Pamela Nigro Dunn during a hearing five months before she was murdered by her husband.[22] This is the same commission that waited for over four years before censuring another judge for similar misconduct.[23] The Massachusetts judiciary has resisted structural reforms aimed at ensuring greater accountability.

At the beginning of this chapter, Eileen McNamara reminds us that despite its regal symbols of authority, the courtroom belongs to the public. Several researchers have suggested that community oversight and the democratization of state institutions will be essential if there is to be real change in legal practices toward woman battering.[24] In Massachusetts, there is already evidence of this. What could be called *internal* and *external* strategies of community involvement in the courts can be seen. By *internal* involvement I mean the cooperative work being done by outside organizations within the courthouse itself. In the Quincy District Court, a woman can participate in support groups run with the assistance of a local shelter, obtain referrals for housing or welfare, or take part in an alcohol treatment program. There is a batterers' counseling group connected with the court as well. One can easily imagine how such services could be provided elsewhere, along with other resources specifically addressing the needs of women in poor, multiracial, and multilingual communities who have been socially isolated by battering. By seeing the court as a place where the holes in the social fabric are most exposed and inviting in the community to help repair them, the nightmare of irrelevance can be averted. Across the state, other projects have been developed between the courts and law schools, bar associations, law firms, and women's organizations to further the goal of justice for abused women.

External strategies have also been pursued. Disturbed by the lack of judicial accountability for mistreatment of battered women, feminist activists in the Boston area organized a grassroots effort to monitor court proceedings involving woman battering. Not surprisingly, many judges have viewed such community action negatively, perhaps because it goes against traditional notions of deference owed to the judiciary. One judge voiced his frustration with restraining orders and with this public spotlight on judicial demeanor:

The problem is the law, as well as the advocates, the activists and the poorly informed and biased general media. . . . As a judge in the trenches, I am constantly aware of the fact that the aforementioned have their guns trained on me.[25]

Evidence presented in this study suggests that the answer to a public crisis of judicial authority, however, is more rather than less democracy. In light of the struggle it has taken to bring the state to bear witness to these crimes, it will be essential to keep the windows open on these encounters between judicial authority and the coercive authority that violent men are collectively holding over women's lives.

Appendix: Research Methods

The two courts investigated for this study were Dorchester District Court and Quincy District Court. The time period of the study was between 1992 and 1994. In the years since then, the presiding judges at both courts have changed, as has undoubtedly much else. It must therefore be noted that this study is framed by those years.

Dorchester District Court serves a largely African American and Latina and Latino population; the court in Quincy serves a largely Anglo-American population. These are two of the busiest lower criminal courts in Massachusetts: in 1992, over 2,000 restraining orders were filed in Dorchester; nearly 1,700 restraining orders were filed in Quincy.[1] This made Dorchester the second-highest court statewide in restraining order filings for 1992; Quincy was the sixth-highest court. Both of these courts have established restraining order offices that are separate from other civil and criminal court business; this is unusual for Massachusetts criminal courts. Both of these courts have become known for having judges who are progressive reformers on issues of women and the law and who are responsible for training other judges in the area of domestic violence law and procedures. Among advocates for battered women, attorneys, and judges, these two courts have been considered among the best district courts in Massachusetts in terms of the seriousness with which they treat woman battering. Quincy District Court has received national attention for its treatment of woman battering. It won the 1992 Ford Foundation Award for Innovations in State and

Local Government and was named a model program by the National Council of Juvenile and Family Court Judges.[2]

Since these are both very busy courts, any hopeful findings about judicial demeanor might indicate that if institutional change could be accomplished here, it could be achieved in any court. On the other hand, this also means that any findings of a detrimental impact of judicial demeanor may point to substantial institutional resistance to women's requests for protection.

Types of Data Gathered for the Study

Random Sampling of Domestic Violence Case Files

The first part of the study is based on a random sample of written records on restraining order cases in two criminal courts in Massachusetts. A random sample of 100 cases filed in 1992 was selected for a profile of women's help-seeking and the kinds of help women actually receive from each court. This sample consists of 50 cases drawn from Dorchester District Court and 50 cases from Quincy District Court. Every fifth nonimpounded case was selected that involved a woman seeking an order against a husband, former husband, boyfriend, or former boyfriend, beginning on a particular date. Court records on restraining orders are officially open to the public in recognition of "the public's general right to examine and evaluate the quality of justice done in its courts."[3]

Qualitative and quantitative data from the original complaint forms and the court orders were gathered to construct a profile of the relationships of the women to the defendants, the kinds of help women sought, and the kinds of help they actually received from the courts. Women's affidavits are also part of the court files. These affidavits are the written statements, signed under penalty of perjury, that women file as part of the restraining order request. In their own words, generally written out in longhand, women detail the range of violence and abuse that prompted them to seek court protection, along with a sense of the strategies they see behind men's violence.

Field Notes and Courtroom Observations

Over a nine-month period in 1992 and 1993, 18 different judges were observed in restraining order hearings, nine at Dorchester

District Court and nine at Quincy District Court (one of these judges was additionally observed at a third court). Of the 18 judges, four were white women, two were African American men, and 12 were white men. It is important to recall that these two courts have taken a high profile in Massachusetts for their responsiveness to battering: judges within each court have played leading roles in training other judges on issues of domestic violence. Field notes were taken concerning judicial demeanor toward women appearing as plaintiffs and toward men appearing as defendants. A total of 147 hearings before these 18 judges were observed over 31 days. Since most of these judges were "visiting" rather than "permanent" members of these courts, the unit of analysis for the courtroom observations is more appropriately judges, and differences between courts will not be emphasized.

The unpredictability of which judge will be hearing restraining orders and the different numbers of orders heard each day made for difficulty in gathering comparable numbers of hearings for each judge; thus more hearings were observed before some judges than others. Furthermore, there was difficulty in hearing everything that judges said in these hearings; all of the judges observed allowed women to stand near or immediately before the bench, even at arm's reach from the judge. There was even greater difficulty hearing what women said as plaintiffs in these hearings. Nonetheless, these observations provided rich descriptive data on the emotional presence of judges in courtroom interactions.

An observation form was used to gather data on particular aspects of demeanor. This form was designed by then-Boston-area attorneys Sarah Buel, Laurie Salame, and Carla DiMare for a court-monitoring project. I assisted in the final drafts of this form and adapted it for use in this study. I added Maureen Mileski's categories of judicial demeanor to the form,[4] along with a new category of "condescending" demeanor.

Interviews with Judges

Eight judges were interviewed in person by the author between March 1992 and February 1994. Two are from Dorchester District Court, two are from Quincy District Court, and four sit at a number of other courts in Massachusetts. Seven of these judges have taken public stands that indicate they view themselves as reformers on the issue of woman battering. Five other judges declined to participate in the interviews. Several of this latter group of judges presented a more traditional judicial stance toward abused women. In an institution where both journalists and researchers are eyed suspiciously, these judges may have sought to avoid any kind of spotlight.

The interviews, all but two of which were tape-recorded, centered around both symbolic and material dimensions of the restraining order process. Judges were asked about judicial demeanor: its importance, in their eyes, in restraining order hearings, the kind of demeanor they wanted to convey to women seeking protection and to men appearing as defendants, and the means by which they sought to convey this demeanor. Issues of child support, criminal penalties for restraining order violations, and judicial accountability were also raised.

Telephone Interviews with Women Who Have Sought Court Protection

Telephone interviews were conducted with 40 women who appeared in court seeking protective orders in 1992: 20 women appeared in Dorchester, and 20 appeared in Quincy. As they are contained in the court documents, phone numbers for the women are also public record. Women who sought court protection from husbands, former husbands, boyfriends, or former boyfriends were telephoned and asked to participate in a telephone interview. All women who filled out requests for orders starting on a particular date were called in each court until 20 interviews were completed, with the following exceptions: women were excluded whose records were impounded, who lacked or did not list telephone numbers, or whose case files were incomplete or missing. Women whose names appeared in the news because their alleged batterers were charged with violent crimes were also not pursued, as it was assumed they were likely being called repeatedly by news reporters, and I didn't want to add to this public attention. There were also a very few women whose numbers were not called because the violence involved, in my reading of the documents, extreme sexual torture. Undoubtedly, many requests for protection involve horrifying violence, and it is clear that the dimensions of the abuse are only barely sketched in these documents. Nonetheless, when evidence of Nazi-like torture was present, women were not called, out of fear that even discussing their court experiences would impose undue burdens on these women.

The guidelines on access to court documents prepared by the Massachusetts Trial Courts emphasize the need of researchers to be mindful of the dignity of individuals involved in domestic abuse cases and their desire for a level of privacy. This study does not include any names, descriptions, or other identifying information concerning the women seeking protection, the men named as defendants, or their families.

The Ethics of Research with Abused Women

Calling a woman about her request for a restraining order can place her at risk. Three types of potential harm exist. First, the conversation—even a brief conversation in which a woman declines to participate—can be upsetting. This is a very sensitive issue to discuss with anyone, let alone a stranger. Women may fear phone calls from strangers, particularly if they are no longer living with their abusive partners; abusive men often harass women by telephone and through myriad other means. Furthermore, shame and stigma continue to surround public perceptions of abused women. Negative images of women who have suffered violence, especially African American women, hold extraordinary power in our culture.[5] Being identified as a woman who sought protection from the courts can therefore be painful.

Second, if an interviewer telephones a woman but reaches an abusive man, there is the potential that the man may become suspicious and angry toward the woman. Isolation is a tactic commonly used by abusive men to control women. Any interviewer needs to be aware of this dynamic and needs strategies for dealing with a suspicious man on the telephone.

A third type of danger concerns women who have children and fear losing their children either to their estranged abusive partner or to child-protection authorities. Women who have been abused by their husbands or boyfriends often report threats that men make to take the children away. Care must therefore be taken to establish trust in the telephone interview. A woman who has children may also have concerns that questions about her alcohol consumption, for example, might elicit information that could be used against her if reported to child protection authorities. Attention to the kinds of questions that might raise these fears is therefore needed.

To protect against these risks, I had the interviews conducted by women who have experience as advocates on the issues of violence against women. Tina Nappi, M.S.W., has worked in a hospital setting with women who have been abused and has been trained in court advocacy with women. Beyond her ability to speak with women about violence and abuse, her background enabled her to provide information and assistance to the women being called. The remainder of the interviews were conducted by Bonnie Zimmer and Danielle London. Bonnie Zimmer, M.S.W., has extensive experience working with women around violence. Danielle London worked as victim and witness advocate with the district attorney's office of a court not involved in the study, specializing in assisting restraining order petitioners. Given the isolation that violence imposes on women, it was hoped that along with gathering information on women's experiences and interpretations, the telephone interviews would serve to connect women with the variety of resources available in the Boston area.

The goal of the introduction to the interview was to make sure that women understood why they were called and that they had every opportunity to refuse participation. Twenty-four women declined to participate after hearing this introduction.

The interviewers were also experienced at talking to suspicious men who answered the phone. After several calls to phone numbers where men answered, the interviewer removed the woman's name and number from the list.

Regarding women's fears that information from the interviews could be used against them, I had several women who had experience in working with women around violence review the interview guide. Any questions that could be interpreted as posing threats to women with regard to child custody or child-protection agencies were removed. There are questions about men's use of drugs and alcohol, for example, but not women's use; questions about men's criminal records but not women's criminal records.

The interview guide was also reviewed with advocates for abused women to ensure that none of the questions would be stigmatizing. In consultation with the interviewers, I decided that tape-recording the telephone interviews might prove intimidating and depersonalizing. The interviewers wrote out responses to the semistructured guide in longhand. Immediately after the interview, the interviewers also made notes about their own observations of the conversation and their feelings about it.

Before 40 interviews had been completed, the three interviewers made a total of over 1,000 telephone calls to over 450 different phone numbers. On average, women were called 10 months after their initial hearings for orders in late 1992. By this time, over 100 phone numbers had been disconnected, but three times as many numbers were disconnected in the area surrounding Dorchester District Court as in the Quincy area. As poverty is more prevalent among the women interviewed in Dorchester, this may indicate how poverty intensifies the chaos violence creates in women's lives.

The introduction to the interview mentions that the interviewer could provide women with local resources, if they desired. Many women requested information and were provided with phone numbers of victim and witness advocates in district attorney's offices, contact people for support groups, and phone numbers of shelters, drug and alcohol programs, Medicaid, and job training sites. Safety planning was also discussed with a number of women. Several women asked about volunteering to work in shelters themselves, and women who seemed interested were told about an upcoming community walk to raise money for shelters. In several cases, the interviewers determined that women's need for support was more important than talking about their court experiences.

The majority of women who were interviewed indicated that they found the conversation itself to be beneficial. Many were isolated and had few people to talk with about the violence and its aftermath. If a willingness to be called again in a future study could serve as a rough indicator of women's feelings about the interview process, it is noteworthy that of those women who were asked, all but one said yes.

Notes

Preface

1. Jeffrey Fagan, "The Criminalization of Domestic Violence: Promises and Limits," National Institute of Justice Research Report (Washington, D.C.: U.S. Department of Justice, January 1996).

2. Rebecca Emerson Dobash and Russell Dobash, "The Negotiation of Daily Life and the 'Provocation' of Violence: A Patriarchal Concept in Support of the Wife Beater," Paper presented at the Ninth World Congress of Sociology, Uppsala, Sweden, 1978.

Chapter 1

1. Judge Settle, in State v. Oliver, 70 N.C. 61, 62 (1874).

2. Settle, Preface to State v. Oliver, 70 N.C. at 60.

3. Joan Meier, "Battered Justice," *Washington Monthly*, May 1987, 38.

4. Meier, "Battered Justice," 38.

5. Eileen McNamara, "Judge Criticized After Woman's Death," *Boston Globe*, September 21, 1986, 1.

6. McNamara, "Judge Criticized After Woman's Death," 1.

7. McNamara, "Judge Criticized After Woman's Death," 1.

8. Eileen McNamara, "Judge Is Viewed as Erring on Abuse Law," *Boston Globe*, September 24, 1986, 13; McNamara, "Dunn to Face Murder Charges on Return to Mass. Today," *Boston Globe*, November 18, 1986, 38; McNamara, "Two Judges Criticized in Review by Zoll," *Boston Globe*, March 11, 1987, 1.

9. Paul Langner, "Dunn Given Life Term in Wife's Slaying," *Boston Globe*, May 20, 1987, 1.

10. WBUR Radio, August 2, 1993.

11. Barbara J. Hart, "State Codes on Domestic Violence: Analysis, Commentary, and Recommendations," *Juvenile and Family Court Journal* 43, no. 4 (1990): 3–80.

12. Massachusetts Supreme Judicial Court, "Annual Report of the State of the Massachusetts Court System," Fiscal Year 1996 (Boston: Supreme Judicial Court, 1997), 149–150.

13. Martha R. Mahoney, "Legal Issues of Battered Women: Redefining the Issue of Separation," *Michigan Law Review* 90, no. 1 (1991): 1–94.

14. Evan Stark and Anne H. Flitcraft, "Spouse Abuse," in *Violence in America: A Public Health Approach*, edited by Mark L. Rosenberg and Mary Ann Fenlet (New York: Oxford University Press, 1991), 123–157.

15. The study reports that 15.9 percent of the injuries to women were caused by either spouses or former spouses, and another 20.9 percent were caused by boyfriends or girlfriends. This adds up to 36.8 percent if these categories are collapsed into intimate partners or former partners. But the relationship between women and their assailants was unknown in 19.3 percent of the cases. Removing these cases gives a figure of 45.6 percent of women's injuries caused by intimate partners or former partners, of those cases where a relationship was reported. Michael R. Rand, "Violence-Related Injuries Treated in Hospital Emergency Departments," Special Report of the Bureau of Justice Statistics (Washington, D.C.: U.S. Department of Justice, August 1997).

16. Stark and Flitcraft, "Spouse Abuse," 142.

17. Diana E. H. Russell, *Rape in Marriage* (Bloomington: Indiana University Press, 1990), 90.

18. Judith Lewis Herman, *Trauma and Recovery* (New York: Basic Books, 1992), 51.

19. Susan Schechter, "Guidelines for Mental Health Practitioners in Domestic Violence Cases" (Washington, D.C.: National Coalition Against Domestic Violence, 1987).

20. Ellen Pence and Michael Paymar, *Education Groups for Men Who Batter: The Duluth Model* (New York: Springer, 1993).

21. Linda Gordon, *Heroes of Their Own Lives: The Politics and History of Family Violence* (New York: Viking, 1988), 285.

22. Gordon, *Heroes of Their Own Lives*.

23. Evan Stark and Anne Flitcraft, *Women at Risk: Domestic Violence and Women's Health* (Thousand Oaks, Calif.: Sage, 1996).

24. Cynthia K. Gillespie, *Justifiable Homicide: Battered Women, Self-Defense, and the Law* (Columbus: Ohio State University Press, 1989); Elizabeth Pleck, *Domestic Tyranny* (New York: Oxford University Press, 1987).

25. Molly Chaudhuri and Kathleen Daly, "Do Restraining Orders Help? Battered Women's Experience with Male Violence and Legal Process," in *Domestic Violence: The Changing Criminal Justice Response*, edited by Eve Buzawa and Carl Buzawa (Westport, Conn.: Auburn House, 1992), 227–252; Peter Finn, "Civil Protection Orders: A Flawed Opportunity for Intervention," in *Woman Battering: Policy Responses*, edited by Michael Steinman (Highland Heights, Ky.: Academy of Criminal Justice Sciences, 1991), 155–190.

26. Lawrence W. Sherman, *Policing Domestic Violence: Experiments and Dilemmas* (New York: Free Press, 1992); Jalna Hanmer, Jill Radford, and Elizabeth A. Stanko, eds., *Women, Policing, and Male Violence: International Perspectives* (London: Routledge, 1989).

27. Robert L. Hampton, ed., *Violence in the Black Family: Correlates and Consequences* (Lexington, Mass.: Lexington Books, 1987); Robert L. Hampton, ed., *Black Family Violence: Current Research and Theory* (Lexington, Mass.: Lexington Books, 1991); Beth E. Richie, *Compelled to Crime: The Gender Entrapment of Battered Black Women* (New York: Routledge, 1996); Susan B. Sorenson and Cynthia A. Telles, "Self-Reports of Spousal Violence in a Mexican-American and Non-Hispanic White Population," *Violence and Victims* 6, no. 1 (1991): 3–15.

28. Beth E. Richie, "Battered Black Women: A Challenge for the Black Com-

munity," *Black Scholar* 16, no. 2 (March-April 1985): 40–44; M. Annette Jaimes and Theresa Halsey, "American Indian Women: At the Center of Indigenous Resistance in North America," in *The State of Native America: Genocide, Colonization, and Resistance*, edited by M. Annette Jaimes (Boston: South End Press, 1992), 311–344; Kimberlé Williams Crenshaw, "Mapping the Margins: Intersectionality, Identity Politics, and Violence Against Women of Color," in *The Public Nature of Private Violence*, edited by Martha Albertson Fineman and Roxanne Mykitiuk (New York: Routledge, 1994), 93–118; Margaretta Wan Ling Lin and Cheng Imm Tan, "Holding Up More Than Half the Heavens: Domestic Violence in Our Communities, A Call for Justice," in *The State of Asian America: Activism and Resistance in the 1990s*, edited by Karin Aguilar-San Juan (Boston: South End Press, 1994), 321–334; Jenny Rivera, "Domestic Violence Against Latinas by Latino Males: An Analysis of Race, National Origin, and Gender Differentials," *Third World Law Journal* 14, no. 2 (1994): 231–257; Gloria Bonilla-Santiago, "Latina Battered Women: Barriers to Service Delivery and Cultural Considerations," in *Helping Battered Women: New Perspectives and Remedies*, edited by Albert R. Roberts (New York: Oxford Press, 1996), 229–234; Valli Kanuha, "Domestic Violence, Racism, and the Battered Women's Movement in the United States," in *Future Interventions with Battered Women and Their Families*, edited by Jeffrey L. Edleson and Zvi C. Eisikovits (Thousand Oaks, Calif.: Sage, 1996), 34–50.

29. Stark and Flitcraft, "Spouse Abuse," 123; Richie, *Compelled to Crime*.

30. Gordon, *Heroes of Their Own Lives*, 257.

31. Robert M. Bohm and Keith N. Haley, *Introduction to Criminal Justice* (Glencoe: McGraw-Hill, 1997), 11.

32. Max Weber, *From Max Weber: Essays in Sociology*, translated and edited by Hans H. Gerth and C. Wright Mills (New York: Oxford University Press, 1946 [1921]), 78.

33. Sylvia Walby, "Theorising Patriarchy," *Sociology* 23, no. 2 (1989): 225.

34. Kenneth Polk, *When Men Kill: Scenarios of Masculine Violence* (Cambridge: Cambridge University Press, 1994).

35. Donald Black, "Crime as Social Control," *American Sociological Review* 48, no. 1 (1983): 39.

36. Elizabeth C. Stanton, Susan B. Anthony, and Matilda J. Gage, "Selections from the *History of Woman Suffrage*," in *The Feminist Papers*, edited by Alice S. Rossi (Toronto: Bantam, 1973), 417.

37. Elizabeth Pleck, "Feminist Responses to 'Crimes Against Women,' 1868–1896," *Signs: Journal of Women in Culture and Society* 8, no. 3 (Spring 1983): 451–470.

38. David Peterson del Mar, *What Trouble I Have Seen: A History of Violence Against Wives* (Cambridge, Mass.: Harvard University Press, 1996), 85.

39. Elizabeth Pleck, "Wife-Beating in Nineteenth-Century America," *Victimology* 4, no. 1 (1979): 60–74; Peterson del Mar, *What Trouble I Have Seen*, 88.

40. Herbert Blumer, "Social Problems as Collective Behavior," *Social Problems* 18, no. 3 (1971): 301.

41. Rebecca Emerson Dobash and Russell P. Dobash, *Women, Violence, and Social Change* (New York: Routledge, 1992); Karlene Faith, "Justice Where Art Thou? And Do We Care? Feminist Perspectives on Justice for Women in Canada," in *Readings in Critical Criminology*, edited by Ronald Hinch (Scarborough, Ontario: Prentice-Hall Canada, 1994), 84–108; Laureen Snider, "The Potential of the Criminal Justice System to Promote Feminist Concerns," in *The Social Basis of*

Law, edited by Elizabeth Comack and Stephen Brickey (Halifax, Nova Scotia: Garamond Press, 1991), 238–260.

42. Eve S. Buzawa and Carl G. Buzawa, *Domestic Violence: The Criminal Justice Response*, 2d ed. (Thousand Oaks, Calif.: Sage, 1996), 164–165.

43. Massachusetts Supreme Judicial Court, "Gender Bias Study of the Court System in Massachusetts" (Boston: Supreme Judicial Court, 1989), 93.

44. Angela Davis, "We Do Not Consent: Violence Against Women in a Racist Society," in *Women, Culture, and Politics* (New York: Vintage, 1990), 35–52.

45. Jenny Rivera, "The Politics of Invisibility," *Georgetown Journal on Fighting Poverty* 3, no. 1 (Fall 1995): 61–65.

Chapter 2

1. Angela Browne, "Reshaping the Rhetoric: The Nexus of Violence, Poverty, and Minority Status in the Lives of Women and Children in the United States," *Georgetown Journal on Fighting Poverty* 3, no. 1 (Fall 1995): 20.

2. S. M. Miller, "Equality, Morality, and the Health of Democracy," in *Myths About the Powerless*, edited by M. Brinton Lykes, Ali Banuazizi, Ramsay Liem, and Michael Morris (Philadelphia: Temple University Press, 1996), 17–33.

3. James Ptacek, "Wifebeaters' Accounts of Their Violence: Loss of Control as Excuse and as Subjective Experience," Master's Thesis, Department of Sociology, University of New Hampshire, 1985; Ptacek, "Why Do Men Batter Their Wives?," in *Feminist Perspectives on Wife Abuse*, edited by Kersti Yllö and Michele Bograd (Newbury Park, Calif.: Sage, 1988), 133–157; Ptacek, "The Clinical Literature on Men Who Batter: A Review and Critique," in *Family Abuse and Its Consequences: New Directions in Family Violence Research*, edited by Gerald T. Hotaling, David Finkelhor, John T. Kirkpatrick, and Murray A. Straus (Newbury Park, Calif.: Sage, 1988), 149–162.

4. Douglas S. Massey and Nancy A. Denton, *American Apartheid* (Cambridge: Harvard University Press, 1993).

5. bell hooks, *Feminist Theory: From Margin to Center* (Boston: South End Press, 1984).

6. Patricia Hill Collins, *Black Feminist Thought: Knowledge, Consciousness, and the Politics of Empowerment* (Boston: Unwin Hyman, 1990).

7. Kimberlé Williams Crenshaw, "Mapping the Margins: Intersectionality, Identity Politics, and Violence Against Women of Color," in *The Public Nature of Private Violence*, edited by Martha Albertson Fineman and Roxanne Mykitiuk (New York: Routledge, 1994), 105.

8. For a discussion of the methods used in this study, see the Appendix.

9. Collins, *Black Feminist Thought*, 187.

10. Robert J. Sampson and William Julius Wilson, "Toward a Theory of Race, Crime, and Urban Inequality," in *Crime and Inequality*, edited by John Hagan and Ruth D. Peterson (Stanford: Stanford University Press, 1995), 37.

11. Michael Tonry, *Malign Neglect: Race, Crime, and Punishment in America* (New York: Oxford University Press, 1995), viii.

12. Darnell F. Hawkins, ed., *Ethnicity, Race, and Crime* (Albany: State University of New York Press, 1995), 8.

13. Richard J. Herrnstein and Charles Murray, *The Bell Curve: Intelligence and Class Structure in American Life* (New York: Free Press, 1994).

14. Naomi Glauberman and Russell Jacoby, eds., *The Bell Curve Debate: His-*

tory, Documents, Opinions (New York: Times Books, 1995); Steven Fraser, ed., *The Bell Curve Wars: Race, Intelligence, and the Future of America* (New York: Basic Books, 1995); Claude S. Fischer et al., *Inequality by Design: Cracking the Bell Curve Myth* (Princeton: Princeton University Press, 1996); Joe L. Kincheloe, Shirley R. Steinberg, and Aaron D. Gresson, eds., *The Bell Curve Examined* (New York: St. Martin's Press, 1996); William T. Dickens, Thomas J. Kane, and Charles Schultze, *Does the Bell Curve Ring True?* (Washington, D.C.: Brookings Institute, 1997); Bernie Devlin, ed., *Intelligence and Success: Is It All in the Genes? Scientists Respond to the Bell Curve* (New York: Springer Verlag, 1997).

15. Beth E. Richie, "Battered Black Women: A Challenge for the Black Community," *Black Scholar* 16, no. 2 (March-April 1985): 40–44.

16. Margaretta Wan Ling Lin and Cheng Imm Tan, "Holding Up More Than Half the Heavens: Domestic Violence in Our Communities, A Call for Justice," in *The State of Asian America: Activism and Resistance in the 1990s*, edited by Karin Aguilar-San Juan (Boston: South End Press, 1994), 321–334.

17. Jenny Rivera, "Domestic Violence Against Latinas by Latino Males: An Analysis of Race, National Origin, and Gender Differentials," *Third World Law Journal* 14, no. 2 (1994): 231–257.

18. Suzanne S. K. Steinmetz and Murray A. Straus, *Violence in the Family* (New York: Harper and Row, 1974).

19. Jennifer Hunt, " 'Abuse Is a Choice; He Didn't Have to Abuse Me,' " *Boston Sunday Globe*, July 27, 1997, F1–F2.

20. Martin D. Schwartz, "Ain't Got No Class: Universal Risk Theories of Battering," *Contemporary Crises* 12 (1988): 373–392.

21. Angela Moore, "Intimate Violence: Does Socioeconomic Status Matter?," in *Violence Between Intimate Partners: Patterns, Causes, and Effects*, edited by Albert P. Cardarelli (Boston: Allyn and Bacon, 1997), 90–100.

22. Schwartz, "Ain't Got No Class," 373.

23. Susan Schechter, *Women and Male Violence: The Visions and Struggles of the Battered Women's Movement* (Boston: South End Press, 1982).

24. Michelle Fine, "Unearthing Contradictions: An Essay Inspired by *Women and Male Violence*," *Feminist Studies* 11, no. 2 (1985): 391–407.

25. Schwartz, "Ain't Got No Class," 374–375.

26. Moore, "Intimate Violence," 95, 96.

27. Lawrence W. Sherman, *Policing Domestic Violence: Experiments and Dilemmas* (New York: Free Press, 1992), 134. Other studies of policing and domestic violence can be found, along with important commentary, in two special journal issues: "Symposium on Domestic Violence," a special issue of the *Journal of Criminal Law and Criminology* 88, no. 1 (1992); and Eve S. Buzawa and Carl G. Buzawa, eds., "The Impact of Arrest on Domestic Assault," a special issue of the *American Behavioral Scientist* 36, no. 5 (1993).

28. Murray A. Straus, Richard J. Gelles, and Suzanne K. Steinmetz, *Behind Closed Doors: Violence in the American Family* (Garden City: Anchor Press/Doubleday, 1980), 148.

29. Rebecca Emerson Dobash and Russell Dobash, *Violence Against Wives: A Case Against the Patriarchy* (New York: Free Press, 1979); Kersti Ylló and Michele Bograd, eds., *Feminist Perspectives on Wife Abuse* (Newbury Park, Calif.: Sage, 1988); Irene Hanson Frieze and Angela Browne, "Violence in Marriage," in *Family Violence*, edited by Lloyd Ohlin and Michael Tonry (Chicago: University of Chicago Press, 1989), 163–218.

30. Schwartz, "Ain't Got No Class," 376.

31. Mary P. Koss, Christine A. Gidycz, and Nadine Wisniewski, "The Scope of Rape: Incidence and Prevalence of Sexual Aggression and Victimization in a National Sample of Higher Education Students," *Journal of Consulting and Clinical Psychology* 55, no. 2 (1987): 162–170; Diana E. H. Russell, *Sexual Exploitation: Rape, Child Sexual Abuse, and Workplace Harassment* (Beverly Hills: Sage, 1984); Frieze and Browne, "Violence in Marriage."

32. Diana E. H. Russell, *Rape in Marriage* (Bloomington: Indiana University Press, 1990).

33. Koss, Gidycz, and Wisniewski, "The Scope of Rape."

34. Liz Kelly, *Surviving Sexual Violence* (Minneapolis: University of Minnesota Press, 1988).

35. Ronet Bachman and Linda E. Saltzman, "Violence Against Women: Estimates from the Redesigned Survey," Special Report of the Bureau of Justice Statistics (Washington, D.C.: U.S. Department of Justice, August 1995).

36. Mary Ann Allard, Randy Albelda, Mary Ellen Colten, and Carol Cosenza, "In Harm's Way? Domestic Violence, AFDC Receipt, and Welfare Reform in Massachusetts," A Report from the University of Massachusetts Boston (Boston: University of Massachusetts, 1997), 16.

37. Richard J. Gelles and Murray A. Straus, *Intimate Violence* (New York: Simon and Schuster, 1988), 250.

38. Allard et al., "In Harm's Way?," 16.

39. Russell, *Rape in Marriage*, 89.

40. Angela Browne and Shari S. Bassuk, "Intimate Violence in the Lives of Homeless and Poor Housed Women," *American Journal of Orthopsychiatry* 67, no. 2 (April 1997): 261–278; Susan Lloyd, "The Effects of Violence on Women's Employment," Paper presented at the Eighteenth Annual Research Conference, Pittsburgh, Pa., 1996; P. Roper and G. Weeks, "Over Half of the Women on Public Assistance in Washington State Reported Physical or Sexual Abuse as Adults," Issue Brief of the Washington State Institute for Public Policy (Olympia, Wash.: Evergreen State College, 1993); P. Curcio, "The Passaic County Study of AFDC Recipients in a Welfare to Work Program: A Preliminary Analysis" (Passaic County, N.J.: Passaic County Board of Social Services, 1996).

41. Ellen L. Bassuk, Linda F. Weintraub, John C. Buckner, Angela Browne, Amy Solomon, and Shari S. Bassuk, "The Characteristics and Needs of Sheltered Homeless and Low-Income Housed Mothers," *Journal of the American Medical Association* 276, no. 8 (August 28, 1996): 640.

42. Joan Zorza, "Woman Battering: A Major Cause of Homelessness," *Clearinghouse Review* 24, no. 4 (1991): 421–429.

43. Jody Raphael, "Prisoners of Abuse: Domestic Violence and Welfare Receipt" (Chicago: Taylor Institute, April 1996).

44. Straus, Gelles, and Steinmetz, *Behind Closed Doors*, 134.

45. Noel A. Cazenave and Murray A. Straus, "Race, Class, Network Embeddedness, and Family Violence: A Search for Potent Support Systems," *Journal of Comparative Family Studies* 10, no. 3 (1979): 281–300.

46. Lettie L. Lockhart, "Spousal Violence: A Cross-Racial Perspective," in *Black Family Violence: Current Research and Theory*, edited by Robert L. Hampton (Lexington, Mass.: Lexington Books, 1991), 85–101.

47. Diego O. Castro, " 'Hot Blood and Easy Virtue': Mass Media and the Making of Racist Latino/a Stereotypes," in *Images of Color, Images of Crime: Read-*

ings, edited by Coramae Richey Mann and Marjorie S. Zatz (Los Angeles: Roxbury, 1998), 142n.2.

48. Murray A. Straus and Christine Smith, "Violence in Hispanic Families in the United States: Incidence Rates and Structural Interpretations," in *Physical Violence in American Families*, edited by Murray A. Straus and Richard J. Gelles (New Brunswick, N.J.: Transaction, 1990), 341–367.

49. Susan B. Sorenson and Cynthia A. Telles, "Self-Reports of Spousal Violence in a Mexican-American and Non-Hispanic White Population," *Violence and Victims* 6, no. 1 (1991): 3–15.

50. Bachman and Saltzman, "Violence Against Women," 1.

51. James F. Short, Jr., *Poverty, Ethnicity, and Violent Crime* (Boulder: Westview Press, 1997).

52. Diana E. H. Russell, "Preface," in *Femicide: The Politics of Woman Killing*, edited by Jill Radford and Diana E. H. Russell (New York: Twayne, 1990), xiv.

53. Michael R. Rand, "Violence-Related Injuries Treated in Hospital Emergency Departments," Special Report of the Bureau of Justice Statistics (Washington, D.C.: U.S. Department of Justice, August 1997); Evan Stark and Anne H. Flitcraft, "Spouse Abuse," in *Violence in America: A Public Health Approach*, edited by Mark L. Rosenberg and Mary Ann Fenlet (New York: Oxford University Press, 1991), 123–157.

54. Reynolds Farley, "Homicide Trends in the United States," in *Homicide Among Black Americans*, edited by Darnell F. Hawkins (Lanham, Md.: University Press of America, 1986), 13–27; Evan Stark, "Rethinking Homicide: Violence, Race, and the Politics of Gender," *International Journal of Health Services* 20, no. 1 (1990): 3–26.

55. Susan A. Wilt, Susan M. Illman, and Maia BrodyField, "Female Homicide Victims in New York City 1990–1994," Draft Report (New York: New York City Department of Health, March 1997).

56. Marcia Smith, "When Violence Strikes Home," *The Nation*, June 30, 1997, 23–24.

57. Massachusetts Department of Public Health, "Homicide in Massachusetts: Trends and Characteristics 1978–1993," 2d ed. (Boston: Massachusetts Department of Public Health, 1995), 33, 21.

58. Sampson and Wilson, "Toward a Theory of Race, Crime, and Urban Inequality."

59. Darnell F. Hawkins, "Devalued Lives and Racial Stereotypes: Ideological Barriers to the Prevention of Family Violence Among Blacks," in *Violence in the Black Family: Correlates and Consequences*, edited by Robert L. Hampton (Lexington, Mass.: Lexington Books, 1987), 189–205.

60. Stark, "Rethinking Homicide: Violence, Race, and the Politics of Gender."

61. Russell, *Rape in Marriage*, 189.

62. Collins, *Black Feminist Thought*, 223.

63. Ptacek, "Why Do Men Batter Their Wives?"; Moore, "Intimate Violence: Does Socioeconomic Status Matter?," 93.

64. Moore, "Intimate Violence: Does Socioeconomic Status Matter?," 100.

65. O. Uzzell and W. Peebles-Wilkins, "Black Spouse Abuse: A Focus on Relational Factors and Intervention Strategies," *Western Journal of Black Studies* 13 (1989): 10–16. Cited in Robert L. Hampton and Richard J. Gelles, "Violence Toward Black Women in a Nationally Representative Sample of Black Families," *Journal of Comparative Family Studies* 25, no. 1 (Spring 1994): 105–120.

66. Etiony Aldarondo, Dennis Tyrell, and Erika Shore, "Uses and Misuses of the Concepts of Ethnicity and Race in Wife Assault Research," Paper presented at the Fifth International Family Violence Research Conference, University of New Hampshire, Durham, New Hampshire, June 30, 1997.

67. Sampson and Wilson, "Toward a Theory of Race, Crime, and Urban Inequality," 40.

68. Martin Gilens, "Race and Poverty in America: Public Misperceptions and the American News Media," *Public Opinion Quarterly* 60 (1996): 515–541.

69. Sampson and Wilson, "Toward a Theory of Race, Crime, and Urban Inequality," 41.

70. Massey and Denton, *American Apartheid.*

71. Cornell West, *Race Matters* (Boston: Beacon Press, 1993), x.

72. Robert L. Hampton, ed., *Violence in the Black Family: Correlates and Consequences* (Lexington, Mass.: Lexington Books, 1987); Robert L. Hampton, ed., *Black Family Violence: Current Research and Theory* (Lexington, Mass.: Lexington Books, 1991).

73. Beth Richie, *Compelled to Crime: The Gender Entrapment of Battered Black Women* (New York: Routledge, 1996).

74. Laura Nader, "Up the Anthropologist: Perspectives Gained from Studying Up," in *Reinventing Anthropology*, edited by Dell Hynes (New York: Pantheon, 1972), 284–311.

75. John Aloysius Farrell, "Nixon Was Known to Be a Wife-Abuser, a Journalist Alleges," *Boston Globe*, April 7, 1998, A13.

76. Michael Omi and Howard Winant, *Racial Formation in the United States: From the 1960s to the 1990s*, 2d ed. (New York: Routledge, 1994), 159.

77. Johnnetta B. Cole, "Commonalities and Differences," in *All American Women: Lines That Divide, Ties That Bind* (New York: Free Press, 1986), 25.

78. William J. Chambliss, "Crime Control and Ethnic Minorities: Legitimizing Racial Oppression by Creating Moral Panics," in *Ethnicity, Race, and Crime*, edited by Darnell F. Hawkins (Albany: State University of New York Press, 1995), 245.

79. Joe R. Feagin and Hernán Vera, *White Racism* (New York: Routledge, 1995), 114.

80. Feagin and Vera, *White Racism*, 122.

81. David C. Anderson, *Crime and the Politics of Hysteria* (New York: Times Books, 1995).

82. Gary LaFree, "Race and Crime Trends in the United States, 1946–1990," in *Ethnicity, Race, and Crime*, edited by Darnell F. Hawkins (Albany: State University of New York Press, 1995), 186.

83. Crenshaw, "Mapping the Margins," 105.

84. Of those sociologists who indicate their racial identities, 85 percent are white, according to the American Sociological Association. The American Psychological Association reports that in 1995, 93 percent of their members who gave information on racial identity were white. Over one-fifth of the members of these organizations do not indicate their racial identities.

85. Massey and Denton, *American Apartheid*, 144–147.

86. Jill Quadagno, *The Color of Welfare: How Racism Undermined the War on Poverty* (New York: Oxford University Press, 1994).

87. Gilens, "Race and Poverty in America."

88. Ruth Brandwein, "The Use of Public Welfare by Family Violence Victims:

Implications of New Federal Welfare 'Reform,' " Paper presented at the Fifth International Family Violence Research Conference, University of New Hampshire, Durham, New Hampshire, July 1, 1997.

89. Desmond Ellis and Walter S. DeKeseredy, "Marital Status and Woman Abuse: The DAD Model," *International Journal of Sociology of the Family* 19 (Autumn 1989): 67–87.

90. NOW Legal Defense and Education Fund, "The G.O.P. Welfare Bills— H.R. 3507 and S. 1795—Hurt Battered Women," Report of the National Task Force on Violence Against Women, July 17, 1996.

91. John Irwin and James Austin, *It's About Time: America's Imprisonment Binge*, 2d ed. (Belmont, Calif.: Wadsworth, 1997), 1.

92. Jerome G. Miller, *Search and Destroy: African-American Males in the Criminal Justice System* (Cambridge: Cambridge University Press, 1996), 55.

93. Chambliss, "Crime Control and Ethnic Minorities"; Steven R. Donziger, ed., *The Real War on Crime: The Report of the National Criminal Justice Commission* (New York: HarperPerennial, 1996); Miller, *Search and Destroy*; Tonry, *Malign Neglect*.

94. Tonry, *Malign Neglect*, 105.

95. Donziger, *The Real War on Crime*.

96. Tonry, *Malign Neglect*, 104.

97. Tonry, *Malign Neglect*, 181–190.

98. Crenshaw, "Mapping the Margins"; Rivera, "Domestic Violence Against Latinas by Latino Males."

99. Representative Major Owens, cited in James Ridgeway, "Send in the Feds," *The Village Voice*, September 9, 1997, 38.

100. Peter T. Elikann, *The Tough-on-Crime Myth: Real Solutions to Cut Crime* (New York: Plenum, 1996), 65.

101. Richie, *Compelled to Crime*, 3.

102. Donziger, *The Real War on Crime*, 160.

103. Browne, "Reshaping the Rhetoric," 20.

Chapter 3

1. Herbert Blumer, "Social Problems as Collective Behavior," *Social Problems* 78, no. 3 (1971): 301–302.

2. Elizabeth Pleck, *Domestic Tyranny* (New York: Oxford University Press, 1987), 4.

3. Pleck, *Domestic Tyranny*, 21–22.

4. Pleck, *Domestic Tyranny*, 22.

5. Pleck, *Domestic Tyranny*, 22.

6. Pleck, *Domestic Tyranny*, 29, 33.

7. Elizabeth Pleck, "Wife-Beating in Nineteenth-Century America," *Victimology* 4, no. 1 (1979): 63.

8. Pleck, "Wife-Beating in Nineteenth-Century America," 65.

9. Elizabeth Pleck, "Feminist Responses to 'Crimes Against Women,' 1868– 1896," *Signs* 8, no. 3 (Spring 1983): 453.

10. Linda Gordon, *Heroes of Their Own Lives: The Politics and History of Family Violence* (New York: Viking, 1988), 254.

11. Pleck, "Feminist Responses to 'Crimes Against Women,' " 451.

12. Paula Giddings, *When and Where I Enter: The Impact of Black Women on Race and Sex in America* (New York: William Morrow, 1984), 64–68.

13. Hazel V. Carby, " 'On the Threshold of Woman's Era': Lynching, Empire, and Sexuality in Black Feminist Theory," *Critical Inquiry* 12, no. 1 (1985): 262–277.

14. Lucy Stone, "Crimes Against Women," *Woman's Journal*, June 16, 1877, 188.

15. Pleck, "Feminist Responses to 'Crimes Against Women,' " 458–459.

16. Frances Power Cobbe, "Wife Torture in England," in *The Politics of Woman Killing*, edited by Jill Radford and Diana E. H. Russell (New York: Twayne, 1992), 46.

17. "Legal Relief for Assaulted Wives," *Woman's Journal*, January 11, 1879, 12.

18. Pleck, *Domestic Tyranny*, 103.

19. Gordon, *Heroes of Their Own Lives*; Pleck, "Wife-Beating in Nineteenth-Century America."

20. Lisa G. Lerman, "Prosecution of Wife Beaters: Institutional Obstacles and Innovations," in *Violence in the Home: Interdisciplinary Perspectives*, edited by Mary Lystad (New York: Brunner/Mazel, 1986), 257.

21. Pleck, "Feminist Responses to 'Crimes Against Women.' "

22. Verta Taylor, "The Continuity of the American Women's Movement: An Elite-Sustained Stage," in *Women and Social Protest*, edited by Guida West and Rhoda Lois Blumberg (New York: Oxford University Press, 1990), 277–301.

23. Pleck, "Feminist Responses to 'Crimes Against Women,' " 470.

24. Kathleen J. Tierney, "The Battered Women Movement and the Creation of the Wife Beating Problem," *Social Problems* 29, no. 3 (1982): 207, 208.

25. Rebecca Emerson Dobash and Russell P. Dobash, *Women, Violence, and Social Change* (New York: Routledge, 1992), 70.

26. Susan Schechter, *Women and Male Violence: The Visions and Struggles of the Battered Women's Movement* (Boston: South End Press, 1982).

27. Lisa G. Lerman, "State Legislation on Domestic Violence," *Response* 4, no. 7 (1981): 1–18; Pleck, *Domestic Tyranny*; Joan Zorza, "The Criminal Law of Misdemeanor Domestic Violence, 1970–1990," *Journal of Criminal Law and Criminology* 83, no. 1 (1992): 46–72.

28. Zorza, "The Criminal Law of Misdemeanor Domestic Violence," 48.

29. Zorza, "The Criminal Law of Misdemeanor Domestic Violence," 54–55.

30. Bruno v. Codd, 90 Misc. 2d 1047, 396 N.Y.S. 2d 974 (Sup. Ct. 1977), cited in Zorza, "The Criminal Law of Misdemeanor Domestic Violence," 58.

31. Zorza, "The Criminal Law of Misdemeanor Domestic Violence," 59.

32. Lerman, "State Legislation on Domestic Violence."

33. Eve S. Buzawa and Carl G. Buzawa, *Domestic Violence: The Criminal Justice Response* (Newbury Park: Sage, 1990), 112.

34. Katherine Triantafillou, "Massachusetts: New Legislation to Help Battered Women," *Judges' Journal* 27, no. 3 (1988): 20–23, 50–52.

35. Interview with Katherine Triantafillou, November 24, 1993.

36. Diana E. H. Russell, *Rape in Marriage* (Bloomington: Indiana University Press, 1990).

37. Triantafillou, "Massachusetts: New Legislation," 52.

38. Battered Women's Working Group, "Violent Crime in the Family: Enforcement of the Massachusetts Abuse Prevention Law" (Boston: Governor's Statewide Anti-Crime Council, 1985), 6.

39. Battered Women's Working Group, "Violent Crime in the Family," n.p.

40. Eileen McNamara, "Judge Tempone Said to Top Complaint List," *Boston Globe*, November 2, 1986, 18.

41. John Hechinger, "Domestic Violence Difficult to Prevent: Legal Orders Called Largely Ineffective," *Boston Globe*, August 17, 1986, 1.

42. Eileen McNamara, "Judge's Action Questioned, Prior Complaint Recounted," *Boston Globe*, September 27, 1986, 1.

43. Eileen McNamara, "Judge Criticized After Woman's Death," *Boston Globe*, September 21, 1986, 1.

44. Eileen McNamara, "Friends Say Charges Malign Judge, Abuse-Case Controversy Seethes Around 'A Sensitive Person,' " *Boston Globe*, October 5, 1986, 1.

45. Eileen McNamara, "Justice Zoll: Caught in Middle, Tries to Balance Concern for Victims, Judges," *Boston Globe*, December 23, 1986, 1.

46. McNamara, "Judge Tempone Said to Top Complaint List," 18.

47. Eileen McNamara, "Chief Judge to Probe in Somerville," *Boston Globe*, October 2, 1986, 1.

48. Eileen McNamara, "Two Judges Withdraw from Cases, Won't Hear Domestic Abuse Matters Pending Probe," *Boston Globe*, October 15, 1986, 1.

49. Eileen McNamara, " 'No Quick Fix' in Abuse Cases, Judge Rules," *Boston Globe*, November 13, 1986, 1, 18.

50. McNamara, " 'No Quick Fix,' " 1, 18.

51. Eileen McNamara, "Dorchester Judge Stripped of Right to Hear Most Cases," *Boston Globe*, November 14, 1986, 1.

52. Eileen McNamara, "Panel to Look for Sex Bias in Courts," *Boston Globe*, December 19, 1986, 25.

53. "Judicial Accountability," *Boston Globe*, October 17, 1986, 18.

54. Massachusetts Supreme Judicial Court, "Gender Bias Study of the Court System in Massachusetts" (Boston: Supreme Judicial Court, 1989), 110, n. 5.

55. John H. Kennedy, "SJC Reprimands Somerville Judge, Mild Sanction Draws Fire from Heffernan's Critics," *Boston Globe*, September 29, 1988, 36.

56. "Judge King's Wrist-Slap Censure," *Boston Globe*, March 30, 1991, 18.

57. Eileen McNamara, "Still No Order in the Court," *Boston Globe*, June 14, 1987, 87.

58. Richard Kindleberger, "Reassigned Judge Credited with Easing of Case Backlog," *Boston Globe*, April 21, 1989, 60.

59. Stacey Kabat, quoted in Elaine Ray, "Domestic Violence: The Sad Statistics," *Boston Globe*, November 17, 1991, 83.

60. Peggy Hernandez, "Domestic Violence on Rise in Mass., Advocates Link Increase in Battering to Economy," *Boston Globe*, November 29, 1991, 1.

61. Peggy Hernandez, "Harshbarger Calls for More Sensitivity to Battering Victims," *Boston Globe*, December 19, 1991, 41.

62. Jordana Hart, "Courts Issued More Restraint Orders in 1991, Rise in Violence Shows Ineffectiveness," *Boston Globe*, February 16, 1991, 1; Alison Bass, "Domestic Violence: Roots Go Deep," *Boston Globe*, June 5, 1992, 1.

63. Massachusetts Supreme Judicial Court, "Annual Report of the Massachusetts Court System," Fiscal Year 1993 (Boston: Supreme Judicial Court, 1994), 2–3.

64. Massachusetts Supreme Judicial Court, Commission to Study Racial and Ethnic Bias in the Courts, "Equal Justice: Eliminating the Barriers" (Boston: Supreme Judicial Court, 1994).

65. Massachusetts Supreme Judicial Court, "Annual Report of the Massachusetts Court System," Fiscal Years 1981–1996 (Boston: Supreme Judicial Court, 1982–1997). Figures reflect total orders filed (as opposed to granted) for District Courts, Probate and Family Courts, and Boston Municipal Court. Figures for 1990 to 1993 are based on calendar year totals for the District Courts and fiscal year figures for the other courts; all other years are fiscal years.

66. Sandy Coleman, "Judges on Call to Stem Violence," *Boston Globe,* January 24, 1993, 1.

67. Barbara Smith, Introduction to the Combahee River Collective pamphlet, "Twelve Black Women: Why Did They Die?," in *Fight Back! Feminist Resistance to Male Violence,* edited by Frédérique Delacoste and Felice Newman (Minneapolis: Cleis Press, 1981), 68.

68. Andrew Kopkind, "Race, Class, and Murder in Boston," *The Nation,* February 5, 1990, 153.

69. Alex S. Jones, "Bias and Recklessness Are Charged in Boston Reporting of Stuart Slaying," *New York Times,* January 14, 1990, 21.

70. Fox Butterfield, "Flurry of Rumors in a Murder Case," *New York Times,* January 8, 1990, A12; Maria Margaronis, "Fright Knight: Race, Sex, and Charles Stuart's White Lie," *Village Voice,* January 30, 1990, 45; Renée Goldsmith Kasinsky, "Patrolling the Facts: Media, Cops, and Crime," in *Media, Process, and the Social Construction of Crime,* edited by Gregg Barak (New York: Garland, 1994), 203–234.

71. Dorothy A. Clark, "Media Coverage of Poverty in Boston's Black Community," in *Perspectives of Poverty in Boston's Black Community* edited by James Jennings (Boston: Boston Persistent Poverty Project, 1992), 59.

72. Cited in Kasinsky, "Patrolling the Facts," 212.

73. Howard Manly and Jean Caldwell, "Domestic Rampage: Police Say Estranged Boyfriend Killed Three, Then Self, in Chicopee," *Boston Globe,* September 30, 1992, 1.

74. "A Call for Help for Jane Doe," *Boston Globe,* June 30, 1992, 14.

75. Bruce McCabe, "A Forum Against Domestic Violence," *Boston Globe,* June 28, 1992, TV Week, 2.

76. John Robinson, "Tears at a Power Breakfast," *Boston Globe,* October 14, 1993, 69.

77. Don Aucoin, "Battering Bills Stuck on the Hill," *Boston Globe,* January 2, 1994, 1.

78. Massachusetts Department of Public Health, "Homicide in Massachusetts: Trends and Characteristics 1978–1993," 2d ed. (Boston: Massachusetts Department of Public Health, December 1995), 19.

79. Blumer, "Social Problems as Collective Behavior," 301.

80. Interview with Katherine Triantafillou, November 24, 1993.

Chapter 4

1. Judge Charles Pelham, Fulgham v. State, 46 Ala. 146, at 146–147 (1871).

2. Massachusetts General Laws, Chapter 209A; revised form, 1991.

3. Barbara Hart, "Safety for Women: Monitoring Batterers' Programs" (Harrisburg, Pa.: Pennsylvania Coalition Against Domestic Violence, 1988), 17.

4. Donald Black, "Crime as Social Control," *American Sociological Review* 48, no. 1 (1983): 34–45.

5. David Adams, "Stages of Anti-sexist Awareness and Change for Men Who Batter," in *Family Violence*, edited by L. Dickstein and C. Nadelson (Washington, D.C.: Appi Press,1988), 61–98; Jeffrey L. Edleson and Richard M. Tolman, *Intervention for Men Who Batter: An Ecological Approach* (Newbury Park, Calif.: Sage, 1992); Edward W. Gondolf, *Men Who Batter: An Integrated Approach for Stopping Wife Abuse* (Holmes Beach, Fla.: Learning Publications, 1985); Ellen Pence and Michael Paymar, *Education Groups for Men Who Batter: The Duluth Model* (New York: Springer, 1993).

6. James Ptacek, "Why Do Men Batter Their Wives?," in *Feminist Perspectives on Wife Abuse*, edited by Kersti Yllö and Michele Bograd (Newbury Park, Calif.: Sage, 1988), 133–157.

7. Massachusetts Trial Court, "A Guide to Public Access to District Court Records" (Salem, Mass.: Administrative Office of the District Court, 1990), 26.

8. Massachusetts Supreme Judicial Court, "Annual Report of the Massachusetts Court System," Fiscal Year 1992 (Boston: Supreme Judicial Court, 1993), 22, 23.

9. Edward W. Gondolf, Joyce McWilliams, Barbara Hart, and Jane Stuehling, "Court Response to Petitions for Civil Protection Orders," *Journal of Interpersonal Violence* 9, no. 4 (1994): 503–517.

10. Adele Harrell, Barbara Smith, and Lisa Newmark, "Court Processing and the Effects of Restraining Orders for Domestic Violence Victims" (Washington, D.C.: Urban Institute, 1993).

11. Molly Chaudhuri and Kathleen Daly, "Do Restraining Orders Help? Battered Women's Experience with Male Violence and Legal Process," in *Domestic Violence: The Changing Criminal Justice Response*, edited by Eve Buzawa and Carl Buzawa (Westport, Conn.: Auburn House, 1992), 227–252; Gondolf et al., "Court Response to Petitions"; Janice Grau, Jeffrey Fagan, and Sandra Wexler, "Restraining Orders for Battered Women: Issues of Access and Efficacy," *Women and Politics* 4, no. 3 (1985): 13–28; Harrell, Smith, and Newmark, "Court Processing"; Anne L. Horton, Kyriacos M. Simonidis, and Lucy L. Simonidis, "Legal Remedies for Spousal Abuse: Victim Characteristics, Expectations, and Satisfaction," *Journal of Family Violence* 2, no. 3 (1987): 265–279.

12. Anita Diamant, "How the Quincy District Court Protects Battered Women," *Boston Globe Magazine*, October 11, 1992, 14–15, 22–29; National Council of Juvenile and Family Court Judges, "Family Violence: State-of-the-Art Court Programs" (Reno, Nev.: National Council of Juvenile and Family Court Judges, 1992).

13. David Adams, "Counseling Men Who Batter: A Profeminist Analysis of Five Treatment Models," in *Feminist Perspectives on Wife Abuse*, edited by Kersti Yllö and Michele Bograd (Newbury Park, Calif.: Sage, 1988), 176–199; Mary Ann Dutton, *Empowering and Healing the Battered Woman: A Model for Assessment and Intervention* (New York: Springer, 1992); Susan Schechter and Lisa T. Gary, "A Framework for Understanding and Empowering Battered Women," in *Abuse and Victimization Across the Life Span*, edited by Martha B. Straus (Baltimore: Johns Hopkins University Press, 1988), 240–253; Pence and Paymar, *Education Groups for Men Who Batter*.

14. Judge Charles Pelham, Fulgham v. State.

15. Harrell, Smith, and Newmark, "Court Processing," 21.

16. Angela Browne, *When Battered Women Kill* (New York: Free Press, 1987), 65.

17. Andrew R. Klein, "Re-Abuse in a Population of Court-Restrained Male Batterers: Why Restraining Orders Don't Work," in *Do Arrests and Restraining Orders Work?*, edited by Eve S. Buzawa and Carl G. Buzawa (Thousand Oaks, Calif.: Sage, 1996), 194.

18. Albert L. Kramer, "Statement to the Massachusetts Joint Committee on the Judiciary: Written Testimony" (Quincy, Mass.: Quincy District Court, 1992).

19. Arlie Russell Hochschild, "The Sociology of Feeling and Emotion: Selected Possibilities," in *Another Voice: Feminist Perspectives on Social Life and Social Science*, edited by Marcia Millman and Rosabeth Moss Kanter (Garden City, N.Y.: Anchor, 1975), 280–307; Hochschild, "Emotion Work, Feeling Rules, and Social Structure," *American Journal of Sociology* 85, no. 3 (1979): 551–575; Hochschild, *The Managed Heart: Commercialization of Human Feeling* (Berkeley: University of California Press, 1983); Hochschild with Anne Machung, *The Second Shift: Working Parents and the Revolution at Home* (New York: Viking, 1989); Hochschild, "The Economy of Gratitude," in *The Family Experience: A Reader in Cultural Diversity*, edited by Mark Hutter (New York: Macmillan, 1991), 499–515.

20. Hochschild, *The Second Shift*.

21. Martha R. Mahoney, "Legal Issues of Battered Women: Redefining the Issue of Separation," *Michigan Law Review* 90, no. 1 (1991): 6.

22. Mahoney, "Legal Issues of Battered Women," 66.

23. Rebecca Emerson Dobash and Russell P. Dobash, "The Nature and Antecedents of Violent Events," *British Journal of Criminology* 24, no. 3 (1984): 269–288; Linda Gordon, *Heroes of Their Own Lives: The Politics and History of Family Violence, Boston 1880–1960* (New York: Viking, 1988); Margo I. Wilson and Martin Daly, "Who Kills Whom in Spouse Killings? On the Exceptional Sex Ratio of Spousal Homicides in the United States," *Criminology* 30, no. 2 (1992): 189–215; Browne, *When Battered Women Kill*; Desmond Ellis, "Woman Abuse Among Separated and Divorced Women: The Relevance of Social Support," in *Intimate Violence: Interdisciplinary Perspectives*, edited by Emilio C. Viano (Washington, D.C.: Hemisphere, 1992), 177–189.

24. Liz Kelly, *Surviving Sexual Violence* (Minneapolis: University of Minnesota Press, 1988), 23.

25. Ellis, "Woman Abuse Among Separated and Divorced Women"; Desmond Ellis and Walter S. DeKeseredy, "Marital Status and Woman Abuse: The DAD Model," *International Journal of Sociology of the Family* 19 (1989): 67–87.

26. Adrienne Rich, "Husband-Right and Father-Right," in *On Lies, Secrets, and Silence: Selected Prose, 1966–1978* (New York: Norton, 1979), 220.

27. Anthony Astrachan, *How Men Feel: Their Response to Women's Demands for Equality and Power* (New York: Anchor Press/Doubleday, 1986).

28. Robert Jay Lifton, *Home from the War: Learning from Vietnam Veterans* (Boston: Beacon Press, 1992).

29. Mahoney, "Legal Issues of Battered Women," 68.

30. Mahoney, "Legal Issues of Battered Women," 19–20.

31. Pence and Paymar, *Education Groups for Men Who Batter*.

32. Emerge, "Violent and Controlling Behavior Toward Children" (Cambridge, Mass.: Emerge, A Counseling and Educational Program for Abusive Men, n.d.).

33. Kramer, "Statement to the Women's Legislative Caucus Hearing on Domestic Violence."

34. Mary Romero, "A Comparison Between Strategies Used on Prisoners of War and Battered Wives," *Sex Roles* 13, nos. 9–10 (1985): 537–547; Judith Lewis Herman, *Trauma and Recovery* (New York: Basic Books, 1992); Larry L. Tifft, *Battering of Women: The Failure of Intervention and the Case for Prevention* (Boulder: Westview Press, 1993).

35. Jane Roberts Chapman, "Violence Against Women as a Violation of Human Rights," *Social Justice* 17, no. 2 (1990): 54–70; Charlotte Bunch and Roxanna Carrillo, "Gender Violence: A Development and Human Rights Issue" (New Brunswick, N.J.: Center for Women's Global Leadership, Douglass College, Rutgers University, 1991); Roxanna Carrillo, *Battered Dreams: Violence Against Women as an Obstacle to Development* (New York: UNIFEM/United Nations Development Fund for Women, 1992); Margaret Schuler, ed., *Freedom from Violence: Women's Strategies from Around the World* (New York: OEF International/UNIFEM, 1992).

36. Ptacek, "Why Do Men Batter Their Wives?"

37. Klein, "Re-Abuse in a Population of Court-Restrained Male Batterers," 195.

38. Donald Cochran, "Over 8,500 Domestic Restraining Orders Filed Since September in Massachusetts" (Boston: Office of the Commissioner of Probation, 1992).

39. Albert Cardarelli, personal communication, 1993.

40. Gordon, *Heroes of Their Own Lives*, 286.

41. Rebecca Emerson Dobash and Russell P. Dobash, "The Negotiation of Daily Life and the 'Provocation' of Violence: A Patriarchal Concept in Support of the Wife Beater," Paper presented at the Ninth World Congress of Sociology, Uppsala, Sweden, 1978; Dobash and Dobash, *Violence Against Wives: A Case Against the Patriarchy* (New York: Free Press, 1979), 127–133.

Chapter 5

1. Judge Harold Flannery, "Gender Bias in the Courtroom and Judicial Intervention," *Boston Bar Journal* (July-August 1989): 21.

2. Massachusetts Trial Court, "Standards of Judicial Practice: Abuse Prevention Proceedings" (Boston: Massachusetts Trial Court, 1986).

3. Erving Goffman, "The Nature of Deference and Demeanor," in *Interaction Ritual: Essays on Face-to-Face Behavior* (New York: Pantheon, 1982 [1967]), 77.

4. Goffman, "The Nature of Deference and Demeanor," 78.

5. Arlie Russell Hochschild, *The Managed Heart: Commercialization of Human Feeling* (Berkeley: University of California Press, 1983).

6. Goffman, "The Nature of Deference and Demeanor," 55.

7. Robert M. Emerson, *Judging Delinquents: Context and Process in Juvenile Court* (Chicago: Aldine, 1969), 208.

8. Hochschild, *The Managed Heart*, 147.

9. John H. Kennedy, "SJC Reprimands Somerville Judge, Mild Sanction Draws Fire from Heffernan's Critics," *Boston Globe*, September 29, 1988, 36.

10. Code of Judicial Conduct, Canon 3(A)(3), cited in Massachusetts Commission on Judicial Conduct, "Annual Report" (Boston: Commission on Judicial Conduct, 1989), 30.

11. Kennedy, "SJC Reprimands Somerville Judge," 36.

12. Kennedy, "SJC Reprimands Somerville Judge," 36.

13. Massachusetts Supreme Judicial Court, "Number of Judges in Massachusetts Courts by Court, Gender, and Race," Public Information Office (Boston: Supreme Judicial Court, 1994) (totals as of February 1, 1994).

14. Figures from the 1990 census, cited in "Equal Justice: Eliminating the Barriers," Final Report of the Commission to Study Racial and Ethnic Bias in the Courts, Massachusetts Supreme Judicial Court (Boston: Supreme Judicial Court, 1994), 9.

15. Maureen Mileski, "Courtroom Encounters: An Observational Study of a Lower Criminal Court," *Law and Society Review* 5, no. 4 (1971): 527.

16. Michel Foucault, *The Use of Pleasure: History of Sexuality*, Vol. 2 (New York: Vintage, 1980).

17. The "Standards of Judicial Practice" state that "there are no formal rules governing procedures under G.L. 209A" (the law establishing restraining orders), Massachusetts Trial Court, "Standards of Judicial Practice," 1:02.

18. Mileski, "Courtroom Encounters," 523.

19. Goffman, "The Nature of Deference and Demeanor," 55.

20. Mileski, "Courtroom Encounters," 524.

21. Mileski, "Courtroom Encounters," 525.

22. Mileski, "Courtroom Encounters," 524.

23. Mileski, "Courtroom Encounters," 523.

24. Nazarro v. Justices of the Southern Essex Division of the District Court & Richard Jones, Supreme Judicial Court No. 86-149, December 17, 1986.

Chapter 6

1. Max Weber, cited in Suzanne Franzway, Dianne Court, and R. W. Connell, *Staking a Claim: Feminism, Bureaucracy, and the State* (Sydney: Allen and Unwin, 1989), 143.

2. Austin T. Philbin, "Domestic Violence and Abuse in Massachusetts: A Survey," *New England Law Review* 24 (Spring, 1990): 713.

3. Max Weber, *From Max Weber: Essays in Sociology*, translated and edited by Hans H. Gerth and C. Wright Mills (New York: Oxford University Press, 1946), 216, 215.

4. Maureen Mileski, "Courtroom Encounters: An Observational Study of a Lower Criminal Court," *Law and Society Review* 5, no. 4 (1971): 473–537.

5. Arlie Russell Hochschild, "Emotion Work, Feeling Rules, and Social Structure," *American Journal of Sociology* 85, no. 3 (1979): 551–575.

6. Mary Ann Dutton, *Empowering and Healing the Battered Woman: A Model for Assessment and Intervention* (New York: Springer, 1992), 11.

7. Kathleen J. Ferraro and John M. Johnson, "How Women Experience Battering: The Process of Victimization," *Social Problems* 30, no. 3 (1983): 325–339.

8. Rebecca Emerson Dobash and Russell P. Dobash, *Violence Against Wives: A Case Against the Patriarchy* (New York: Free Press, 1979).

9. Franzway, Court, and Connell, *Staking a Claim*, 29; emphasis added.

10. Arlie Russell Hochschild, *The Managed Heart: Commercialization of Human Feeling* (Berkeley: University of California Press, 1983), 167.

11. Cynthia Enloe developed this pattern of dependence and denial of dependence on women's work in relation to the military; Dorothy E. Smith identified this pattern in relation to mothers and their children's schooling. Cynthia Enloe, *Does Khaki Become You? The Militarization of Women's Lives* (Boston: South

End Press, 1983); Dorothy E. Smith, *The Everyday World as Problematic: A Feminist Sociology* (Boston: Northeastern University Press, 1987).

12. Judith Lewis Herman, *Trauma and Recovery* (New York: Basic Books, 1992), 40.

13. Herman, *Trauma and Recovery*, 8.

14. Toni Locy and Sean P. Murphy, "Presiding Judge Dolan Says He'll Quit Dorchester Bench," *Boston Globe*, April 14, 1994, 32.

15. Kimberlé Crenshaw, "Race, Gender, and Violence Against Women," in *Family Matters: Readings on Family Lives and the Law*, edited by Martha Minow (New York: New Press, 1993), 231–232.

16. In their analysis of the treatment of rape victims by the courts in Australia, Franzway, Court, and Connell describe how "the woman is not assumed to be an honourable citizen."

17. Carol Smart, *Feminism and the Power of Law* (London: Routledge, 1989), 144.

18. Ralph Ellison, *Invisible Man* (New York: Vintage, 1972), xii.

19. Patricia Hill Collins, *Black Feminist Thought: Knowledge, Consciousness, and the Politics of Empowerment* (Boston: Unwin Hyman, 1990), 70.

20. Shulamit Reinharz, "Feminist Distrust: Problems of Context and Content in Sociological Work," in *The Self in Social Inquiry: Research Methods*, edited by David N. Berg and Kenwyn K. Smith (Newbury Park, Calif.: Sage, 1985), 170.

21. Gary D. LaFree, *Rape and Criminal Justice: The Social Construction of Sexual Assault* (Belmont, Calif.: Wadsworth, 1989), 217–228.

22. Of the 160 judges at the district court level in 1994, only 14 percent were women, and 6 percent were people of color; Public Information Office, Massachusetts Supreme Judicial Court, 1994.

Chapter 7

1. See the discussion of the sample in the Appendix for more details.

2. Judith Lewis Herman, *Trauma and Recovery* (New York: Basic Books, 1992), 51, 61.

3. Evan Stark and Anne H. Flitcraft, "Violence Among Intimates: An Epidemiological Review," in *Handbook of Family Violence*, edited by Vincent B. Van Hasselt, Randall L. Morrison, Alan S. Bellack, and Michel Hersen (New York: Plenum Press, 1988), 304.

4. Herman, *Trauma and Recovery*, 70.

5. Herman, *Trauma and Recovery*, 76.

6. Mary Ann Dutton, *Empowering and Healing the Battered Woman: A Model for Assessment and Intervention* (New York: Springer, 1992), 59.

7. Liz Kelly, *Surviving Sexual Violence* (Minneapolis: University of Minnesota Press, 1988); Diana E. H. Russell, *Rape in Marriage* (Bloomington: Indiana University Press, 1990).

8. Catharine A. MacKinnon, "Violence Against Women: A Perspective," *Aegis: Magazine on Ending Violence Against Women* 33 (1982): 51–57.

9. Kelly, *Surviving Sexual Violence*, 133.

10. Herman, *Trauma and Recovery*, 77.

11. Data on contact with family members were missing in three cases.

12. Based on data from the 1990 census, 18.7 percent of the total Boston population lives below the official poverty line; for black Bostonians, the figure is 24.2

percent. Peter Medoff and Holly Sklar, *Streets of Hope: The Fall and Rise of an Urban Neighborhood* (Boston: South End Press, 1994), 320. The rate of poverty in Quincy is much lower: according to the Office of the Quincy City Clerk (1991), 8.1 percent of Quincy residents are poor.

13. Boston Foundation, "In the Midst of Plenty: A Profile of Boston and Its Poor" (Boston: Boston Foundation, 1989), 51.

14. Douglas S. Massey and Nancy A. Denton, *American Apartheid* (Cambridge: Harvard University Press, 1993), 15.

15. Massey and Denton, *American Apartheid*, 76.

16. Ellen Goodman, "Simpson Case Divides Us by Race," *Boston Globe*, July 7, 1994, 73.

17. Figures from the Office of the Massachusetts Coalition of Battered Women Service Groups, 1994.

18. Lee H. Bowker, *Beating Wife-Beating* (Lexington, Mass.: Lexington Books, 1983); Edward L. Gondolf and Ellen R. Fisher, *Battered Women as Survivors: An Alternative to Treating Learned Helplessness* (Lexington, Mass.: Lexington Books, 1988).

19. Robert M. Emerson, *Judging Delinquents: Context and Process in Juvenile Court* (Chicago: Aldine, 1969), 172.

20. Arlie Russell Hochschild, *The Managed Heart: Commercialization of Human Feeling* (Berkeley: University of California Press, 1983), 76.

21. Hochschild, *The Managed Heart*, 57.

22. Herman, *Trauma and Recovery*, 165.

23. These questions were asked before judges or judicial demeanor was raised in the interviews; women had only been told that the interview concerned their experiences with restraining orders.

24. Evan Stark and Anne H. Flitcraft, "Personal Power and Institutional Victimization: Treating the Dual Trauma of Woman Battering," in *Post-Traumatic Therapy and Victims of Violence*, edited by Frank M. Ochberg (New York: Brunner/Mazel, 1988), 116–117.

25. Stark and Flitcraft, "Personal Power and Institutional Victimization," 117.

26. Erving Goffman, *Stigma: Notes on the Management of Spoiled Identity* (New York: Touchstone/Simon and Schuster, 1986 [1963]), 3.

27. Patricia Hill Collins, *Black Feminist Thought: Knowledge, Consciousness, and the Politics of Empowerment* (Boston: Unwin Hyman, 1990).

28. Herman, *Trauma and Recovery*, 1.

29. Battered Women Fighting Back, "Victims Murdered Due to Domestic Violence in 1992" (Boston: Battered Women Fighting Back [now called Peace at Home], 1993).

30. Herman, *Trauma and Recovery*, 57. Herman uses this phrase in a description of rape, but it also applies to battering.

31. Kathleen J. Ferraro and John M. Johnson, "How Women Experience Battering: The Process of Victimization," *Social Problems* 30, no. 3 (1983): 325–339.

32. Nazarro v. Justices of the Southern Essex Division of the District Court & Richard Jones, Supreme Judicial Court No. 86-149, December 17, 1986.

33. Massachusetts General Laws, ch. 209A, sec. 6c.

34. Nancy E. Isaac, Donald Cochran, Marjorie E. Brown, and Sandra L. Adams, "Men Who Batter: Profile from a Restraining Order Database," *Archives of Family Medicine* 3 (1994): 50–54.

35. Molly Chaudhuri and Kathleen Daly, "Do Restraining Orders Help? Bat-

tered Women's Experience with Male Violence and Legal Process," in *Domestic Violence: The Changing Criminal Justice Response,* edited by Eve Buzawa and Carl Buzawa (Westport, Conn.: Auburn House, 1992), 246.

36. Arlie Russell Hochschild (with Anne Machung), *The Second Shift: Working Parents and the Revolution at Home* (New York: Viking, 1989), 221.

Chapter 8

1. Eileen McNamara, "Who Judges the Judges?," Ford Hall Forum, Faneuil Hall, Boston, Mass., October 20, 1988.

2. Andrew Klein, personal communication, 1993.

3. Andrew R. Klein, "Re-Abuse in a Population of Court-Restrained Male Batterers: Why Restraining Orders Don't Work," in *Do Arrests and Restraining Orders Work?,* edited by Eve S. Buzawa and Carl G. Buzawa (Thousand Oaks, Calif.: Sage, 1996), 195; Donald Cochran, "Over 8,500 Domestic Restraining Orders Filed Since September in Massachusetts" (Boston: Office of the Commissioner of Probation, 1992); Nancy E. Isaac, Donald Cochran, Marjorie E. Brown, and Sandra L. Adams, "Men Who Batter: Profile from a Restraining Order Database," *Archives of Family Medicine* 3 (1994): 52.

4. Carol Smart, *Feminism and the Power of Law* (London: Routledge, 1989), 144.

5. Peter S. Canellos, "Angry and Alone, America's Poorest Drift Further Away," *Boston Globe,* February 6, 1994, 1.

6. Canellos, "Angry and Alone," 24–25.

7. Ellen Pence and Michael Paymar, *Educational Groups for Men Who Batter: The Duluth Model* (New York: Springer, 1993), 2.

8. Ellen Pence, "In Our Best Interest: A Process for Personal and Social Change" (Minneapolis, Minn.: Minnesota Program Development, 1987), 10.

9. Jill Davies, Eleanor Lyon, and Diane Monti-Catania, *Safety Planning for Battered Women: Complex Lives, Difficult Choices* (Thousand Oaks, Calif.: Sage, 1998), 2.

10. Davies et al., *Safety Planning for Battered Women,* 3.

11. Davies et al., *Safety Planning for Battered Women,* 6.

12. Domestic Violence Court Advocacy Research Project, "A Guide to Domestic Violence Court Advocacy in Massachusetts" (Boston: Massachusetts Office of Victim Assistance, 1993), AI/VI–VII.

13. Linda Gordon, *Heroes of Their Own Lives: The Politics and History of Family Violence* (New York: Viking, 1988), 285.

14. Available from the Domestic Violence Project, Inc., 6308 8th Avenue, Kenosha, WI 53143. Along with the Duluth "Power and Control Wheel," the medical wheels served as inspiration for the judicial authority wheels.

15. Michelle Fine and Lois Weis, *The Unknown City: The Lives of Poor and Working-Class Young Adults* (Boston: Beacon Press, 1998), 154–160, 170–174.

16. Canellos, "Angry and Alone."

17. Michael Tonry, *Malign Neglect: Race, Crime, and Punishment in America* (New York: Oxford University Press, 1995); Jerome G. Miller, *Search and Destroy: African-American Males in the Criminal Justice System* (Cambridge: Cambridge University Press, 1996); Elliot Currie, *Crime and Punishment in America* (New York: Metropolitan Books, 1998).

18. Human Rights Watch, *All Too Familiar: Sexual Abuse of Women in U.S. State Prisons* (New York: Human Rights Watch, 1996).

19. James Gilligan, *Violence: Our Deadly Epidemic and Its Causes* (New York: Grosset/Putnam, 1996); Terry A. Kupers, "Trauma and Its Sequelae in Male Prisoners: Effects of Confinement, Overcrowding, and Diminished Services," *American Journal of Orthopsychiatry* 66, no. 2 (April 1996): 189–196.

20. bell hooks, *Feminist Theory: From Margin to Center* (Boston: South End Press, 1984).

21. Massachusetts Supreme Judicial Court, "Gender Bias Study of the Court System in Massachusetts" (Boston: Supreme Judicial Court, 1989).

22. John H. Kennedy, "SJC Reprimands Somerville Judge, Mild Sanction Draws Fire from Heffernan's Critics," *Boston Globe*, September 29, 1988, 36.

23. "Judge King's Wrist-Slap Censure," *Boston Globe*, March 30, 1991, 18.

24. Susan Caringella-MacDonald, "Parallels and Pitfalls: The Aftermath of Legal Reform for Sexual Assault, Marital Rape, and Domestic Violence Victims," *Journal of Interpersonal Violence* 3, no. 2 (June 1988): 186; Rebecca Emerson Dobash and Russell P. Dobash, *Women, Violence, and Social Change* (London: Routledge, 1992), 212.

25. Letter to the editor, *Massachusetts Lawyers Weekly*, October 25, 1993, 11.

Appendix

1. Massachusetts Supreme Judicial Court, "Annual Report of the Massachusetts Trial Court," Fiscal Year 1992, 22, 23.

2. National Council of Juvenile and Family Court Judges, "Family Violence: State-of-the-Art Court Programs" (Reno, Nev.: National Council of Juvenile and Family Court Judges, 1992).

3. Massachusetts Trial Court, "A Guide to Public Access to District Court Records" (Boston: Massachusetts Trial Court, 1990), 26.

4. Maureen Mileski, "Courtroom Encounters: An Observational Study of a Lower Criminal Court," *Law and Society Review* 5, no. 4 (May 1971): 473–537.

5. Patricia Hill Collins, *Black Feminist Thought: Knowledge, Consciousness, and the Politics of Empowerment* (Boston: Unwin Hyman, 1990), 187.

References

Books and Periodicals

Adams, David. "Counseling Men Who Batter: A Profeminist Analysis of Five Treatment Models." In *Feminist Perspectives on Wife Abuse*, edited by Kersti Yllö and Michele Bograd, 176–199. Newbury Park, Calif.: Sage, 1988.

———. "Stages of Anti-sexist Awareness and Change for Men Who Batter." In *Family Violence*, edited by L. Dickstein and C. Nadelson, 61–98. Washington, D.C.: Appi Press, 1988.

Aldarondo, Etiony, Dennis Tyrell, and Erika Shore. "Uses and Misuses of the Concepts of Ethnicity and Race in Wife Assault Research." Paper presented at the Fifth International Family Violence Research Conference, University of New Hampshire, Durham, New Hampshire, June 30, 1997.

Allard, Mary Ann, Randy Albelda, Mary Ellen Colten, and Carol Cosenza. "In Harm's Way? Domestic Violence, AFDC Receipt, and Welfare Reform in Massachusetts." Report from the University of Massachusetts Boston. Boston: University of Massachusetts, 1997.

Anderson, David C. *Crime and the Politics of Hysteria*. New York: Times Books, 1995.

Astrachan, Anthony. *How Men Feel: Their Response to Women's Demands for Equality and Power*. New York: Anchor Press/Doubleday, 1986.

Aucoin, Don. "Battering Bills Stuck on the Hill." *Boston Globe*, January 2, 1994, 1.

Bachman, Ronet, and Linda E. Saltzman. "Violence Against Women: Estimates from the Redesigned Survey." Special Report of the Bureau of

Justice Statistics. Washington, D.C.: U.S. Department of Justice, August 1995.

Bass, Alison. "Domestic Violence: Roots Go Deep." *Boston Globe*, June 5, 1992, 1.

Bassuk, Ellen L., Linda F. Weintraub, John C. Buckner, Angela Browne, Amy Solomon, and Shari S. Bassuk. "The Characteristics and Needs of Sheltered Homeless and Low-Income Housed Mothers." *Journal of the American Medical Association* 276, no. 8 (August 28, 1996): 640–646.

Battered Women Fighting Back. "Victims Murdered Due to Domestic Violence in 1992." Boston: Battered Women Fighting Back [now called Peace at Home], 1993.

Battered Women's Working Group. "Violent Crime in the Family: Enforcement of the Massachusetts Abuse Prevention Law." Boston: Governor's Statewide Anti-Crime Council, 1985.

Black, Donald. "Crime as Social Control." *American Sociological Review* 48, no. 1 (1983): 34–45.

Blumer, Herbert. "Social Problems as Collective Behavior." *Social Problems* 18, no. 3 (1971): 298–306.

Bohm, Robert M., and Keith N. Haley. *Introduction to Criminal Justice*. Glencoe: McGraw-Hill, 1997.

Bonilla-Santiago, Gloria. "Latina Battered Women: Barriers to Service Delivery and Cultural Considerations." In *Helping Battered Women: New Perspectives and Remedies*, edited by Albert R. Roberts, 229–234. New York: Oxford University Press, 1996.

Boston Foundation. "In the Midst of Plenty: A Profile of Boston and Its Poor." Boston: Boston Foundation, 1989.

Bowker, Lee H. *Beating Wife-Beating*. Lexington, Mass.: Lexington Books, 1983.

Brandwein, Ruth. "The Use of Public Welfare by Family Violence Victims: Implications of New Federal Welfare 'Reform.'" Paper presented at the Fifth International Family Violence Research Conference, University of New Hampshire, Durham, New Hampshire, July 1, 1997.

Browne, Angela. "Reshaping the Rhetoric: The Nexus of Violence, Poverty, and Minority Status in the Lives of Women and Children in the United States." *Georgetown Journal on Fighting Poverty* 3, no. 1 (Fall 1995): 17–23.

———. *When Battered Women Kill*. New York: Free Press, 1987.

Browne, Angela, and Shari S. Bassuk. "Intimate Violence in the Lives of

Homeless and Poor Housed Women." *American Journal of Orthopsy-chiatry* 67, no. 2 (April 1997): 261–278.

Bunch, Charlotte, and Roxanna Carrillo. "Gender Violence: A Development and Human Rights Issue." New Brunswick, N.J.: Center for Women's Global Leadership, Douglass College, Rutgers University, 1991.

Butterfield, Fox. "Flurry of Rumors in a Murder Case." *New York Times*, January 8, 1990, A12.

Buzawa, Eve S., and Carl G. Buzawa. *Domestic Violence: The Criminal Justice Response*. 2d ed. Thousand Oaks, Calif.: Sage, 1996.

———, eds. "The Impact of Arrest on Domestic Assault." Special issue of the *American Behavioral Scientist* 36, no. 5 (1993).

"A Call for Help for Jane Doe." *Boston Globe*, June 30, 1992, 14.

Canellos, Peter S. "Angry and Alone, America's Poorest Drift Further Away." *Boston Globe*, February 6, 1994, 1, 24–25.

Carby, Hazel V. " 'On the Threshold of Woman's Era': Lynching, Empire, and Sexuality in Black Feminist Theory." *Critical Inquiry* 12, no. 1 (1985): 262–277.

Caringella-MacDonald, Susan. "Parallels and Pitfalls: The Aftermath of Legal Reform for Sexual Assault, Marital Rape, and Domestic Violence Victims." *Journal of Interpersonal Violence* 3, no. 2 (June 1988): 174–189.

Carrillo, Roxanna. *Battered Dreams: Violence Against Women as an Obstacle to Development*. New York: UNIFEM/United Nations Development Fund for Women, 1992.

Castro, Diego O. " 'Hot Blood and Easy Virtue': Mass Media and the Making of Racist Latino/a Stereotypes." In *Images of Color, Images of Crime: Readings*, edited by Coramae Richey Mann and Marjorie S. Zatz, 134–144. Los Angeles: Roxbury, 1998.

Cazenave, Noel A., and Murray A. Straus. "Race, Class, Network Embeddedness, and Family Violence: A Search for Potent Support Systems." *Journal of Comparative Family Studies* 10, no. 3 (1979): 281–300.

Chambliss, William J. "Crime Control and Ethnic Minorities: Legitimizing Racial Oppression by Creating Moral Panics." In *Ethnicity, Race, and Crime*, edited by Darnell F. Hawkins, 235–258. Albany: State University of New York Press, 1995.

Chapman, Jane Roberts. "Violence Against Women as a Violation of Human Rights." *Social Justice* 17, no. 2 (1990): 54–70.

Chaudhuri, Molly, and Kathleen Daly. "Do Restraining Orders Help?

Battered Women's Experience with Male Violence and Legal Process."
In *Domestic Violence: The Changing Criminal Justice Response*, edited by Eve Buzawa and Carl Buzawa, 227–252. Westport, Conn.: Auburn House, 1992.

Clark, Dorothy A. "Media Coverage of Poverty in Boston's Black Community." In *Perspectives of Poverty in Boston's Black Community*,
edited by James Jennings, 49–61. Boston: Boston Persistent Poverty
Project, 1992.

Cobbe, Frances Power. "Wife Torture in England." In *The Politics of
Woman Killing*, edited by Jill Radford and Diana E. H. Russell, 46–52.
New York: Twayne, 1992.

Cochran, Donald. "Over 8,500 Domestic Restraining Orders Filed Since
September in Massachusetts." Boston: Office of the Commissioner of
Probation, 1992.

Cole, Johnnetta B. "Commonalities and Differences." In *All American
Women: Lines That Divide, Ties That Bind*, 1–30. New York: Free
Press, 1986.

Coleman, Sandy. "Judges on Call to Stem Violence." *Boston Globe*, January 24, 1993, 1.

Collins, Patricia Hill. *Black Feminist Thought: Knowledge, Consciousness, and the Politics of Empowerment*. Boston: Unwin Hyman, 1990.

Crenshaw, Kimberlé Williams. "Mapping the Margins: Intersectionality,
Identity Politics, and Violence Against Women of Color." In *The Public Nature of Private Violence*, edited by Martha Albertson Fineman
and Roxanne Mykitiuk, 93–118. New York: Routledge, 1994.

———. "Race, Gender, and Violence Against Women." In *Family Matters: Readings on Family Lives and the Law*, edited by Martha
Minow, 230–232. New York: New Press, 1993.

Curcio, P. "The Passaic County Study of AFDC Recipients in a Welfare
to Work Program: A Preliminary Analysis." Passaic County, N.J.: Passaic County Board of Social Services, 1996.

Currie, Elliot. *Crime and Punishment in America*. New York: Metropolitan Books, 1998.

Davies, Jill, Eleanor Lyon, and Diane Monti-Catania. *Safety Planning for
Battered Women: Complex Lives, Difficult Choices*. Thousand Oaks,
Calif.: Sage, 1998.

Davis, Angela. "We Do Not Consent: Violence Against Women in a Racist Society." In *Women, Culture, and Politics*, 35–52. New York: Vintage, 1990.

Devlin, Bernie, ed. *Intelligence and Success: Is It All in the Genes? Scientists Respond to the Bell Curve.* New York: Springer Verlag, 1997.

Diamant, Anita. "How the Quincy District Court Protects Battered Women." *Boston Globe Magazine,* October 11, 1992, 14–15, 22–29.

Dickens, William T., Thomas J. Kane, and Charles Schultze. *Does the Bell Curve Ring True?* Washington, D.C.: Brookings Institute, 1997.

Dobash, Rebecca Emerson, and Russell P. Dobash. "The Nature and Antecedents of Violent Events." *British Journal of Criminology* 24, no. 3 (1984): 269–288.

———. "The Negotiation of Daily Life and the 'Provocation' of Violence: A Patriarchal Concept in Support of the Wife Beater." Paper presented at the Ninth World Congress of Sociology, Uppsala, Sweden, 1978.

———. *Violence Against Wives: A Case Against the Patriarchy.* New York: Free Press, 1979.

———. *Women, Violence, and Social Change.* New York: Routledge, 1992.

Domestic Violence Court Advocacy Research Project. "A Guide to Domestic Violence Court Advocacy in Massachusetts." Boston: Massachusetts Office of Victim Assistance, 1993.

Donziger, Steven R., ed. *The Real War on Crime: The Report of the National Criminal Justice Commission.* New York: HarperPerennial, 1996.

Dutton, Mary Ann. *Empowering and Healing the Battered Woman: A Model for Assessment and Intervention.* New York: Springer, 1992.

Edleson, Jeffrey L., and Richard M. Tolman. *Intervention for Men Who Batter: An Ecological Approach.* Newbury Park, Calif.: Sage, 1992.

Elikann, Peter T. *The Tough-on-Crime Myth: Real Solutions to Cut Crime.* New York: Plenum, 1996.

Ellis, Desmond. "Woman Abuse Among Separated and Divorced Women: The Relevance of Social Support." In *Intimate Violence: Interdisciplinary Perspectives,* edited by Emilio C. Viano, 177–189. Washington, D.C.: Hemisphere, 1992.

Ellis, Desmond, and Walter S. DeKeseredy. "Marital Status and Woman Abuse: The DAD Model." *International Journal of Sociology of the Family* 19 (Autumn 1989): 67–87.

Ellison, Ralph. *Invisible Man.* New York: Vintage, 1972.

Emerge. "Violent and Controlling Behavior Toward Children." Cambridge, Mass.: Emerge, A Counseling and Educational Program for Abusive Men, n.d.

Emerson, Robert M. *Judging Delinquents: Context and Process in Juvenile Court.* Chicago: Aldine, 1969.

Enloe, Cynthia. *Does Khaki Become You? The Militarization of Women's Lives.* Boston: South End Press, 1983.

Fagan, Jeffrey. "The Criminalization of Domestic Violence: Promises and Limits." National Institute of Justice Research Report. Washington, D.C.: U.S. Department of Justice, January 1996.

Faith, Karlene. "Justice Where Art Thou? And Do We Care? Feminist Perspectives on Justice for Women in Canada." In *Readings in Critical Criminology*, edited by Ronald Hinch, 84–108. Scarborough, Ontario: Prentice-Hall Canada, 1994.

Farley, Reynolds. "Homicide Trends in the United States." In *Homicide Among Black Americans*, edited by Darnell F. Hawkins, 13–27. Lanham, Md.: University Press of America, 1986.

Farrell, John Aloysius. "Nixon Was Known to Be a Wife-Abuser, a Journalist Alleges." *Boston Globe*, April 7, 1998, A13.

Feagin, Joe R., and Hernán Vera. *White Racism.* New York: Routledge, 1995.

Ferraro, Kathleen J., and John M. Johnson. "How Women Experience Battering: The Process of Victimization." *Social Problems* 30, no. 3 (1983): 325–339.

Fine, Michelle. "Unearthing Contradictions: An Essay Inspired by *Women and Male Violence.*" *Feminist Studies* 11, no. 2 (1985): 391–407.

Fine, Michelle, and Lois Weis. *The Unknown City: The Lives of Poor and Working-Class Young Adults.* Boston: Beacon Press, 1998.

Finn, Peter. "Civil Protection Orders: A Flawed Opportunity for Intervention." In *Woman Battering: Policy Responses*, edited by Michael Steinman, 155–190. Highland Heights, Ky.: Academy of Criminal Justice Sciences, 1991.

Fischer, Claude S., et al., eds. *Inequality by Design: Cracking the Bell Curve Myth.* Princeton: Princeton University Press, 1996.

Flannery, Judge Harold. "Gender Bias in the Courtroom and Judicial Intervention." *Boston Bar Journal* (July-August 1989): 21.

Foucault, Michel. *The Use of Pleasure: History of Sexuality.* Vol. 2. New York: Vintage, 1980.

Franzway, Suzanne, Dianne Court, and R. W. Connell. *Staking a Claim: Feminism, Bureaucracy, and the State.* Sydney: Allen and Unwin, 1989.

Fraser, Steven, ed. *The Bell Curve Wars: Race, Intelligence, and the Future of America.* New York: Basic Books, 1995.

Frieze, Irene Hanson, and Angela Browne. "Violence in Marriage." In *Family Violence,* edited by Lloyd Ohlin and Michael Tonry, 163–218. Chicago: University of Chicago Press, 1989.

Gelles, Richard J., and Murray A. Straus. *Intimate Violence.* New York: Simon and Schuster, 1988.

Giddings, Paula. *When and Where I Enter: The Impact of Black Women on Race and Sex in America.* New York: William Morrow, 1984 .

Gilens, Martin. "Race and Poverty in America: Public Misperceptions and the American News Media." *Public Opinion Quarterly* 60 (1996): 515–541.

Gillespie, Cynthia K. *Justifiable Homicide: Battered Women, Self-Defense, and the Law.* Columbus: Ohio State University Press, 1989.

Gilligan, James. *Violence: Our Deadly Epidemic and Its Causes.* New York: Grosset/Putnam, 1996.

Glauberman, Naomi, and Russell Jacoby, eds. *The Bell Curve Debate: History, Documents, Opinions.* New York: Times Books, 1995.

Goffman, Erving. "The Nature of Deference and Demeanor." In *Interaction Ritual: Essays on Face-to-Face Behavior,* 47–95. New York: Pantheon, 1982 [1967].

———. *Stigma: Notes on the Management of Spoiled Identity.* New York: Touchstone/Simon and Schuster, 1986 [1963].

Gondolf, Edward W. *Men Who Batter: An Integrated Approach for Stopping Wife Abuse.* Holmes Beach, Fla.: Learning Publications, 1985.

Gondolf, Edward L., and Ellen R. Fisher. *Battered Women as Survivors: An Alternative to Treating Learned Helplessness.* Lexington, Mass.: Lexington Books, 1988.

Gondolf, Edward W., Joyce McWilliams, Barbara Hart, and Jane Stuehling. "Court Response to Petitions for Civil Protection Orders." *Journal of Interpersonal Violence* 9, no. 4 (1994): 503–517.

Goodman, Ellen. "Simpson Case Divides Us by Race." *Boston Globe,* July 7, 1994, 73.

Gordon, Linda. *Heroes of Their Own Lives: The Politics and History of Family Violence.* New York: Viking, 1988.

Gorov, Lynda, and John Ellement. "Most Women's Deaths Laid to Intimates." *Boston Globe*, January 3, 1993, 21, 25.

Grau, Janice, Jeffrey Fagan, and Sandra Wexler. "Restraining Orders for Battered Women: Issues of Access and Efficacy." *Women and Politics* 4, no. 3 (1985): 13–28.

Hampton, Robert L., ed. *Black Family Violence: Current Research and Theory.* Lexington, Mass.: Lexington Books, 1991.

———. *Violence in the Black Family: Correlates and Consequences.* Lexington, Mass.: Lexington Books, 1987.

Hampton, Robert L., and Richard J. Gelles. "Violence Toward Black Women in a Nationally Representative Sample of Black Families." *Journal of Comparative Family Studies* 25, no. 1 (Spring 1994): 105–120.

Hanmer, Jalna, Jill Radford, and Elizabeth A. Stanko, eds. *Women, Policing, and Male Violence: International Perspectives.* London: Routledge, 1989.

Harrell, Adele, Barbara Smith, and Lisa Newmark. "Court Processing and the Effects of Restraining Orders for Domestic Violence Victims." Washington, D.C.: Urban Institute, 1993.

Hart, Barbara J. "Safety for Women: Monitoring Batterers' Programs." Harrisburg, Pa.: Pennsylvania Coalition Against Domestic Violence, 1988.

———. "State Codes on Domestic Violence: Analysis, Commentary, and Recommendations." *Juvenile and Family Court Journal* 43, no. 4 (1990): 3–80.

Hart, Jordana. "Courts Issued More Restraint Orders in 1991, Rise in Violence Shows Ineffectiveness." *Boston Globe*, February 16, 1991, 1.

Hawkins, Darnell F. "Devalued Lives and Racial Stereotypes: Ideological Barriers to the Prevention of Family Violence Among Blacks." In *Violence in the Black Family: Correlates and Consequences*, edited by Robert L. Hampton, 189–205. Lexington, Mass.: Lexington Books, 1987.

———, ed. *Ethnicity, Race, and Crime.* Albany: State University of New York Press, 1995.

Hechinger, John. "Domestic Violence Difficult to Prevent: Legal Orders Called Largely Ineffective." *Boston Globe*, August 17, 1986, 1.

Herman, Judith Lewis. *Trauma and Recovery.* New York: Basic Books, 1992.

Hernandez, Peggy. "Domestic Violence on Rise in Mass., Advocates Link

Increase in Battering to Economy." *Boston Globe,* November 29, 1991, 1.

———. "Harshbarger Calls for More Sensitivity to Battering Victims." *Boston Globe,* December 19, 1991, 41.

Herrnstein, Richard J., and Charles Murray. *The Bell Curve: Intelligence and Class Structure in American Life.* New York: Free Press, 1994.

Hochschild, Arlie Russell. "The Economy of Gratitude." In *The Family Experience: A Reader in Cultural Diversity,* edited by Mark Hutter, 499–515. New York: Macmillan, 1991.

———. "Emotion Work, Feeling Rules, and Social Structure." *American Journal of Sociology* 85, no. 3 (1979): 551–575.

———. *The Managed Heart: Commercialization of Human Feeling.* Berkeley: University of California Press, 1983.

———. "The Sociology of Feeling and Emotion: Selected Possibilities." In *Another Voice: Feminist Perspectives on Social Life and Social Science,* edited by Marcia Millman and Rosabeth Moss Kanter, 280–307. Garden City, N.Y.: Anchor, 1975.

Hochschild, Arlie Russell, with Anne Machung. *The Second Shift: Working Parents and the Revolution at Home.* New York: Viking, 1989.

hooks, bell. *Feminist Theory: From Margin to Center.* Boston: South End Press, 1984.

Horton, Anne L., Kyriacos M. Simonidis, and Lucy L. Simonidis. "Legal Remedies for Spousal Abuse: Victim Characteristics, Expectations, and Satisfaction." *Journal of Family Violence* 2, no. 3 (1987): 265–279.

Human Rights Watch. *All Too Familiar: Sexual Abuse of Women in U.S. State Prisons.* New York: Human Rights Watch, 1996.

Hunt, Jennifer. " 'Abuse Is a Choice; He Didn't Have to Abuse Me.' " *Boston Sunday Globe,* July 27, 1997, F1–F2.

"In Memoriam." *Boston Globe,* December 31, 1993, 18.

"In Memoriam." *Boston Globe,* December 31, 1994, 14.

"In Memoriam." *Boston Globe,* December 31, 1995, 84.

"In Memoriam." *Boston Globe,* December 31, 1996, A14.

Irwin, John, and James Austin. *It's About Time: America's Imprisonment Binge.* 2d ed. Belmont, Calif.: Wadsworth, 1997.

Isaac, Nancy E., Donald Cochran, Marjorie E. Brown, and Sandra L. Adams. "Men Who Batter: Profile from a Restraining Order Database." *Archives of Family Medicine* 3 (1994): 50–54.

Jaimes, M. Annette, and Theresa Halsey. "American Indian Women: At the Center of Indigenous Resistance in North America." In *The State of Native America: Genocide, Colonization, and Resistance*, edited by M. Annette Jaimes, 311–344. Boston: South End Press, 1992.

Jones, Alex S. "Bias and Recklessness Are Charged in Boston Reporting of Stuart Slaying." *New York Times*, January 14, 1990, 21.

"Judge King's Wrist-Slap Censure." *Boston Globe*, March 30, 1991, 18.

"Judicial Accountability." *Boston Globe*, October 17, 1986, 18.

Kanuha, Valli. "Domestic Violence, Racism, and the Battered Women's Movement in the United States." In *Future Interventions with Battered Women and Their Families*, edited by Jeffrey L. Edleson and Zvi C. Eisikovits, 34–50. Thousand Oaks, Calif.: Sage, 1996.

Kasinsky, Renée Goldsmith. "Patrolling the Facts: Media, Cops, and Crime." In *Media, Process, and the Social Construction of Crime*, edited by Gregg Barak, 203–234. New York: Garland, 1994.

Kelly, Liz. *Surviving Sexual Violence*. Minneapolis: University of Minnesota Press, 1988.

Kennedy, John H. "SJC Reprimands Somerville Judge, Mild Sanction Draws Fire from Heffernan's Critics." *Boston Globe*, September 29, 1988, 36.

Kincheloe, Joe L., Shirley R. Steinberg, and Aaron D. Gresson, eds. *The Bell Curve Examined*. New York: St. Martin's Press, 1996.

Kindleberger, Richard. "Reassigned Judge Credited with Easing of Case Backlog." *Boston Globe*, April 21, 1989, 60.

Klein, Andrew R. "Re-Abuse in a Population of Court-Restrained Male Batterers: Why Restraining Orders Don't Work." In *Do Arrests and Restraining Orders Work?*, edited by Eve S. Buzawa and Carl G. Buzawa, 192–213. Thousand Oaks, Calif.: Sage, 1996.

Kopkind, Andrew. "Race, Class, and Murder in Boston." *The Nation*, February 5, 1990, 149, 153–154.

Koss, Mary P., Christine A. Gidycz, and Nadine Wisniewski. "The Scope of Rape: Incidence and Prevalence of Sexual Aggression and Victimization in a National Sample of Higher Education Students." *Journal of Consulting and Clinical Psychology* 55, no. 2 (1987): 162–170.

Kramer, Albert L. "Statement to the Massachusetts Joint Committee on the Judiciary: Written Testimony." Quincy, Mass.: Quincy District Court, 1992.

———. "Statement to the Women's Legislative Caucus Hearing on Domestic Violence, March 2: Oral Testimony." Quincy, Mass.: Quincy District Court, 1992.

Kupers, Terry A. "Trauma and Its Sequelae in Male Prisoners: Effects of Confinement, Overcrowding, and Diminished Services." *American Journal of Orthopsychiatry* 66, no. 2 (April 1996): 189–196.

LaFree, Gary. "Race and Crime Trends in the United States, 1946–1990." In *Ethnicity, Race, and Crime*, edited by Darnell F. Hawkins, 169–193. Albany: State University of New York Press, 1995.

———. *Rape and Criminal Justice: The Social Construction of Sexual Assault*. Belmont, Calif.: Wadsworth, 1989.

Langner, Paul. "Dunn Given Life Term in Wife's Slaying." *Boston Globe*, May 20, 1987, 1.

"Legal Relief for Assaulted Wives." *Woman's Journal*, January 11, 1879, 12.

Lerman, Lisa G. "Prosecution of Wife Beaters: Institutional Obstacles and Innovations." In *Violence in the Home: Interdisciplinary Perspectives*, edited by Mary Lystad, 250–295. New York: Brunner/Mazel, 1986.

———. "State Legislation on Domestic Violence." *Response* 4, no. 7 (1981): 1–18.

Letter to the editor. *Massachusetts Lawyers Weekly*, October 25, 1993, 11.

Lifton, Robert Jay. *Home from the War: Learning from Vietnam Veterans*. Boston: Beacon Press, 1992.

Lin, Margaretta Wan Ling, and Cheng Imm Tan. "Holding Up More Than Half the Heavens: Domestic Violence in Our Communities, A Call for Justice." In *The State of Asian America: Activism and Resistance in the 1990s*, edited by Karin Aguilar-San Juan, 321–334. Boston: South End Press, 1994.

Lloyd, Susan. "The Effects of Violence on Women's Employment." Paper presented at the Eighteenth Annual Research Conference, Pittsburgh, Pa., November 1996.

Lockhart, Lettie L. "Spousal Violence: A Cross-Racial Perspective." In *Black Family Violence: Current Research and Theory*, edited by Robert L. Hampton, 85–101. Lexington, Mass.: Lexington Books, 1991.

Locy, Toni, and Sean P. Murphy. "Presiding Judge Dolan Says He'll Quit Dorchester Bench." *Boston Globe*, April 14, 1994, 32.

MacKinnon, Catharine A. "Violence Against Women: A Perspective." *Aegis: Magazine on Ending Violence Against Women* 33 (1982): 51–57.

Mahoney, Martha R. "Legal Issues of Battered Women: Redefining the Issue of Separation." *Michigan Law Review* 90, no. 1 (1991): 1–94.

Manly, Howard, and Jean Caldwell. "Domestic Rampage: Police Say Estranged Boyfriend Killed Three, Then Self, in Chicopee." *Boston Globe*, September 30, 1992, 1.

Margaronis, Maria. "Fright Knight: Race, Sex, and Charles Stuart's White Lie." *Village Voice*, January 30, 1990, 45.

Massachusetts Commission on Judicial Conduct. "Annual Report." Boston: Commission on Judicial Conduct, 1989.

Massachusetts Department of Public Health. "Homicide in Massachusetts: Trends and Characteristics 1978–1993." 2d ed. Boston: Massachusetts Department of Public Health, 1995.

Massachusetts Supreme Judicial Court. "Annual Report of the Massachusetts Court System." Fiscal Years 1981–1996. Boston: Supreme Judicial Court, 1982–1997.

Massachusetts Supreme Judicial Court. "Equal Justice: Eliminating the Barriers." Final Report of the Commission to Study Racial and Ethnic Bias in the Courts. Boston: Supreme Judicial Court, 1994.

Massachusetts Supreme Judicial Court. "Gender Bias Study of the Court System in Massachusetts." Boston: Supreme Judicial Court, 1989.

Massachusetts Supreme Judicial Court, Public Information Office. "Number of Judges in Massachusetts Courts by Court, Gender, and Race." Boston: Supreme Judicial Court, 1994.

Massachusetts Trial Court. "A Guide to Public Access to District Court Records." Salem, Mass.: Administrative Office of the District Court, 1990.

Massachusetts Trial Court. "Standards of Judicial Practice: Abuse Prevention Proceedings." Boston: Massachusetts Trial Court, 1986.

Massey, Douglas S., and Nancy A. Denton. *American Apartheid*. Cambridge: Harvard University Press, 1993.

McCabe, Bruce. "A Forum Against Domestic Violence." *Boston Globe*, June 28, 1992, TV Week, 2.

McNamara, Eileen. "Chief Judge to Probe in Somerville." *Boston Globe*, October 2, 1986, 1.

———. "Dorchester Judge Stripped of Right to Hear Most Cases." *Boston Globe*, November 14, 1986, 1.

———. "Dunn to Face Murder Charges on Return to Mass. Today." *Boston Globe*, November 18, 1986, 38.

———. "Friends Say Charges Malign Judge, Abuse-Case Controversy Seethes Around 'A Sensitive Person.' " *Boston Globe*, October 5, 1986, 1.

———. "Judge Criticized After Woman's Death." *Boston Globe*, September 21, 1986, 1.

———. "Judge Is Viewed as Erring on Abuse Law." *Boston Globe*, September 24, 1986, 13.

———. "Judge's Action Questioned, Prior Complaint Recounted." *Boston Globe*, September 27, 1986, 1.

———. "Judge Tempone Said to Top Complaint List." *Boston Globe*, November 2, 1986, 18.

———. "Justice Zoll: Caught in Middle, Tries to Balance Concern for Victims, Judges." *Boston Globe*, December 23, 1986, 1.

———. " 'No Quick Fix' in Abuse Cases, Judge Rules." *Boston Globe*, November 13, 1986, 1, 18.

———. "Panel to Look for Sex Bias in Courts." *Boston Globe*, December 19, 1986, 25.

———. "Still No Order in the Court." *Boston Globe*, June 14, 1987, 87.

———. "Two Judges Criticized in Review by Zoll." *Boston Globe*, March 11, 1987, 1.

———. "Two Judges Withdraw from Cases, Won't Hear Domestic Abuse Matters Pending Probe." *Boston Globe*, October 15, 1986, 1.

———. "Who Judges the Judges?" Ford Hall Forum, Faneuil Hall, Boston, Mass., October 20, 1988.

Medoff, Peter, and Holly Sklar. *Streets of Hope: The Fall and Rise of an Urban Neighborhood*. Boston: South End Press, 1994.

Meier, Joan. "Battered Justice." *Washington Monthly* (May 1987): 37–45.

Mileski, Maureen. "Courtroom Encounters: An Observational Study of a Lower Criminal Court." *Law and Society Review* 5, no. 4 (1971): 527.

Miller, Jerome G. *Search and Destroy: African-American Males in the Criminal Justice System*. Cambridge: Cambridge University Press, 1996.

Miller, S. M. "Equality, Morality, and the Health of Democracy." In *Myths About the Powerless*, edited by M. Brinton Lykes, Ali Banuazizi, Ramsay Liem, and Michael Morris, 17–33. Philadelphia: Temple University Press, 1996.

Moore, Angela. "Intimate Violence: Does Socioeconomic Status Matter?" In *Violence Between Intimate Partners: Patterns, Causes, and Effects*, edited by Albert P. Cardarelli, 90–100. Boston: Allyn and Bacon, 1997.

Nader, Laura. "Up the Anthropologist: Perspectives Gained from Studying Up." In *Reinventing Anthropology*, edited by Dell Hynes, 284–311. New York: Pantheon, 1972.

National Council of Juvenile and Family Court Judges. "Family Violence: State-of-the-Art Court Programs." Reno, Nev.: National Council of Juvenile and Family Court Judges, 1992.

NOW Legal Defense and Education Fund. "The G.O.P. Welfare Bills—H.R. 3507 and S. 1795—Hurt Battered Women." Report of the National Task Force on Violence Against Women, July 17, 1996.

Omi, Michael, and Howard Winant. *Racial Formation in the United States: From the 1960s to the 1990s*. 2d ed. New York: Routledge, 1994.

Pence, Ellen. "In Our Best Interest: A Process for Personal and Social Change." Minneapolis, Minn.: Minnesota Program Development, 1987.

Pence, Ellen, and Michael Paymar. *Education Groups for Men Who Batter: The Duluth Model*. New York: Springer, 1993.

Peterson del Mar, David. *What Trouble I Have Seen: A History of Violence Against Wives*. Cambridge, Mass.: Harvard University Press, 1996.

Philbin, Austin T. "Domestic Violence and Abuse in Massachusetts: A Survey." *New England Law Review* 24 (Spring 1990): 713–725.

Pleck, Elizabeth. *Domestic Tyranny*. New York: Oxford University Press, 1987.

———. "Feminist Responses to 'Crimes Against Women,' 1868–1896." *Signs: Journal of Women in Culture and Society* 8, no. 3 (Spring 1983): 451–470.

———. "Wife-Beating in Nineteenth-Century America." *Victimology* 4, no. 1 (1979): 60–74.

Polk, Kenneth. *When Men Kill: Scenarios of Masculine Violence*. Cambridge: Cambridge University Press, 1994.

Ptacek, James. "The Clinical Literature on Men Who Batter: A Review and Critique." In *Family Abuse and Its Consequences: New Directions in Family Violence Research*, edited by Gerald T. Hotaling, David Finkelhor, John T. Kirkpatrick, and Murray A. Straus, 149–162. Newbury Park, Calif.: Sage, 1988.

———. "Why Do Men Batter Their Wives?" In *Feminist Perspectives on Wife Abuse*, edited by Kersti Yllö and Michele Bograd, 133–157. Newbury Park, Calif.: Sage, 1988.

———. "Wifebeaters' Accounts of Their Violence: Loss of Control as Excuse and as Subjective Experience." Master's Thesis, Department of Sociology, University of New Hampshire, 1985.

Quadagno, Jill. *The Color of Welfare: How Racism Undermined the War on Poverty*. New York: Oxford University Press, 1994.

Rand, Michael R. "Violence-Related Injuries Treated in Hospital Emergency Departments." Special Report of the Bureau of Justice Statistics. Washington, D.C.: U.S. Department of Justice, August 1997.

Raphael, Jody. "Prisoners of Abuse: Domestic Violence and Welfare Receipt." Chicago: Taylor Institute, April 1996.

Ray, Elaine. "Domestic Violence: The Sad Statistics." *Boston Globe*, November 17, 1991, 83.

Reinharz, Shulamit. "Feminist Distrust: Problems of Context and Content in Sociological Work." In *The Self in Social Inquiry: Research Methods*, edited by David N. Berg and Kenwyn K. Smith, 153–172. Newbury Park, Calif.: Sage, 1985.

Rich, Adrienne. "Husband-Right and Father-Right." In *On Lies, Secrets, and Silence: Selected Prose, 1966–1978*, 215–222. New York: Norton, 1979.

Richie, Beth E. "Battered Black Women: A Challenge for the Black Community." *Black Scholar* 16, no. 2 (March-April 1985): 40–44.

———. *Compelled to Crime: The Gender Entrapment of Battered Black Women*. New York: Routledge, 1996.

Ridgeway, James. "Send in the Feds." *Village Voice*, September 9, 1997, 38.

Rivera, Jenny. "Domestic Violence Against Latinas by Latino Males: An Analysis of Race, National Origin, and Gender Differentials." *Third World Law Journal* 14, no. 2 (1994): 231–257.

———. "The Politics of Invisibility." *Georgetown Journal on Fighting Poverty* 3, no. 1 (Fall 1995): 61–65.

Robinson, John. "Tears at a Power Breakfast." *Boston Globe*, October 14, 1993, 69.

Romero, Mary. "A Comparison Between Strategies Used on Prisoners of War and Battered Wives." *Sex Roles* 13, nos. 9–10 (1985): 537–547.

Roper, P., and G. Weeks. "Over Half of the Women on Public Assistance

in Washington State Reported Physical or Sexual Abuse as Adults."
Issue Brief of the Washington State Institute for Public Policy. Olympia, Wash.: Evergreen State College, 1993.

Russell, Diana E. H. "Preface." In *Femicide: The Politics of Woman Killing*, edited by Jill Radford and Diana E. H. Russell, xiv–xv. New York: Twayne, 1990.

——. *Rape in Marriage*. Bloomington: Indiana University Press, 1990.

——. *Sexual Exploitation: Rape, Child Sexual Abuse, and Workplace Harassment*. Beverly Hills: Sage, 1984.

Sampson, Robert J., and William Julius Wilson. "Toward a Theory of Race, Crime, and Urban Inequality." In *Crime and Inequality*, edited by John Hagan and Ruth D. Peterson, 37–54. Stanford: Stanford University Press, 1995.

Schechter, Susan. "Guidelines for Mental Health Practitioners in Domestic Violence Cases." Washington, D.C.: National Coalition Against Domestic Violence, 1987.

——. *Women and Male Violence: The Visions and Struggles of the Battered Women's Movement*. Boston: South End Press, 1982.

Schechter, Susan, and Lisa T. Gary. "A Framework for Understanding and Empowering Battered Women." In *Abuse and Victimization Across the Life Span*, edited by Martha B. Straus, 240–253. Baltimore: Johns Hopkins University Press, 1988.

Schuler, Margaret, ed. *Freedom from Violence: Women's Strategies from Around the World*. New York: OEF International/UNIFEM, 1992.

Schwartz, Martin D. "Ain't Got No Class: Universal Risk Theories of Battering." *Contemporary Crises* 12 (1988): 373–392.

Sherman, Lawrence W. *Policing Domestic Violence: Experiments and Dilemmas*. New York: Free Press, 1992.

Short, James F., Jr. *Poverty, Ethnicity, and Violent Crime*. Boulder: Westview Press, 1997.

Smart, Carol. *Feminism and the Power of Law*. London: Routledge, 1989.

Smith, Barbara. Introduction to the Combahee River Collective pamphlet, "Twelve Black Women: Why Did They Die?" In *Fight Back! Feminist Resistance to Male Violence*, edited by Frédérique Delacoste and Felice Newman, 68–69. Minneapolis: Cleis Press, 1981.

Smith, Dorothy E. *The Everyday World as Problematic: A Feminist Sociology*. Boston: Northeastern University Press, 1987.

Smith, Marcia. "When Violence Strikes Home." *The Nation*, June 30, 1997, 23–24.

Snider, Laureen. "The Potential of the Criminal Justice System to Promote Feminist Concerns." In *The Social Basis of Law*, edited by Elizabeth Comack and Stephen Brickey, 238–260. Halifax, Nova Scotia: Garamond Press, 1991.

Sorenson, Susan B., and Cynthia A. Telles. "Self-Reports of Spousal Violence in a Mexican-American and Non-Hispanic White Population." *Violence and Victims* 6, no. 1 (1991): 3–15.

Stanton, Elizabeth C., Susan B. Anthony, and Matilda J. Gage. "Selections from the *History of Woman Suffrage*." In *The Feminist Papers*, edited by Alice S. Rossi, 413–470. Toronto: Bantam, 1973.

Stark, Evan. "Rethinking Homicide: Violence, Race, and the Politics of Gender." *International Journal of Health Services* 20, no. 1 (1990): 3–26.

Stark, Evan, and Anne H. Flitcraft. "Personal Power and Institutional Victimization: Treating the Dual Trauma of Woman Battering." In *Post-Traumatic Therapy and Victims of Violence*, edited by Frank M. Ochberg, 115–151. New York: Brunner/Mazel, 1988.

———. "Spouse Abuse." In *Violence in America: A Public Health Approach*, edited by Mark L. Rosenberg and Mary Ann Fenlet, 123–157. New York: Oxford University Press, 1991.

———. "Violence Among Intimates: An Epidemiological Review." In *Handbook of Family Violence*, edited by Vincent B. Van Hasselt, Randall L. Morrison, Alan S. Bellack, and Michel Hersen, 293–317. New York: Plenum Press, 1988.

———. *Women at Risk: Domestic Violence and Women's Health*. Thousand Oaks, Calif.: Sage, 1996.

Steinmetz, Suzanne S. K., and Murray A. Straus. *Violence in the Family*. New York: Harper and Row, 1974.

Stone, Lucy. "Crimes Against Women." *Woman's Journal*, June 16, 1877, 188.

Straus, Murray A., Richard J. Gelles, and Suzanne K. Steinmetz. *Behind Closed Doors: Violence in the American Family*. Garden City: Anchor Press/Doubleday, 1980.

Straus, Murray A., and Christine Smith. "Violence in Hispanic Families in the United States: Incidence Rates and Structural Interpretations." In *Physical Violence in American Families*, edited by Murray A. Straus and Richard J. Gelles, 341–367. New Brunswick, N.J.: Transaction, 1990.

"Symposium on Domestic Violence." *Journal of Criminal Law and Criminology* 88, no. 1 (1992).

Taylor, Verta. "The Continuity of the American Women's Movement: An Elite-Sustained Stage." In *Women and Social Protest*, edited by Guida West and Rhoda Lois Blumberg, 277–301. New York: Oxford University Press, 1990.

Tierney, Kathleen J. "The Battered Women Movement and the Creation of the Wife Beating Problem." *Social Problems* 29, no. 3 (1982): 207, 208.

Tifft, Larry L. *Battering of Women: The Failure of Intervention and the Case for Prevention.* Boulder: Westview Press, 1993.

Tonry, Michael. *Malign Neglect: Race, Crime, and Punishment in America.* New York: Oxford University Press, 1995.

Triantafillou, Katherine. "Massachusetts: New Legislation to Help Battered Women." *Judges' Journal* 27, no. 3 (1988): 20–23, 50–52.

Uzzell, O., and W. Peebles-Wilkins. "Black Spouse Abuse: A Focus on Relational Factors and Intervention Strategies." *Western Journal of Black Studies* 13 (1989): 10–16.

Walby, Sylvia. "Theorising Patriarchy." *Sociology* 23, no. 2 (1989): 213–234.

Weber, Max. *From Max Weber: Essays in Sociology.* Translated and edited by Hans H. Gerth and C. Wright Mills. New York: Oxford University Press, 1946 [1921].

West, Cornell. *Race Matters.* Boston: Beacon Press, 1993.

Wilson, Margo I., and Martin Daly. "Who Kills Whom in Spouse Killings? On the Exceptional Sex Ratio of Spousal Homicides in the United States." *Criminology* 30, no. 2 (1992): 189–215.

Wilt, Susan A., Susan M. Illman, and Maia BrodyField. "Female Homicide Victims in New York City 1990–1994." Draft Report. New York: New York City Department of Health, March 1997.

"Year of the Woman: In Memoriam." *Boston Globe*, December 31, 1992, 14.

Yllö, Kersti, and Michele Bograd, eds. *Feminist Perspectives on Wife Abuse.* Newbury Park, Calif.: Sage, 1988.

Zorza, Joan. "The Criminal Law of Misdemeanor Domestic Violence, 1970–1990." *Journal of Criminal Law and Criminology* 83, no. 1 (1992): 46–72.

———. "Woman Battering: A Major Cause of Homelessness." *Clearinghouse Review* 24, no. 4 (1991): 421–429.

Legal Cases

Bruno v. Codd, 90 Misc. 2d 1047, 396 N.Y.S. 2d 974 (Sup. Ct. 1977).

Fulgham v. State, 46 Ala. 146 (1871).

Nazarro v. Justices of the Southern Essex Division of the District Court & Richard Jones, Supreme Judicial Court No. 86-429, December 17, 1986.

State v. Oliver, 70 N.C. 60 (1874).

Index